LESSONS IN IRISH SEXUALITY

By the same author

*Moral Monopoly: The Rise and Fall of the
Catholic Church in Modern Ireland*
(Second, revised edition, University College Dublin Press 1998)

Lessons in Irish Sexuality

TOM INGLIS

University College Dublin Press
Preas Choláiste Ollscoile Bhaile Átha Cliath

First published 1998 by University College Dublin Press,
Newman House, St Stephen's Green, Dublin 2, Ireland

ISBN 1 900621 16 9

Cataloguing in Publication data available from the British Library

Typeset in 11/13 Garamond in Bantry, Ireland by Elaine Shiels
Printed in Ireland by Colour Books, Dublin

Contents

Acknowledgements

The sexual world in which I grew up is very different from what it is today. We are all struggling – whether as parents, teachers, children or young people – to understand ourselves as sexual human beings, and the importance of sexuality in everyday life. We try as adults to pass on to the new generation of young people what we have learnt and understood about the world. Yet when it comes to speaking or writing about ourselves and sexuality, we seem to stagger and stumble. I am a sociologist and this is my attempt to explain some of the issues involved in teaching children and young people about relationships and sexuality. I have not resolved any of these issues. Indeed I end up asking more questions than I answer. But I am sure of one thing. We have in recent years in Ireland begun to break the silence in which sex was shrouded for so long. We need to continue to break the silence, to raise issues, and ask questions to which we may not have all the answers. This is what this book is about.

There are many people who have helped me along the way. The teachers, parents and pupils of the school in which I did my interviews were very generous with their time, commitment and support. I learnt a great amount from them. Mark Murphy was my research assistant for those interviews and, as always, did a wonderfully professional job. I would like to thank all those who responded to my call for help, in particular Nora Brennan, Emer Egan, Owen Metcalfe, Stephanie Walsh. A book such as this is founded on long hours of debate and discussion. I am particularly grateful to my colleagues in the Department of Sociology in University College Dublin who helped clarify my ideas. I would also like to thank many friends and members of my family who debated and discussed the issues with me, in particular Michael Cussen, Manus Charleton, Carol MacKeogh and Susie Parr. Eoin O'Mahony, Susan Gilmartin and Tom Hobson read and commented on earlier drafts. Tom, especially, was most generous with his time and comments. Stephen and Barbara Mennell have, once again, not only been great editors, but a source of tremendous encouragement and support.

Finally, I come to those who are closest and dearest to me. Aileen MacKeogh is the best wife, partner in life and lover that I could have. It is her love which provided me with the sexual and emotional security I needed to write this book. My daughter Olwen is a major source of inspiration, from whom I continue to learn so much. The book is dedicated with love to my son Arron.

Tom Inglis
Dublin, June 1998

For Arron

1
Introduction

On 16 May 1997 the body of a newborn baby was found in a village graveyard in Portarlington, Co. Laois. It was concealed in a bag of kitchen rubbish. The following day a teenage girl admitted that she was the mother. The discovery of dead, newborn babies is a frequent occurrence in Ireland. For example, in December 1993, the body of a dead baby boy was found in the Phoenix Park in Dublin. The next month another body was found. This time it was a baby girl. Her body was found along the banks of the River Feale in Co. Kerry. A month later again, in February 1994, the decomposed body of another baby was found in the Royal Canal in Co. Kildare. A year later, in May 1995, the body of another newborn baby was washed up by the tide off the coast of Kerry. The discovery of these dead babies was, for many people, a reminder of what happened to Joanne Hayes and Anne Lovett, and to hundreds of other single Irish women who have given birth outside marriage. The accumulation of dead, newborn babies was to have an unintended consequence. It was, to borrow terminology from another episode in Irish history, the grotesque, bizarre, unprecedented and, most of all, unacceptable discovery of two dead babies within a month in 1994 which became the necessary impetus for the state, in particular the then Minister for Education Niamh Breathnach, to set about organising a relationships and sexuality education programme for Irish schools. Times had changed. Where there had once been ridicule and scorn for the unmarried mother, there was now growing sympathy and understanding. It is difficult for people to be sexually responsible when they are not just sexually illiterate, but ignorant of the basic facts of life.

There was a feeling perhaps that what had happened to these young women was not just something that could have happened to many others, but that finding dead newborn babies was just the tip of a much bigger, grotesque iceberg. The belief that ignorance was bliss when it came to sex was falling on stony ground. Some unacceptable contradictions also began to emerge. Some of the priests, brothers and fathers, who had taught children what they deemed they needed to know about sex, were the ones who had been quietly sexually abusing and terrorising them. The denial of sex had gone too far. The denial of a proper programme of relationships and sexuality education could be linked to the denial of the right of a teenage girl who had become pregnant through rape to travel to Britain for an abortion. Many liberals felt that Ireland had become the laughing stock of the Western world.

Indeed for many people the very idea of the Irish and sex is a joke. We have a reputation for being ignorant, incompetent, shy and awkward when it comes to sex. After years of sexual oppression, we are seen to associate sex with feelings of guilt, shame and embarrassment.[1] There may be some truth in the way others see us. I grew up in a good Catholic home in the suburbs of Dublin in the 1950s and 1960s. I also went to a good Catholic school where I was taught all I supposedly needed to know about sex, sexuality and personal relationships – nothing. My father taught me little or nothing. In fact, any time sex came up in conversation, on the radio or, worst of all, on television, he got up from his chair and walked out of the room. My mother never spoke to me about sex. However, one day she did decide to take matters in hand and left a Catholic Truth Society pamphlet in the bathroom which I discovered just before I was to take a bath. I read the pamphlet, but it left me more confused than knowledgeable. It was not until I was thirteen that I discovered from a school-friend that a man putting his seed into a woman was different from peeing into her.[2]

There is evidence that I was not alone in my naïveté about sex and the facts of life. Humphreys found considerable ignorance in his research in Dublin in the 1960s. As one of his respondents noted: 'I used to think of marriage as a mere matter of companionship. I thought that children just came somehow, I knew not how. It never occurred to me that children or the purpose of marriage had anything to do with sex.'[3] Sweetman discovered similar naïveté and ignorance in the 1970s. People whom she interviewed admitted to having a very limited knowledge about sex: 'I became pregnant with the first child and I don't even know how. The same with the second child. When I was having the third this woman lent me this book *Everywoman*. That was the first I ever really learnt about sex.'[4] In a national sample survey of almost 3,000 women, Wiley and Merriman found that slightly less than half (49 per cent) had received sex education. The proportion of women who had received sex education diminished dramatically with age – for example 88 per cent of those between 18–24 years, compared with 15 per cent of those between 55–60 years. Moreover, the overall proportion (63 per cent) of those who thought this education had been adequate was also higher among younger women (75 per cent). The results of this survey suggested a possible link between sexual ignorance and births outside marriage. Almost seven in ten (69 per cent) of those who had not received sex education agreed that a woman could not get pregnant during first intercourse. This compared with only three in ten (31 per cent) of those who had received sex education.[5]

A study of unmarried mothers showed that half had received no sex education at home, and one fifth had not received any sex education at all. More than half (54 per cent) did not know or could offer no opinion on when they were most likely to conceive in their menstrual cycle.[6] In a study of crisis pregnancies among women it was found that the majority of women had used no form of contraception. As the authors concluded, social and personal factors militated against the use of contraception.

In the past, social attitudes to sexual activity and contraceptive use in Ireland have been shaped by Catholic social teaching which deems sexual intercourse outside marriage to be sinful and immoral. In the case of many of the women interviewed, their parents presumed that they would follow such teaching so sexual intimacy and the use of contraceptives were not discussed within their families.[7]

There is, then, considerable evidence which suggests that many young Irish people have grown up, left school and become mature adults without knowing enough about the biological facts of sex, the nature of human sexuality and, consequently, without being confident and competent in their sexual relations. In reviewing existing provision, the Expert Advisory Group on Relationships and Sexuality Education (RSE) established by the Minister for Education in 1994, concluded that sex education was 'generally uneven, uncoordinated and sometimes lacking'.[8]

Teaching young people about relationships and sexuality

The Department of Education's programme Relationships and Sexuality Education (RSE) commenced in Autumn 1997. The programme was a designated part of the national curriculum. It was designed around a series of resource materials which can be adapted to the religious and cultural ethos of each particular school. There was considerable opposition to the programme. Earlier in 1997 – just two weeks before the newborn baby was found in the rubbish bag in Portarlington – twenty-three teachers in a primary school in Co. Kerry wrote to their local Catholic bishop and to all the other schools in the diocese indicating that they would have nothing do with the new programme which they said 'debases the meaning, mystery and sanctity of human sexuality for the child'.[9] The teachers insisted that sex education was the sole responsibility of parents. Their position was similar to a lay Catholic group which had been actively disseminating anti-RSE material to schools.[10] This group argued that their position was supported by guidelines issued by the Catholic Church, specifically the Pontifical Council for the Family in its *The Truth and Meaning of Human Sexuality*.[11]

But the Catholic Church does not speak with one voice on this issue. There are Irish bishops who would distance themselves from what emerges from the Vatican. Similarly, there are priests, nuns and brothers who would distance themselves from their bishops. The general position adopted by the Irish Catholic hierarchy has been that, while they maintain that sex education is primarily the responsibility of parents, they accept that most parents need the help and support of teachers and schools. What they have emphasised, however, is the importance of putting sex education firmly within the context of Catholic moral teaching.

The position of the state and, in particular, the Department of Education is that it is necessary, indeed obligatory, for each primary and secondary school to teach a programme of relationships and sexuality education. This is the first part of a much broader programme of Social, Personal and Health Education (SPHE) which, it is envisaged, will be introduced gradually over the next few years. The state, through the National Council for Curriculum and Assessment (NCCA), produced a detailed interim curriculum and set of guidelines for both primary and secondary schools. The guidelines provided a detailed description of the overall programme, specifying what should be taught in each lesson, in each class, for every year from Junior Infants to final year in secondary school. The guidelines also provided information about suitable books and videos which schools might use as resource materials.[12] The state also produced, in association with all the main interest groups involved, a set of policy guidelines as to how the RSE programme should be introduced into each school. The interest groups included the National Parents' Council, the Catholic Primary Schools Managers Association, and the Church of Ireland Board of Education as well as associations representing schools and teachers' unions. The policy guidelines made clear that while it was necessary for each school to introduce an RSE programme, it was not necessary for schools to introduce the specific programme which the NCCA had produced.[13] The policy guidelines recognised and accepted that most Irish schools had a particular religious ethos. Consequently, the state decided that the decision as to what would be contained within the specific RSE programme of each school would be delegated to the teachers, parents and authorities of that school. Together they would choose a committee which would decide what would be contained within their own RSE programme. This was an important opt-out clause. In effect, RSE became a mandatory programme without a mandatory curriculum. It was in reality a recognition by the state of the special position of the Catholic Church in Irish society and, specifically, in Irish education. It was, consequently, another Irish solution to the problem of the state trying to resolve an issue pertaining to the Catholic Church and sexual morality.

The Catholic Church, then, did not reject the curriculum and guidelines for RSE set out by the Department of Education. In fact, most Catholic bishops – who have jurisdiction for Catholic education in their dioceses – accepted the general course outline set out in the NCCA's curriculum guidelines. They accepted the specific topics and the order in which they should be taught. For example, in primary schools, they agreed that children should be taught about self-esteem, their bodies, the creation of life, relationships with others, family life, growing up, physical development and sexual intercourse. However, many bishops have recommended that what Catholic pupils in their schools are taught about in relation to these issues – in other words the specific content – should be drawn from the religious education programme, the *Children of God* series, which has been granted formal Church approval. In other words, the position of the Church is that it agrees with sexuality education as long as it is corresponds with Catholic teaching, ethos and philosophy. It is perfectly acceptable to teach children about sexual intercourse as long as it is within Church teaching. It has taken the Department of Education's guidelines and within each specific lesson has given appropriate readings and practices from the *Children of God* series. The manual reminds teachers and parents that in a Catholic School, this is the way children should be taught about relationships and sexuality.

Wider context and issues

Drawing back from the present programme of Relationships and Sexuality Education (RSE) and placing it within a broader historical context, we can see that the attempt to implement relationships and sexuality education in Irish schools is part of a continuing struggle involving the separation of Church and state in Irish society. RSE can be seen as a part of a slow, steady, but ongoing struggle by the state to take the ownership and control of education away from the churches, particularly the Catholic Church, and to assume authority for shaping the minds, hearts and bodies of Irish children. The view of the state, supported by those who take a progressive or liberal attitude to education, morality and sexuality, is that young people need to be rescued from the traditional teachings of the Church which are deemed to be inadequate to meet the realities of modern social life. In other words, it is no longer practical or desirable to try to keep young people pure, chaste and innocent. What is necessary is to help them recognise and accept the needs, stresses and strains of being sexually responsible, and to appreciate the consequences if they are not.

On the other hand, resistance to RSE can be seen as an attempt to maintain the traditional moral fabric of Irish society, which is being eroded by consumerism and materialism. It is about protecting the private life of the family from encroachment by the state, and preventing the spread of liberal individualism in which the common good is sacrificed in order to allow some people to do and say what they please. The demand by the state to teach children about sex is seen to lead to the unnecessary sexualisation of children at a young age. It is deemed to be a capitulation to the commercial interests of those who seek to make young people consumers as early as possible, particularly by suggesting that they need the products they produce to be deemed acceptable and attractive by their peers. It is argued that the hidden message of many television programmes and teenage magazines, especially the advertisements, is that to be 'with it' – to be socially acceptable – it is necessary to have up-to-date fashions, wear appropriate make-up, follow successful sports stars, buy the latest pop music and, in general, to be properly branded. In other words, the process of sexualising young people early in life is part of the disease of materialism, consumerism and liberalism which reduces young people, as well as everyone else, to relationships revolving around producing, buying and exchanging commodities. These processes of sexualisation and commodification are seen as part of an increasing secularisation of Irish society which reduces personalities and social life to a godless, spiritually barren, hedonistic consumption of goods and services.

The introduction of RSE raises fundamental issues not just about the relationship between Church and state in Ireland, but about regulation and control of the market. The capitalist market is based on freedom of choice. Individuals should, it is argued, be left to decide what goods and services they themselves decide they need and want. In Ireland, the state, and people who have a liberal attitude to sex, have moved to accepting that if adult men and women wish to buy and then, in privacy, read, gaze at, and perhaps even masturbate to soft pornography, they should be allowed to do so. Or, at least, they should not be prohibited through state legislation from doing so.

Raising questions about the state and the growth of market relations, however, necessarily raises fundamental questions about the role and function of the media in modern society. It could well be argued that the media have penetrated into the heart of Irish homes and, regardless of what is taught by parents, teachers, priests or bishops, have created the need for relationships and sexuality education. Through television, radio, films, videos, and magazines, sex is displayed and promoted, giving rise to the desire to be sexually knowledgeable, attractive and experienced. Furthermore, it is through the media that capitalist market relations – that is seeing, understanding and relating to ourselves and others in terms of the consumption of goods and services – have penetrated into the heart of family and community life, and have come to dominate the most private, intimate sphere of human relations. The media, through the commercial interests which they represent and on which they are dependent for advertising revenue, promote continual, excessive consumption. They also promote a knowledge and understanding of ourselves, particularly a sexuality, which fits into such a lifestyle. If issues or questions are raised about this lifestyle, they are debated and discussed through the media themselves and not just, for example, within the Catholic Church.[14] Increasingly it is the media which set the agenda for public debate and discussion about what is right, wrong, good and bad not just about sex, but about modern lifestyle in general. In this respect, commercial interests, the market, and the media have become the major opposition to the world-view and ethics promoted by the Catholic Church and religion in general. It is these commercial forces which have developed a monopoly over the way Irish people see, know, understand and realise themselves as individuals.

From a liberal individual perspective, this penetration of traditional culture, the erosion of the Catholic Church's monopoly over morality, the ending of the silence and feelings of shame and guilt about anything to do with sex, is a good thing. Understanding sex, love, passion and desire is central to understanding who and what we are – our emotions, anxieties, fears, pleasures and tastes. Talking about them openly and honestly in private and public life, is an important process of discovering who we are, and how we came to be the way we are. Teaching young people about sex, sexuality and personal relationships is seen as central to becoming critically reflective, individually moral responsible adults.

Relationships and Sexuality Education also raises questions about the design and content of non-examination educational programmes, the way young people are taught in school, and the level of participation and control which they have over what and how they learn. In the past, when talk about sex in schools was strictly regulated, if it were mentioned at all it was either within a natural scientific or a religious, ethical perspective. In other words, sex and sexuality were separated. Within a natural scientific perspective, sex had to do with young people learning the biological facts of life. Young people learnt about the human reproductive system in the same way as they would learn about how other animals reproduce. On the other hand, learning about sexuality was confined to learning about what was right and wrong, good and bad, appropriate and inappropriate sexual behaviour.

There was little or no discussion of actual sexual behaviour – of how, for example, Irish people actually behaved sexually rather than how they should have behaved. In other words, it was not treated in a sociological or political manner. There was little or no attempt to provide a knowledge and understanding about sexuality. But, perhaps most important of all, little attention was given to the personal experiences, needs and interests of the young people themselves. They were regarded as not being in a position to say what it was that they needed to learn about sexuality. If relationships and sexuality education involves children and young people learning about sex in terms of gender relations and power, then it could be argued that it becomes crucial *how* they learn to read and understand the sexual world in which they live. In other words, the pedagogical strategy used – what children and young people are taught at what age, how they are taught, by whom, when and where – becomes critical. I would argue, using an insight derived from adult education, that if children are not enabled to learn to read their sexual world for themselves, the teaching they receive may dominate and oppress rather than liberate and emancipate them.[15] Teaching children about the sociology and politics of sex – about how people think and behave sexually, and about who influences and controls what they do and say – is very different from teaching them the biology of sex or, for example, the sexual moral rules and regulations of the Catholic Church. Adult education theory suggests that if young people are to become self-confident, emotionally stable, critically reflective, sexually responsive, responsible, mature adults, then a radically different approach is needed which focuses on their needs and interests, and gives them a much greater say over what they want to learn, when and how.

Yet there is still a very strong argument which holds that young people, particularly children in primary school, are not sufficiently mature to know what they need to learn. The question is to what extent this holds for young people in secondary schools. But even if an adult education approach were deemed desirable, there might still be problems in implementing it. How could parents and teachers allow young people, even if they are in their late teens, to decide what and how they want to learn about sexuality? How could a Catholic school permit young people to learn about contraception, sterilisation and abortion? Most important of all, how could teachers who are committed to the ethos and message of the Catholic Church, who have a traditional approach to implementing school curricula, and who perhaps have a distaste if not a fear of talking about sexuality, engage in non-directive, open-ended learning processes with children who are committed to sexual liberation?

Contemporary attitudes and practices

The generation gap between teachers and parents and young people is reflected in the changes in sexual attitudes, values and practices which have taken place, particularly since the 1970s. A national survey in 1973–74 found that 71 per cent of the Catholic respondents thought that a man and a woman having sex relations before marriage was always wrong. This, in effect, was most of the people, since 96 per cent of the Republic of Ireland's population was Catholic. In the same survey, more than six in ten (62 per cent) thought that using contraceptives was wrong.[16]

Attitudes to pre-marital sex have changed dramatically. In Mícheál MacGréil's survey in 1988–89, only 27 per cent of the respondents felt that pre-marital sex was always wrong. There was, however, strong evidence of a generation gap. Twenty per cent of those under 35 years thought that premarital sex was always wrong, compared with 85 per cent of those over 65 years.[17] But it is not just that people's own attitudes are changing. They also see a major change in other people's attitudes and practices. A survey in 1992 found that 63 per cent of respondents thought that sex outside marriage was very common, and 73 per cent thought that teenagers were much more sexually active compared to twenty years ago.[18]

It was not until the 1990s that researchers felt confident enough to ask people about their own sexual behaviour. The same survey in 1992 found that 70 per cent of single men and 55 per cent of single women were sexually active. More significantly, one third of the single men, compared with nine per cent of single women, had more than one sexual partner in the previous twelve months.[19] The trend towards sex outside marriage and with different partners seems to be growing. A survey in 1997 found that 21–24 year olds had had, on average, 13 different sexual partners. More significantly, half (54 per cent) of those aged 17–20 years had had sex with more than one partner.[20] There is also evidence that young Irish people are having sex at an earlier age. In 1992, almost half (48 per cent) of the 18–24 years who had had sexual intercourse, had done so by the time they were eighteen years. In comparison, only four per cent of those aged 50–64 years had had sexual intercourse by this age.[21] Again, the picture changed in the five years to 1997. The 1997 survey found that of those aged 17–20 years, exactly half had had sex before they were sixteen years old. The average age of first sexual intercourse was 15.9 years. This compared with 18.8 years among those aged 35–39 years.

Not only are Irish people beginning to have sex at a younger age, the 1997 survey showed that young people are having sex regularly. More than four in ten (43 per cent) of the 17–20 year olds were having sex at least once a week. Moreover, there is definite evidence that Irish people do not confine sex to marriage. Only 10 per cent of single people had never had sex, and more than half (52 per cent) were having sex at least once a week.[22]

These changes link with the rise in the number of births outside marriage in Ireland since 1960, but particularly since 1980. In 1980, one in twenty births was outside marriage. By 1996, this had risen to one in four. This represents one of the fastest growths in Europe (see table 1).

The Irish level of births outside marriage is coming closer to the levels in the United Kingdom, France and Denmark where more than one-third of births are outside marriage. Within the overall trend, there has been a dramatic rise in the number of births to teenagers outside marriage. While the number of births to women aged under twenty years has not changed significantly since 1972, the proportion of these which have occurred outside marriage has increased from three per cent in 1972 to 89 per cent in 1992. The direction of the changes in Irish sexual attitudes and practices corresponds to what has been happening in general in Western society, where the age at first intercourse has been decreasing and the proportion sexually active by age 18 years rising.[23]

In this changed context many respondents to an ESRI survey in 1991 felt that there was a need for more sex education. It showed that only one-fifth of young people expressed satisfaction with their preparation in school for adult life roles and relationships with friends of the opposite sex.[24] Almost two-thirds (63 per cent) of those interviewed in a survey in 1992 thought that children did not get enough sex education in schools. Seven in ten thought it was a good idea to have information

Table 1: Births Outside Marriage Rate for European Union Member
Countries 1960–1992

	Percentage of Births Outside Marriage of Natural Births			
Country	1960	1970	1980	1994
Greece	1.2%	1.1%	1.5%	2.9%
Netherlands	1.4%	2.1%	4.1%	13.1%
Ireland	1.6%	2.7%	5.0%	19.7% *
Belgium	2.1%	2.8%	4.1%	12.6%
Spain	2.3%	1.4%	3.9%	10.5%
Italy	2.4%	2.2%	4.3%	7.3%
Luxembourg	3.2%	4.0%	6.0%	12.9%
United Kingdom	5.2%	8.4%	11.5%	32.0%
France	6.1%	6.8%	11.4%	34.9%
Germany	6.3%	5.5%	7.6%	15.4%
Denmark	7.8%	11.0%	33.2%	46.8%
Portugal	9.5%	7.3%	9.2%	17.0%

Sources: *Eurostat 1989 Demographic Statistics*, 3C, Table 6, pp. 78–238; *Eurostat Statistics in Focus: Population and Social Conditions* 1995 No. 8; *Vital Statistics 1996*, CSO, Dublin: Government Publications 1997, 99.

* 1996 = 24.8%

about sex in newspapers, magazines and television. These findings correspond with the results of another survey in the same year which found that only 20 per cent of the respondents listed teachers as their main source of accurate information about the facts of life; 23 per cent said it was their mother, but 48 per cent said it was from friends or reading books and magazines. It would also appear that children are learning the facts of life much earlier. Over half (54 per cent) of 17–20 year olds said that they became aware of the facts of life by the time they were twelve years old, whereas only one third of those aged 40–49 years were aware of the facts of life by this age (see table 2). In the 1997 survey, two in three of those interviewed believed that sex education should start before the age of 12. Finally, five years previously, when respondents were asked about the role of religion in sex education, 78 per cent thought that they should be kept separate.[25]

Table 2.   Selection of Findings of Young Adults (17–20 years) Sexual
Attitudes and Lifestyles in 1992 and 1997.

	%
Sexuality Education:	
Main source of accurate information about facts of life (1992):	
Friends	26%
Mother	23%
Teacher (religious)	19%
Teacher (lay)	12%
Aware of facts of life at 12 years old	54%
Main source of knowledge about AIDS(1992):	
Television/Films	42%
Teachers (religious and lay)	25%
Main source of knowledge about contraception(1992):	
Friends	24%
Books/magazines/newspapers	20%
Television/films	10%
Teachers (religious and lay)	22%
Consider that teaching about sex, contraception should be independent of religious instruction	72%
Sexual Lifestyle (1997):	
Sex with one partner in past twelve months	22%
Sex with two or more partners	52%
None/not sexually active	19%
Had sex before 16 years old	50%
Have sex at least once a week	43%
Sexual Attitudes (1992):	
Proportion agreeing that:	
They are worried about catching HIV/AIDS	65%
It is mainly homosexuals and drug addicts who are really at risk from HIV/AIDS	38%
Single women who carry condoms are sensible	86%
They have ever carried condoms	29%

Source: Irish Marketing Surveys, Durex Survey, 1992 and 1997

Historical development of sex education

It is important to place the current demand for sexuality education within an even broader historical context. To understand the public debate and discussion, and the struggle between various interest groups for and against RSE, we need to be able to stand back from contemporary issues and debates and ask bigger, broader questions such as: 'Why at this particular point in Irish history, or indeed in the history of Western society, do we see it as necessary that young people be educated about sexuality and social and personal relationships?' What changes have taken place which necessitate that the mystery of relationships and sexuality be opened up and laid bare for young people?

The way in which young people learn about sex and sexuality varies as much across cultures as it has over time. It can be a vague knowledge which is acquired informally by watching animals, seeing adults courting, making love and, perhaps, having sex. [How many people in Western society first see adults having sex on television?] Children and young people often learn about sex by finding out bits and pieces of information through stories, jokes, intimations and allusions, which are shared and then put together like a jigsaw. In this process, some pieces of information may be missing but, on the other hand, the unique, individual mystery of sex is maintained. More recently, there has been a move towards formal lessons, and full, frank and open discussions. But why the need now for formal lessons? Norbert Elias has argued that as society becomes more complex, the need for discovering and implementing new forms of social integration increases. Social integration revolves around people behaving in a civilised manner. This means behaving in a transparent, predictable, trustworthy, restrained way so as not to frighten or offend others. Since sex is the most basic and primary of animal instincts, it is the aspect of human behaviour which has the potential to instil the greatest fear and disgust. Increased social complexity brought about through urbanisation, commerce and travel requires greater physical and emotional restraint in all areas of human conduct, but particularly in sexual behaviour. Respect for the dignity of others, particularly their bodies, becomes paramount. The rules concerning when it is permissible to embrace, kiss, touch and even look at members of the opposite sex may have become less formal, but they have also become far more complex. This, consequently, brings pressure for formal learning.

Elias pointed out that the Western notion of sex education dates back to at least the sixteenth century and the writings of Erasmus.[26] His *Colloquies* (1522) went through numerous editions and were widely translated. It became a standard textbook in schools. Although written for an elite social class, there is frankness in the approach which people today might find offensive, if not immoral. It presents fictitious dialogues between courting men and women, including a conversation between a young man and a prostitute. Elias points out that the *Colloquies* were written from a secular point of view and dealt factually and realistically with the world in which children lived.[27] It was eventually declared heretical by the Catholic Church.

For the next four hundred years, in a process supported and in many cases engineered by the Catholic Church, not only did children become separated from adult life, they were deliberately kept ignorant of its sexual aspects. By the nineteenth century the depiction of lust by Erasmus was seen as despicable and something from which children had to be protected. Sex became wrapped in a veil of silence, protecting standards of shame and the functioning of civil society. In 1857, Von Raumer argued in his *The Education of Girls* that matters of sex

should not be touched upon at all in the presence of children, least of all in a secret way which is liable to arouse curiosity. Children should be left for as long as it is at all possible in the belief that an angel brings her mother her little children.[28]

But, as Michel Foucault pointed out, the silencing of sex in the family and public life did not make it go away. Rather it brought a whole new attention to sex and made it much more complicated than it ever had been. Sex became a major problem. It had to be guarded against, particularly in women and young children. It became the subject of intense study. Foucault went so far as to argue that instead of sex being silenced or eliminated, it was in fact – through its control – brought into every area of public and private life.[29] He argued that from the eighteenth century, sex became the subject of public and private scrutiny. What was obvious and natural became the subject of rigorous analysis and examination. The implementation of a new regime of sexuality began with the detailed examination of the sexual sins of penitents in confession; the inculcation of shame and guilt about the body; the designation of women as being saturated with sex (overcome through their being made first into virgins and then, like Our Lady, chaste mothers); the rigorous denial of sex in children; the bringing of sexual issues and problems into the doctor's surgery; and, finally, the incarceration of the sexually deviant.[30] Foucault reminds us that although sex was denied in much of modern Irish life, it presided everywhere in its absence. It was in the bedrooms and bathrooms of every Irish home. It was present in every strategy of separation and supervision of girls from boys. It pervaded the pubs among the bachelor drinking groups. It was in every shy, awkward look, speech and touch of Irish men and women. Foucault emphasises that within the overall implementation of sexuality there were many different ways of speaking and writing about it, some of which served to reinforce and others to undermine the existing structures of power.

Carlson has identified four different discourses or perspectives about sexuality – that is, four different ways in which people in Western societies have written, spoken, understood and learnt about sex. Discourses are produced and recorded in books, reports, newspapers, films, television and radio programmes, plays, art and so forth. Although they have an important oral dimension, particularly in relation to everyday life, it is useful to consider discourses as having some kind of material existence, and being capable of being catalogued and stored in libraries, museums and archives. The discourses Carlson identified were:

(1) *a traditionalist discourse* which portrays sex primarily in terms of sin and sickness;
(2) *a progressive discourse* which centres on secular, scientific, utilitarian, state management of sexual problems;
(3) *a libertarian discourse* which emphasises sexual pleasure, diversity and individual sexual rights;
(4) *a radical Freudian discourse* which stresses the importance of creating non-repressive sexuality in a post-capitalist, post-patriarchal society.[31]

Examining the way sex was written about in the 1920s – the beginning of the progressive era – Carlson argues that it was significantly different from the traditionalist discourse of the late nineteenth century, epitomised by Victorian puritanism. A libertarian view of sexuality first began to emerge in the United States in the 1940s. It was characterised by laissez-faire capitalism and minimalist state intervention. It centred on an ethic of *reciprocity* and *consensuality* – meaning that I must grant you the same freedom of choice you grant me, and that individuals must enter into relations as consenting adults who agree on the terms of their relationship.[32] In the 1960s a new perspective on sex, inspired by the writings of Reich and Marcuse, emphasised how sexual liberation was dependent on ending the type of social relations endemic in patriarchal capitalism.

The emergence of these perspectives or discourses should not be seen as a rational, linear development from one viewpoint to the next, but more in terms of historical shifts or ruptures in the way in which sex was written and thought about. The emergence of a new perspective does not eliminate those which preceded it. In any one society, such as Ireland, and at any point in time, such as the 1990s, there will be elements of all the different perspectives. The dominance of one perspective over another is determined by the struggle by representatives of different interest groups and organisations to have their way of seeing, understanding, speaking, writing and – most of all in the present context – teaching young people, about sex as the most truthful and moral and, consequently, the most politically and socially acceptable. The proponents of the different viewpoints argue that their interpretation of sex and sexuality should be the one which informs public policy, social legislation, school curricula and pedagogical practice. Let me give a brief overview of the argument.

Much of what was written and spoken about sexuality in Ireland during the nineteenth and twentieth centuries was dominated by the teachings and ethos of the Catholic Church. This is not to deny that there were examples of progressive, liberal and even radical perspectives. Brian Merriman's *The Midnight Court* and James Joyce's *Ulysses* were radical in their time. But these instances were few and far between, and owing to strict censorship and the monopoly which the Church held over morality, tended to be driven underground. The crucial sociological question is to what extent the official perspective of the Catholic Church held sway over what was said and done by people in ordinary, everyday public life and, more significantly perhaps, between husbands and wives, courting couples and lovers. Gradually, from the late 1960s, the Church's dominance in the field of sexuality began to be challenged, primarily through the media. Different voices and opinions began to be aired. Censorship began to be relaxed. The discussion of sexual behaviour and the depiction of erotic scenes and photographs became increasingly common in books, films, television, newspapers and magazines. Over the next thirty years, progressive and liberal viewpoints about sexuality existed side by side with the traditional perspective of the Catholic Church.

The Catholic Church began to soften its hard line on sexuality. There were fewer hell and damnation sermons about fornication. Priests were no longer self-confident in prying into deviant sexual behaviour during home visitations. But the Church also began to write and teach about sexuality. It began to recognise and accept the importance of sensual, erotic feelings between husbands and wives in marriage. In other words, where there used to be just one standard message about sexuality, there was now a wide variety of messages. As well as the liberal voice of the media, there were numerous interest groups, particularly within the women's movement, which were developing a progressive view of sexuality. The state relaxed the censorship laws. Some traditional sources, including priests and nuns, began to express progressive if not liberal opinions. Again the crucial sociological question is how these different, sometimes contradictory, viewpoints were manifested in everyday life. Did ordinary people begin to feel comfortable and relaxed about their sexuality, their sexual identity and orientation? Were they able to talk about sex with each other without feeling shameful and becoming embarrassed? When, where, how and among whom did these changes take place?

I will return to these issues in chapter 6. But it is necessary to make one more important point here. Most individuals, including young people, are skilled social actors. They recognise the sources and power behind the different perspectives on sexuality. They operate successfully within the different contexts in which sexuality is discussed. They know what is appropriate and inappropriate to do and say within the different contexts. How young people talk about sexuality varies according to whether they are a couple being intimate, in a group, in a classroom or with their parents. It is the way the different perspectives are lived out and embodied by each individual in all the different social contexts that their sexual identity, orientations and preferences are formed.[33]

It is important to say something briefly about some of the terms and definitions which I use in the book. When I use the term 'children' it generally refers to boys and girls up to the age of 12 years, and 'young people' refers to those up to the age of 18 years. For the most part, this fits into the difference between primary and secondary schools. In general, I use the term sex in the narrow sense of the physical and biological dimensions to human sexual activity. In this sense, sex education has to do with teaching children and young people the 'facts of life'. I tend to use the term sexuality to cover the broader dimensions associated with being a sexual human being, particularly psychological (personality, drives, desires), cultural (the way sex is seen, understood, written and talked about) and social (the institutional forces which attempt to limit and control what is said and done about sex).

I have mentioned that within Irish culture we can identify four different perspectives or currents of opinion on sexuality. These are different ways of seeing, understanding and thinking about sex and sexuality. In many respects they can be seen as competing viewpoints within an overall social field. There are, of course, many different social fields in Irish society. For example, there is a religious field and, as within the field of sexuality, we can identify different, often competing viewpoints about the nature of religion and being religious. Now, as well as different perspectives, there are also within the field of sexuality, different institutional forces and interest groups which take and defend positions about sexuality. As I have suggested already, the Catholic Church tends to speak and write within a traditional discourse or perspective, the state within a progressive perspective, and the media within a liberal perspective. But not only do institutions and interest groups change the way they write and talk about sexuality over time, there are often individuals within them who have a dissenting viewpoint. In other words, just as there are traditionalists within the media, there are liberals within the Church.

The different perspectives are encountered by people in their everyday life. The perspectives are seen, heard and assessed, adapted and adopted as part of the way people see, understand, react to, engage in and embody sexuality. It becomes part of the automatic way people have of reading, understanding and reacting to sex and sexuality. It becomes part of their *habitus*. By habitus, I mean a lasting, general and adaptable way of thinking and acting in conformity with a systematic view of the world. People's habitus becomes part of their 'second nature'. It is like an invisible pair of glasses which enables them to decipher and respond to what is being said and done in the sexual world in which they live. One of the important issues in Irish sexuality, addressed in later chapters, is how the different institutional discourses or perspectives shape young people's sexual habitus.[34]

The book begins by examining the nature of traditional Catholic opinions regarding sex education. The Church has moved slowly from a position which held that modesty and innocence needed to be protected, to one which accepted instruction on the facts of life within a scientific, biological perspective, to one which has increasingly accepted the need for instruction on social and sexual relationships. However, the emphasis is on the spiritual mystery of sex and, consequently, on an avoidance of explicit discussion. It is also based on instruction rather than a liberating learning approach which enables children to reveal, read, interpret and critically reflect about the sexual world in which they live.

Chapter 3 examines the progressive perspective of the state and other agencies. The beginnings of the state's challenge to the Catholic Church's monopoly over sexuality and morality is to be found in its promotion of the Stay Safe Programme. This was introduced into primary schools – again on a school by school basis – from the beginning of the 1990s. In an analysis of the Relationships and Sexuality Programme, it is argued that the state, like the Catholic Church, speaks with different voices in relation to sex. The Department of Health has been far more radical than the Department of Education in its approach to sex education. Caught in between the traditional viewpoint of the Catholic Church, which owns and controls most of the schools in the country, and the liberal viewpoint of popular culture and the media, the state has tended to lean towards accommodating a traditional viewpoint. While the official position is that each school develops its own policies regarding the exact nature of the programme adopted, there is in the resource material an emphasis on sexual orthodoxy within marriage and on the dangers rather than the experiences and pleasures of sex.

The fourth chapter examines the liberal perspective on sexuality and sexuality education in Ireland. This, it is argued, is mainly articulated within the media through the dialogue, scenes and lifestyles portrayed in soaps, serials and films and the concerns, attitudes and practices of the characters. It is also articulated through advertisements, the feature articles and advice columns of magazines, and various reports, debates and discussions on radio and television. There has been a gradual loosening within the media and popular culture of the strings which tied sexuality and sexual expression to the teachings of the Catholic Church. What was for so long hidden, unspoken and inexpressible is now displayed in public, talked about in the media. Sexual expression has become part of people's intimate understanding of themselves. The rigid censorship of books and films, which existed until the late 1960s, has been relaxed. Nude bodies and sex scenes have become the norm in film, video and television. Not only are pornographic magazines on sale throughout the country, but many of the top-selling women's and men's magazines are laden with sex in the feature articles, short stories, advertisements and advice columns. More significantly, in relation to teaching children about relationships and sexuality, the magazines orientated towards young teenage girls are also laden with sex.

Chapter 5 looks at the nature of radical sexual discourse. This viewpoint links political freedom to sexual freedom. It is relatively underdeveloped in Ireland. It is based on the assumption that the struggle for self-realisation is linked to the struggle for sexual freedom which, in turn, is linked to changing the political and economic structures within which people live their lives. We have, it might be argued, become alienated not just from ourselves but also from each other, from being human, and from nature in general through living within patriarchal families in state capitalist societies. A radical sexual perspective advocates the fulfilment of sexual interests not so much as self-indulgent pleasure, but as political activity. This can be inside or outside marriage and love, and often involves a positive exploration of desire and pleasure. Sexual freedom means being able to break the normative barriers of sex and accept and explore different sexual preferences and orientations, whether heterosexual, homosexual, lesbian or bisexual.

It would be wrong to think that the typology of the different ways of thinking, speaking and writing about sexuality described in the previous chapters is neatly adhered to in everyday life. Depending on the context, what is written, read and said by pupils, teachers and parents will vary between the different perspectives. Indeed the central argument of this book is that there is neither any single perspective about sexuality in Ireland, nor any readily identifiable single truth. In chapter 6, I look at the field of Irish sexuality in terms of the different social forces which come together to shape young people's sexuality, and the way that different voices emanate within traditional, progressive or liberal institutions. I also examine some examples of the attempt to shape public opinion about RSE through the media.

In Chapter 7, I examine the different voices and way that people think and talk about sexuality and specifically about the Relationships and Sexuality Education programme. The chapter is based on a description and analysis of three focus-group interviews conducted separately with teachers, parents and pupils in a secondary school in a small town in Ireland. In Chapter 8, I examine how the conflicts and contradictions in the way people think, talk and write about sexuality are linked to changes the balance of institutional power between the Catholic Church, the state, and the media. When the Catholic Church held a monopoly over sexual morality, people tended to speak with a unified voice within a traditional perspective. The entry of the state and the media into the field of sexuality has meant that not only are there different perspectives and voices, but there are contradictions between them, and opposition and conflict between the speakers and writers.

2

Being Taught to be Chaste and Modest

If Irish Catholics are shy, awkward and embarrassed about sex, it may well be that, more than others in Western society, they are modest, chaste and pure of heart. It may also be that for a long time they did not have access to, or competence in, a way of speaking which enabled them to express and communicate their sexual feelings, experiences, emotions and desires. Indeed, as we saw in the last chapter, many did not have access to a knowledge or understanding of the basic facts of life. What knowledge and understanding of sex did exist was caught in a space between an informal, popular cultural form of banter, teasing, repartee and jokes, and a more formal religious moral discourse based on Catholic Church teaching.[1]

Writing in 1923 an anonymous Irish priest made the following comment about sex education:

Is it not a fact that, as a rule, the first, and often times the sole, information . . . which a pure-minded boy gets of the mystery of human generation is from the polluted lips of some corrupt boy, or from a vulgar expression heard on the street, or from some other such source of contagion.[2]

The priest obviously felt that there was a need to counteract such vulgar knowledge. The problem was to write and talk about sex in a delicate way which would not pollute the chastity and modesty of innocent children. Consequently, he suggested that if a boy asked his mother where he came from she might answer as follows:

'My dear child,' the mother might say, 'all children come from Almighty God. Everything in the world comes from God. You see how God makes the blossoms grow on trees and plants. You have seen an apple-tree, first there is the flower, then the bud becomes larger and larger and grows into fruit, and when the fruit is ripe it is taken from the tree. In the same way Almighty God made you grow within me. For nine months you were like a blossom under my heart, growing bigger and bigger. You were part of myself. You could not live without me. I took food, some of it was changed into blood, and that blood fed you. If you were taken away from me during that time you would have died at once; and if I died during that time you would have died with me, because you were part of myself. I could not see you, but I knew you were there, and I prayed for you. And when you grew big enough to be able to live by yourself, the doctor (or nurse) was sent for, and then you came into the world to live your own life without me; and that is what is meant by saying you were born.'[3]

The central feature of this approach to sex education is the constitution of human sexuality and reproduction within the natural law of God. Human birth is part of the miracle of life. God, so to speak, makes children grow within women. The explanation is characterised as much by what is absent. There is no mention of any human intervention in the process. Men, at least in the initial stages of learning, are written out of the process. Pregnancy and birth are something which happen to women as part of God's plan. Although the explanation is couched in a biological analogy, there is a marked absence of any scientific language. No technical terms are used, nor parts of the body named. Human reproduction becomes wrapped in mysterious, vague, romantic imagery. The priest goes on to suggest that this explanation will help the child understand the only difficult part in the prayer *Hail Mary* – 'Blessed is the fruit of thy womb Jesus'.

The advice given by the Irish priest was not unique. The author refers the reader to English and French sources for his ideas. Furthermore, while the explanation may have been Catholic, the general ethos of protecting children's innocence and treating sex as a matter of extreme delicacy was no different from that given in Protestant Victorian Britain.[4] Nothing is known about the circulation, readership or practical implementation of the priest's advice. There were very few Irish publications on sex education from the turn of the century. Any texts which were published tended to come from the Catholic Truth Society of England and Wales. Indeed, the priest was aware that many of his readers would think that he was going too far in even raising sex education as an issue. Yet he was bold enough to criticise mothers who forbade priests to talk to their boys about the sixth commandment.[5]

He attacks the strategy of silence on sex for fear any talk would cause scandal. This strategy, he felt, was gratuitously dubbed prudence. 'But', he asked, 'when did prudence become such a negative virtue as, practically, to resolve itself into saying nothing for fear of making a mistake.'[6]

A traditionalist approach revolves around confining sex and sexuality to married love. The natural innocence of children and young people needs to be protected. All forms of sensuality are sources of temptation. Chastity, modesty, temperance and self-control are, therefore, the central features of being sexual. Sexual love is about self-denial and surrender to one's spouse. Anything outside the pure intentions of married sexual love is a threat to the natural order of things and can lead to social and moral disease and decay. As Carlson points out, the traditionalist discourse or perspective sees the sublimation of sexuality as essential to civilised society, and views those who control their sexual urges and live a more celibate life as more virtuous and more likely to be productive, efficient and self-disciplined. Such people were also seen as less prone to diseases and to wasting away. A traditionalist viewpoint also idealises the patriarchal family with its clearly defined roles, particularly for women as mothers. Although there can be a very practical, means-end dimension to the traditionalist discourse, Carlson emphasises that its 'core values and precepts . . . upheld a moralistic conception of sexuality and sin having deep roots in Judeo-Christian culture'.[7]

The proposal from the priest in 1922 for some kind of sex education did not gain much acceptance. In fact, the trend in Catholic thought was in the opposite direction – that is towards a prohibition on all talk or discussion about sex with children. This stance was verified in 1945 in Pope Pius XII's encyclical on *Christian Education of Youth*.

Adopting a policy which is as foolish as it is fraught with danger, there are many who advocate and promote a method called by the unpleasant name of 'sex education'. They are under the false impression that it is possible by merely natural arts, and without any of the safeguards of religion and piety, to forearm adolescents against unchastity and sensuality. They therefore initiate and instruct them alike, without distinction of sex and even in public, concerning these delicate matters; worse still, they expose them to premature occasions of sin in order – so they argue – to accustom their minds to such things and so harden them against the dangers of puberty.[8]

This strategy of silence and prudence about all matters concerning sex was not new. It had emerged centuries earlier as part of what Elias termed the civilising process and what Ariès referred to as the constitution of childhood.[9] Sex could only be mentioned indirectly and obliquely, in case it offended or excited the passions and consequently became an occasion of sin. One way of achieving this was to subsume all matters concerning sex within a religious discourse. In writing a handbook on sex and innocence for parents and educators in 1949, O'Hea noted that if asked how a baby is born, the mother should refer to the Jesus and Mary story.

Very soon after Our Lady had grown from being a child into being a young woman . . . God sent an angel to tell her that she was going to have a baby and that the baby was going to be God's own son and that Mary was going to be its mother. On that day this little baby started living inside Mother Mary's body. It was baby Jesus.[10]

O'Hea argued that 'a balanced instruction of the child in matters connected with sex' did not require a knowledge of child psychology or physiology, but rather an ability to answer directly any questions which children ask. Consequently, if a child wanted further information about sexual intercourse, he suggested that it could be described as follows: 'The very giving of themselves to each other completely in marriage as husband and wife causes a tiny baby to start growing deep down inside its mother.'[11]

Maintaining modesty and chastity

Innocence was a virtue which was protected through modesty and purity. The naked body was a source of sin. Having glossed over the facts of life, the Irish priest mentioned previously went on to talk of modesty. 'Animals do not wear clothes; but we must wear clothes, not only to keep us warm, but also because it would be a sin to walk about without clothes.'[12] The child is told that if he sees his father naked and does not turn his eyes away and takes a pleasure in looking, he is committing a sin of impurity. The sin of immodesty leads to the greater sin of impurity. In talking of keeping company, he warns boys that girls will have a 'dangerous attraction for you' and that they have to be careful for they will be burned as 'surely as the moth that flies into the candle'. He warns them never to touch girls except to shake hands and 'to avoid being alone with any of them, especially in a place where you cannot be seen by human eyes'.[13] The danger of immodesty and impurity grows when boys and girls become men and women, and only recedes when they are united in the sacrament of marriage.[14]

The advice given by the Irish priest centred on the confinement of sex to marriage and, within marriage, to procreation. Learning about sex was based on the regulation and control of desire. This was done through knowing and fulfilling fundamental prohibitions. The first prohibition, then, was contact between the sexes. The best solution outside marriage was a strict segregation and supervision of the sexes. Girls were set apart as another species. Boys had to learn that contact with them was always problematical. Any feelings towards the opposite sex were intrinsically dangerous. Sensuous feelings were particularly fraught with danger. They brought people back to the world of animality. It was, according to Pope Pius XI, the duty of mothers to protect their sons and daughters from this fate.

You have to prepare your sons and daughters so that they may pass with unfaltering steps, like those who pick their way among serpents, through that time of crisis and physical change: and may pass through it without losing anything of the joy of innocence, preserving intact that natural instinct of modesty with which Providence has girt them as a check upon wayward passion. That sense of modesty, which in its spontaneous abhorrence from the impure is akin to the sense of religion in these days: but you, mothers, will take care that they do not lose it through indecency in dress or self-adornment, through unbecoming familiarities or immoral spectacles: on the contrary you will seek to make it more delicate and alert, more upright and sincere. You will keep a watchful eye on their steps, you will not suffer the whiteness of their souls to be stained and contaminated by corrupt and corrupting company, advising them to commend themselves to the sure and motherly protection of the Immaculate Virgin.[15]

In the game of love and lust, it was the task of single women to remain chaste and virginal, and certainly not to become pregnant. It was the task of mothers to make sure that they instilled a sense of modesty in their daughters and that they did not lose it. Boys and girls, then, needed to be kept in check through rigorous supervision, the most successful form of which was self-monitoring and self-discipline. However, the only real security was within the public eye. Consequently, if boys found themselves alone in the dangerous company of girls, they were encouraged to find an excuse to leave as soon as they could. In other words, supervision and control were most successful when they moved from external constraints, and the need for direct supervision by parents, teachers and religious, to internalised self-restraint where boys and girls practised modesty and purity.[16]

Nevertheless, there was a strain of thought within Catholic theology which held that any contact whatsoever between girls and boys was problematical. This had its origins in the moral theology of Alphonsus Liguori. He believed that, as a rule, friendship between a boy and girl was dangerous.

I think that as a rule it is difficult for them to remain outside the pale of a proximate occasion of mortal sin. Experience proves this statement, for out of a hundred young people, hardly two or three will be found who are free from mortal sin in these circumstances, if not in the beginning, at least later on as the friendship develops.[17]

The only justification for girls and boys 'keeping company' or courting was when there was a specific intention to marry. If there was no intention of marrying, then keeping company with a member of the opposite sex was a mortal sin. Even when there was a specific intention of marrying, it was recommended that courting couples should not be left on their own. Moral theologians specified very clearly what was, and was not, permissible between courting and engaged couples. For engaged couples, 'brief and modest kisses are proper'. However, 'long and lone conversations in secluded spots, are wrong'.[18] It was the duty of the confessor to root out the practices of these couples and the intentions behind them.

When young men or young women accuse themselves of external sins against purity with the other sex, they should be asked if they are encouraging any familiarity. If they admit that they are, they should be questioned further as to the prospects of marriage. If there are no such prospects, and *a fortiori*, if there is no intention of marriage, the confessor must insist absolutely (*omnino exigendum est*) that the intimacy be broken off; because the young people are, with a sufficient cause, in the occasion of sinning mortally.

If the intention and prospect of marriage are present, but only remotely (after the father's death, when employment or a home is secured), one must further enquire whether the real occasion of sin is the intimacy itself, or some other circumstances of the case (e.g. not taking the matter seriously (*inconsiderato*), indulging in intoxicating drink), so that sins are occasioned, not so much by meeting, as *per accidens*, by those circumstances.[19]

As in all matters to do with Catholic moral teaching, there is a question of the extent to which the formal proscriptions of the Church were embodied in the practices of the laity. Writing in the 1930s, at the height of the drive against modern courtship practices, Fr MacGuaire felt that the Church's teachings were being regularly and openly defied. The extent of compliance or defiance of Church teaching is a matter of historical investigation. However, for a long time it had been in the economic as well as the religious and social interests of parents to secure their children's compliance with Church teaching.

The historical context

The regulation of dating, and the prohibition of any form of sensuality, could be seen as essential ingredients in the formation of a moral, civilised society. The regulation of sex and desire was also central to the maintenance of the institutions of marriage and the family. The strict regulation of dating, dances and all contact between the sexes had been essential in the social system which prevailed in Ireland throughout the nineteenth and much of the twentieth century. In this system, which was crucial to maintaining a decent standard of living, sex was confined to marriage, and marriage was generally confined to one 'inheriting' son and one 'dowried' daughter. Other sons and daughters had to be persuaded against, or prevented from, getting involved in relationships, especially when they had not been identified as 'the marrying kind'. And even those who were deemed to be eligible to marry often had to postpone their marriage for many years.

The Catholic Church provided the religious moral discourse which enabled parents and families to institute practices which were essential to confining sex to marriage and, in particular, to ensuring that unwanted pregnancies did not necessitate unwanted marriages.[20] The success of the strategy was reflected in the low level of births outside marriage. From the middle of the nineteenth century to the middle of the twentieth century these were generally less than three per cent of all births.[21]

In the late nineteenth and early twentieth centuries, as postponed marriage and permanent celibacy became a dominant feature of Irish social life, the impact of sexual disciplinary practices began to be debated. In 1905, the liberal Unionist Sir Horace Plunkett claimed that there was excessive chastity and segregation of the sexes, and that this was presided over by priests.[22] This brought an immediate lengthy response from Michael O'Riordan, Rector of the Irish College in Rome. He did not deny that priests exercised close supervision and control of dances. However, he argued that this was not because of dancing *per se*, but because of the evils associated with it.[23] Nevertheless, bitter attacks on priests, and the depiction of them being the sexual moral policemen of Ireland, continued:

The bare thought of company-keeping or courtship filled them [priests] with horror. After several changes, theologians had fixed the number of Deadly Sins as seven; Irish parish priests in practice made courtship an eighth. For lovers to walk the roadside in rural Ireland when the average priest was abroad was a perilous adventure. He challenged engaged couples, on occasions he challenged married couples.[24]

What is interesting is how this public debate about sexuality in the public sphere was so short-lived. By the foundation of the Irish Free State in the 1920s, the field of sexuality and debate and discussion of sex had been monopolised by the Catholic Church. Sex became confined to the religious teachings of the Church, except when it was discussed within the realms of biology and medicine. The monopoly of the discourse on sexuality was cemented with the Censorship of Films Act (1923) and the Censorship of Publications Act (1929). There was particular concern at the time about contraception and so the 1929 Act made it illegal to publish any material which advocated the use of contraceptives. Six years later another Act made it illegal to import or sell contraceptives. The state and the main political parties were happy to form an alliance with the Catholic Church which cemented their monopoly over sexual morality. It was like a happy marriage – each partner had a distinct role to play, but by and large each supported the other. For example, the Catholic bishops, having failed through their preaching to prevent Catholics from attending 'evil' dance-halls, managed to persuade the government to bring in a Public Dance Hall Act in 1933.[25]

The segregation of the sexes became embodied in social practices in the home, schools, churches, pubs and dance-halls. Boys and girls, men and women, remained physically distant from one another. Catholic writers described courtship as 'an occasion of mortal sin' and dance-halls as a 'moral and national menace'.[26] It was difficult for men and women to meet and communicate – let alone to have a sexual relationship – apart from under the supervisory gaze of parents, priests, neighbours and friends. Courting couples were often forced to resort to the cold comfort of fields. Irish history is replete with mythical tales of teachers, nuns and brothers supervising dances, and of priests beating the hedge-rows late at night to drive out hidden lovers. It was not until the car arrived that a certain amount of warmth and privacy could be guaranteed.

The legacy of repressed sexuality

Whatever the prevalence of these practices, foreign observers of Irish society were agreed about the outcome. From his anthropological study of an island off the West coast in the 1960s, John Messenger was able to conclude that 'probably the most prominent trait of Inis Beag (and Irish) personality is sexual puritanism'.[27] He believed that sexual fantasy and repression were rampant and that in terms of sexual knowledge Inis Beag was 'one of the most sexually naïve of the world's societies'.[28] A few years later, Hugh Brody undertook a study of a different community in the West of Ireland. He did not paint such a bleak picture of repression as Messenger. Sexuality, he claimed, tended to be covert. But he concluded that 'sexual relationships – from small flirtations to copulation – were rare indeed among the younger parishioners'.[29] Moreover,

the young people who anticipate emigration have transferred any expectation of sexual gratification – in or outside marriage – from home and countryside to cities far away from home. Equally, those who have decided to stay at home do so in the full realization that the decision almost certainly entails a life of chastity.[30]

In her study of another community in the West of Ireland in the 1970s, Scheper-Hughes argued that people's strong preoccupation with sexual purity was associated with obsessive concern about bodily functions and rigid vigilance over bodily boundaries.[31] She did not refer to the sexual repression of the Irish, but rather to their emotional distance and sexual 'flatness'. The Irish, she claimed, were often shy, withdrawn and uneasy in the company of others. Mothers were excessively preoccupied with controlling their children's sexual behaviour. This corresponds with Stivers's interpretation: 'A puritanical sexual code is upheld by the mother in the Irish family: in fact, sin in general comes close to being equated with sexual sin in particular.'[32] In their pioneering study, *Family and Community in Ireland*, Arensberg and Kimball devoted a chapter to the family and sex. They noted that it was only among married men and women that 'any kind of sexual interest, officially at least, was permitted or even deemed to exist'. Nevertheless, they reported regular laughter and guffaws at various everyday sexual references. They concluded that the earthiness and ribaldry of the people was not an antithesis to their strict moral code. Rather it reinforced it. 'It gives', they claimed, 'its pietistic and too-respectable, churchly and town-bourgeois aspects an authentic, indigenous touch.'[33] In his study of Dubliners in the 1960s, Humphreys linked the prevailing ascetic sexual morality to the 'intensified reliance upon the teaching power of the Church as voiced by the clergy'.[34] The attitude of the Irish countryman to sex was not, he claimed, so different from those living in Dublin. 'He inclines to a jaundiced view of sex and a generally ascetic outlook which places a high premium upon continence, penance and, in most spheres of life, on abstemiousness.'[35] He concluded that Dubliners were frequently ignorant and ill-at-ease about sex. 'Though more open than the countryman on the subject of sex, they too feel that sex is somehow evil and suspect.'[36]

The results of the repression of sexual interests among Irish people have yet to be properly described and analysed. Foster has linked the agrarian outrages carried out in the second half of the nineteenth century with the existence of large numbers of sexually frustrated bachelors.[37] Murphy has argued that if you have a society where celibacy is the norm and where, at the same time, there is a powerful priest caste, then not only will there be an absence of sexual stimuli, but sex itself recedes into the background. In this situation, Murphy claims, other compensations and sublimations for this biologically abnormal situation develop – like nationalism and religion.[38] The suppression of sexual interests among men was primarily achieved through drinking, particularly within bachelor drinking groups.[39] These groups became the primary force segregating the sexes. The ritual sublimation of desire through drinking was also a means of males bonding and developing and maintaining their emotional independence from women, even in marriage. As in many other societies, the pub became a sanctuary for men, a place where they could displace their sexual frustration through a repetitive, compulsive pattern of drinking.

In other words, the primary mechanism through which sexuality was controlled in Irish society was, on the one hand, a segregation of the sexes and, on the other – if and when males and females did meet – an inculcation of the virtues of chastity, modesty and temperance. These virtues came to be associated with shyness, awkwardness and embarrassment with members of the opposite sex. Those men and women who did have the courage to demonstrate love and affection in public had to learn to put up with the inevitable teasing, behind-the-back comments and snide remarks which followed.

In the supposed cycle of events after the Famine, the segregation of the sexes led to the control of sex. The control of sex helped the control of marriage. The control of marriage helped the control of population and, finally, the control of population help improved the overall standard of living. For the 120 years after the Famine, low rates of marriage became the established pattern. From 1871–1971, the population declined by almost one million from 3.9 to 3 million. The marriage rate remained under 5.0 per 1000 population until the turn of this century and then grew slowly to over 7.0 in 1971.[40]

The strategy of increasing the standard of living through controlling population growth was thus based on restricting the numbers of sons and daughters who could get married. The success of the tactics used – the segregation of the sexes, the inculcation of chastity and modesty and so forth – is reflected in the demographic characteristics of the Irish population.

The practice of not marrying reached a peak in the first half of the twentieth century. The number of bachelors and spinsters in Ireland was one of the highest in the Western world. In 1937, almost a quarter(24 per cent) of women and three in ten(29 per cent) of men aged 45 years or more had never married. It was not that Ireland was completely different from some other Western countries – for example Iceland, Finland and Sweden – it was rather that it was more extreme. Where Ireland was different was that in the 1930s, the number of bachelors was higher than the number of spinsters. This was opposite to the trend in most other Western societies where the number of spinsters was greater than the number of bachelors. The other inter-esting feature is that, in comparison with other countries, the number of spinsters and particularly bachelors in Ireland remained high through to the late 1980s. In 1987, the proportion (22 per cent) of males aged 45 years who had never married was two and a half times more than it was in Italy, Spain and France. The question has also to be asked whether, in comparison with Irish bachelors, bachelors from these countries could be accurately described as permanently celibate. Finally, it is important to note that the level of bachelors and spinsters was

Table 3. Permanent Celibacy in Selected Countries
1930s, 1960s and 1980s.

| | Percentage Single Persons Aged 45 Years and Over | | | | | |
| | *Females* | | | *Males* | | |
Country and Exact Years	(19)30s	60s	80s	(19)30s	60s	80s
Northern Ireland (1936,1966,1981)	25	21	16	22	18	15
Ireland (1937,1966,1985)	24	23	17	29	28	22
Iceland (1940,1966,1984)	24	20	13	17	20	15
Finland (1930,1965,1985)	21	16	14	22	9	11
Sweden (1930,1965,1985)	21	15	9	14	14	12
Scotland (1931,1966,1985)	21	18	12	15	12	9
Norway (1930,1960,1984)	20	18	8	12	13	11
Switzerland (1930,1960,1986)	18	17	12	13	12	8
Austria (1934,1967,1982)	16	13	11	11	7	7
England,Wales (1931,1966,1985)	16	12	8	10	8	8
Belgium (1930,1961,1981)	14	10	8	11	8	8
Netherlands (1930,1967,1985)	14	11	7	10	7	9
Italy (1936,1966,1981)	12	13	11	9	8	8
Spain (1940,1960,1981)	12	14	12	8	7	8
France (1936,1967,1985)	10	10	8	8	8	9
USA (1930,1967,1985)	9	6	4	10	4	6

Sources: Kennedy, R. *The Irish*, Table 49, p. 142: United Nations, *Demographic Yearbook, 1960*, Table 10; 1968, Table 7; 1987, Table 29.

high both in the Republic and in Northern Ireland, and that it was low in Italy, Spain and France. This suggests that the high incidence of bachelors and spinsters was not so much due directly to moral dominance of the Catholic Church and an established norm of celibacy, but rather to the Church providing the necessary means of attaining preferred ends – increased standards of living along with large family sizes.

In most families those sons and daughters who were not selected for marriage had a choice of remaining sexually inactive, or emigrating. They could remain on the farm, or at home, as single and celibate, or they could emigrate. In the 120 years from 1841 Ireland had the highest rate of emigration in Western Europe. Even those destined to marry had often to wait well into their thirties before they could get married. There had been a steady rise in the practice of late or postponed marriage from the middle of the nineteenth century. By 1936, it had reached a peak. At that stage, three-quarters of the men and over half of the women aged 25–34 years were still single. In 1936, the number of single men in Ireland was over four times higher than in France. However, within the next fifty years this gap almost completely closed. For example, while the proportion of single men in Ireland in 1936 was 20 per cent higher than in the other countries listed in table 4, by the 1980s there were seven other countries with more single men. Indeed Sweden with 63 per cent of single men in the 25–34 age group, was 28 per cent higher than Ireland. In other words, there was a considerable shift in the pattern of marriage in Western society in the latter half of the twentieth century. What must be asked again, however, is what proportion of the single men and women in these countries can be said, or would describe themselves, as postponing marriage? More importantly, in terms of a traditional perspective on sexuality, what proportion are not in long-term relationships and not engaging in sexual activity?

It is also important to remember that the imposition of restrictions and constraints on marriage was not something imposed unwillingly on the Irish by the Catholic Church. The curtailment of sexual and erotic interests through the postponement or avoidance of marriage was the primary means of fulfilling their interests in improving the standard of living. The Catholic Church provided the strong moral code which enabled people to segregate the sexes socially and to prevent romantic, emotional entanglements. This was central to the Catholic Church developing a monopoly over morality in general and sexual morality in particular. The teachings of the Church, their enforcement within families, schools and churches, their inculcation within individuals through a series of strategies based on creating shame, embarrassment, guilt and awkwardness about sex, had a lasting legacy which only began to dissolve in the 1980s.

What happened in Ireland was that the whole field of sexuality was constructed and dominated by the Catholic Church through the last two centuries. Talk about sexuality (as opposed to sex which was the jurisdiction of the medical profession) was generally confined to the

Table 4. Postponed Marriage in Selected Countries
1930s, 1960s and 1980s.

| | Percentage Single Among Persons Aged 25–34 Years | | | | | |
| | *Females* | | | *Males* | | |
Country and Exact Years	(19)30s	60s	80s	(19)30s	60s	80s
Ireland (1936,1966,1985)	55	31	22	74	50	35
Northern Ireland (1937,1966,1981)	47	20	16	55	29	26
Finland (1930,1965,1985)	44	19	30	50	28	44
Sweden (1930,1958,1985)	43	16	47	54	30	63
Norway (1930,1958,1986)	43	15	25	51	32	42
Scotland (1931,1966,1985)	41	13	23	44	21	32
Austria (1934,1967,1982)	41	19	22	53	30	36
Iceland (1940,1966,1984)	40	14	28	55	26	40
Switzerland (1930,1960,1986)	39	23	30	46	35	44
Spain (1940,1960,1981)	35	28	17	46	35	27
England, Wales (1931,1966,1985)	33	12	19	35	21	31
Italy (1936,1966,1981)	32	21	17	41	38	32
Netherlands(1930,1967,1985)	30	12	23	36	22	37
Belgium (1930,1967,1985)	22	12	12	29	20	20
USA (1930,1967,1985)	18	7	20	29	14	30
France (1936,1967,1985)	15	14	21	17	27	31

Sources: Kennedy, R. *The* Irish, Table 48, p.141; United Nations, *Demographic Yearbook, 1960*, Table 10; 1968, Table 7; 1987, Table 29.

language of the Church and specifically – in terms of when, where and how sexuality was talked about – to the confessional. It was within confession that the announcement of desire, the examination of passion, and the depiction of pleasures of the flesh, were permitted. Priests became the experts with sole jurisdiction in this area. Beyond the confessional there was a silence. This silence was imposed in homes, schools, the media and other institutions. It was this silence which created and maintained the practices of postponed marriage and permanent celibacy.

In the supposed cycle of things, the restriction of marriage was deemed to be the linchpin in the strategy of controlling population, thereby increasing the standard of living. Given that a comparatively high proportion of people did not marry, and that those who did marry married later in life, then it might be supposed that fewer children would have been born and there would have been a natural decrease in the population. This, in the next generation, would have meant less pressure to postpone marriage, not to marry at all, or to emigrate. However, this was not to be the case. The hitch in the supposed cycle of events was that even though the numbers who married in Ireland were smaller, and even though they married later than most, those who did marry literally out-bred their counterparts in other countries who married earlier and in greater numbers (see table 5).

What is remarkable about the level of marital fertility in Ireland in the 1960s was that at 195.5 it was 40 points higher than its nearest rival New Zealand(154.6). Even a traditionally Catholic country like Spain(142.1) was more than 50 points behind. Over the next twenty years, even though the level of marital fertility in Ireland fell by 65 points, it still remained well in advance of other countries, since many of them also experienced sharp declines.

There is evidence of successful attempts at birth spacing and stopping, but this tended to be confined to the middle classes, those living in urban areas and those living in religiously heterogeneous areas.[41] Even as late as the 1970s, when artificial contraceptives became legally available, birth control within marriage was still a major problem. Successful attempts tended to take place towards the end of the woman's fertile years. Yet evidence indicates that these attempts were not discussed between husbands and wives.[42] The persistence of high levels of marital fertility could be linked to the desire to have large families. But this desire cannot be separated from the strong pro-natal, anti-contraceptive teachings of the Catholic Church. Nor can it be separated from the persisting ignorance about the facts of life, and an inability of husbands and wives to communicate their fears, needs and desires and, consequently, to negotiate when and how they wanted to have sex.

Table 5. Marital Fertility Rate 1960–64 and 1978–85
in Selected Countries

Country and Exact Year of Marital Fertility Rate	Number of Legimate Births per 1,000 Married Women Aged 19–49 Years	
	1960s	*1980s*
Ireland, 1961,1984	195.5	130.6
New Zealand 1961,1981	154.6	82.5
Portugal 1960,1981	148.9	86.6
Spain 1960,1978	142.1	113.1
Netherlands 1963,1985	138.4	74.2
United States 1960,1984	132.7	72.8
Australia 1961,1981	131.9	88.5
Poland 1960,1984	130.1	105.6
Scotland 1964,1985	124.5	74.0
Finland 1963,1985	119.8	77.3
France 1963,1985	118.5	78.2
Switzerland 1960,1983	117.2	76.0
Austria 1961,1982	116.4	70.8
Norway 1960,1984	109.8	70.0
England & Wales, 1964,1985	108.3	73.7
Belgium 1961,1981	106.3	74.2
Denmark 1963,1985	103.2	47.3
Sweden 1963,1985	86.9	59.9

Sources: United Nations, *Demographic Yearbook*, 1964, Table 16, pp. 530–535;
1986, Table 34, pp. 875–877.

Ending the silence on sex

The Catholic Church dominated the field of Irish sexuality well into
the second half of the twentieth century. In public life and the media,
sexuality tended not to be discussed. Anything said or written was
within the ethos and language of the Catholic Church. If sexuality was
mentioned, it was referred to discreetly and obliquely. It was a delicate,
sensitive issue. To talk about it directly could weaken and destroy innocent
minds and souls. The Church was the authority on sexuality. Sex was

a viper which operated in society. Lust and passion led to occasions of sin during which people could become possessed with evil desires. Sex was the problematic side of love. Chastity, modesty and purity were the natural allies of love. Sex was something which could enhance married love, but could destroy it, like it could other relationships. Outside marriage it was best kept at bay through the diligent institution of forms of external control and internal self-restraint. Sex was seen as a potential threat not just to the health, welfare and sanity of the individual, but to social order as a whole. The media changed all of this.

In 1962, shortly after the foundation of RTÉ, an incident took place on the *Late Late Show* which became known as 'The Bishop and the Nightie' incident, and became a landmark in the history of Irish television. As part of the programme, husbands and wives in the audience were asked what they knew about each other. One woman was asked what colour nightie she had worn on her wedding night, and when she said she could not recall and that perhaps she had not worn any, there was laughter and a round of applause from the audience. Bishop Tom Ryan had been watching the programme and was infuriated by this. He sent a telegram to RTÉ saying he was disgusted and gave a sermon on the episode and the show the following day. The newspapers on the Sunday covered the incident in full and it became a major issue of public debate, particularly in the media. There are many reasons why the incident attained mythical status. It was, as Kenny argues, an announcement that honeymoon nights were not just about bridal bouquets and perfumed lingeries, but fundamentally about something more primitive – sex. What could not be countenanced in thought, word or deed had been announced. The bishop in his protest could not even announce it and said 'Everybody will know what I am referring to'. As much as the woman's spontaneous public expression about herself and her pleasure matched a new era in Irish social life, so too did the spontaneous disgust of the bishop at the reference to sex match the old era. A woman had confessed her sexual secrets to a man. But the host, Gay Byrne, was no priest and the television was no dark confessional.[43]

As sex began to seep into Irish public life, the nature of the perspective in sex instructional material began to change quite dramatically – even within the Catholic Church. In a traditional Catholic perspective, the primary mechanism of social control was the confessional in which penitents were subjected to close examination of their sexual morality.

This was combined with a strict censorship and surveillance of sex in the family and community. As long as sexuality could be confined to the confessional and the marital bedroom where nature would take its course, there was little or no need for sex education. In his *M is for Marriage*, Fr Daniel Lord gives detailed instructions to husbands and wives about how they should relate and communicate with each other: how to talk, develop interests, share worries and concerns, and how to be charming and good mannered to each other. He encourages husbands to buy their wives a meal out, to compliment her on her cooking, admire her new hat or hair-do, and to buy her an occasional present. The suggestion seems to be that a good marriage is founded not so much on good communication, but on fulfilling traditional, almost magical, formulae. There is no mention of sex, as if it was not a mutual pleasure, worry or concern.[44] Many of the Catholic Truth Society's pamphlets were originally American publications. Before being printed here, they had to be given the imprimatur of an Irish bishop. The pamphlets often contained material about dating and marriage practices which reflected American more than Irish society – particularly *rural* Irish society – in the 1950s and 1960s. Fr John Gorey's pamphlet *May I Keep Company?*, like many of its successors, is in the form of dialogue between a priest and a courting couple. They are warned to avoid moonlight strolls, secret meetings and anywhere that they are likely to cast off restraint. 'It is possible', they are told, 'to have a very private *tête-à-tête* while all the time remaining in the public eye.' The pamphlet was an attempt to counteract the pernicious messages emerging within the media, particularly the way courting couples were portrayed. 'The cinema and the sex novel of today', the priest says, 'insinuate into a boy's mind that the natural thing for him is to have girl-friends. They propose as the natural relaxation and recreation for a boy, sentimental flirtations with all their usual accompaniment of sensuous fondlings and passionate love-making.'[45]

This advice was repeated in a pamphlet by Fr Daniel Lord on *What to do on a Date* published in Ireland in 1962, again as a reprint of an earlier American edition.[46] There was a shift in balance from external towards internalised self-restraint. Lord accepted that the couple were now allowed to be left on their own. But in order to avoid occasions of sin, they were encouraged to engage in a number of healthy activities such as hiking, visiting art museums, churches, and so forth.

In 1964, in a *Catholic Truth Society of Ireland* publication, Francis Filas called for proper sex education which he saw as the responsibility of parents. He called for the use of 'refined, technical language', but did not give any specific advice as to how instruction might be given.[47] Four years later, Gill & Son published, with the Diocesan Censor's approval, a reprint of Mary and John Ryan's *Love and Sexuality*. This was another American publication which warned against instilling shame and guilt about the body in children, especially during toilet training. It also called for the proper scientific names to be given to genital organs, again without actually naming them in the text itself.[48]

In 1979, a handbook for sex education was published which gave explicit details on all matters of sex. It used scientific language such as vagina, uterus, penis, and so forth to describe the sexual organs. It also gave a vivid description of how the male sperm cells get inside the mother's body.[49] However, this book was published in Ireland by a secular publisher without an imprimatur for the Archbishop of Dublin and was a reprint of a German publication. It was not until 1981 that a Catholic handbook, *Education in Sexuality* was published which made explicit references to sexual organs such as the penis, vagina, ovaries, and to sexual intercourse.[50]

The first two chapters of the *Education in Sexuality* pamphlet concerned the theology and principles of sexuality and sex education. The suggested format was that pupils were introduced to the biological differences between boys and girls, and the contribution of males and females in the creation of life. The creative process was described as emerging from a loving relationship between a man and a woman which develops into marriage. It pointed out that parenthood is a major responsibility and that while natural methods of family planning were acceptable, artificial methods were morally unacceptable. It discussed masturbation, pornography and homosexuality, but only in terms of them being sexually deviant.[51] The pamphlet is presented as a definitive statement concerning the nature of sex and sexuality. There are facts to be learnt. There is little or no encouragement for debate and discussion. There is no expectation of any input or questions from the pupils.

In 1981 the Catholic Archdiocese of Dublin issued its programme, *Education in Sexuality,* for use in secondary schools. The programme emphasised that the main responsibility for sex education belonged to parents, and that the function of the school was to support them in this task. This approach was followed by the rest of the Irish hierarchy in 1985 in their Pastoral letter *Love is for Life*.[52]

Formal teaching of the Catholic Church

The overall position and policy of the Catholic Church regarding relationships and sexuality education is best identified in the Pontifical Council for the Family's *The Truth and Meaning of Human Sexuality: Guidelines for Education within the Family*. The aim of the Council in producing the guidelines is to overcome the 'materialistic hedonism', and the 'depersonalized, recreational and pessimistic information' produced about sexuality in society, particularly within the mass media. This, the Council argues, is where the family plays a crucial role, since the type of programmes run in schools, based on agnostic, positivist theories which have a utilitarian view of people, can 'lead to the deformation of consciences'. Sex education is, then, not just a basic right, but the duty of parents. It must always be carried out, whether in the home, or at school, under their guidance and control.[53]

Sexuality, the Council argues, has to be understood not in terms of concupiscence – the satisfying of one's appetites – but in relation to the type of self-giving which characterises true human love. It is love between husband and wife that elevates sexuality above animality to a truly human quality.[54] Chastity is seen as central to sexuality. It is only through chastity, it argues, that sexuality can be successfully integrated within the person. It is chastity which enables sexuality to be based on love and self-giving and frees it from self-centred slavery. Consequently, Pope John Paul II announced that 'married people are called to live in conjugal chastity; while others practise chastity in continence'. The duty of parents is to instil decency and modesty in their children. In this regard, they should be watchful that certain immoral fashions and attitudes, propagated through misuse of the media, do not violate the integrity of the home.[55]

The Council indicates that there are four main principles regarding information about sexuality. The first is that each child is unique and must receive individualised formation. This effectively means the child's parents, preferably mothers with their daughters, and fathers with their sons, fulfil the role of educators. The only role envisaged for the school or teacher is in the case of single parent families when, for example, the father wishes a female teacher to instruct his daughter. The second principle is that the moral dimension must always be part of the parents' explanations. Third, formation in chastity and timely information regarding sexuality must be provided in the broadest context of education for love. Finally, parents should provide this information with great delicacy, but clearly and at the appropriate time.[56]

Perhaps the most crucial part of the Council's guidelines is the section detailing the type of education appropriate for each stage of the child's development. The first stage – from about five years to puberty – is the years of innocence. Children normally have no interest in sexuality and the tranquillity and serenity of this period 'must never be disturbed by unnecessary information about sex'. The Council warns against planned and determined attempts to impose premature sex information on children. Where children have been led astray by their peers or the mass media, it may be necessary for parents to give limited sexual information to correct immoral and erroneous information.

During puberty, the Council argues, parents are bound to give more detailed explanations about sexuality. 'Therefore, normally, one should discuss the cycles of fertility and their meaning. But it is still not necessary to give detailed explanations about sexual union, unless this is explicitly requested.' In answering children's questions, parents are told to offer well-reasoned arguments about the great value of chastity. Particular attention should be given to counteracting the tendency in consumer society to trivialise sex, and to reduce it to a consumer object. In this regard, parents should teach their children the value of modesty.

Instruction for both girls and boys should aim at pointing out the beauty of motherhood and the wonderful reality of procreation, as well as the deep meaning of virginity. In this way they will be helped to go against the hedonistic mentality which is very widespread today and particularly, at such a decisive stage, in preventing the '*contraceptive mentality*', which unfortunately is very common and which girls will have to face later in marriage.[57]

The Council insists that the first and most important task of parents of adolescents is to help them discern their personal vocation in life whether for the priesthood and religious life, or as a married or celibate person. Since sexual problems become more evident at this time, parents should help their children 'to love the beauty and strength of chastity through prudent advice, highlighting the inestimable value of prayer and frequent fruitful recourse to the sacraments for a chaste life, especially personal confession.' It is important that adolescents learn that the unitive and procreative functions of married love cannot be separated. In particular, the Council argues, it must be emphasised that masturbation 'constitutes a very serious disorder that is illicit in itself . . .'. Similarly, while adolescents should learn to accept homosexual persons with respect, compassion and sensitivity, it is crucial to remember that as Christians, 'homosexual persons are called to chastity'.[58]

The final stage is when young people move towards adulthood and the world of higher education and work. The Council indicates that while there is nothing specific to learn about sex during this phase – unless they are preparing for marriage which is a different issue and beyond its remit – it is important for parents to keep an open dialogue with their children.

While it is stressed that the sex educational needs of no two children will be the same, there are some issues which the Council deems inappropriate at certain stages. For example, while it is appropriate to explain the immoral nature of abortion to children before adolescence, it is not appropriate to discuss issues such as sterilisation and contraception. Even then, they should only be discussed, like abortion, 'in conformity with the teaching of the Catholic Church'.[59]

The Council concludes with some practical guidelines for parents. It recommends that parents attentively follow every form of sex education that is given to their children outside the home, and to remove them if this education does not correspond with their own principles.

Another abuse occurs whenever *sex education* is given to children by teaching them all the intimate details of genital relationships, even in a graphic way. Today this is often motivated by wanting to provide education for 'safe sex', above all in relation to the spread of AIDS. In this situation, parents must also reject the promotion of so-called 'safe sex' or 'safer sex', a dangerous and immoral policy based on a deluded theory that the condom can provide adequate protection against AIDS. Parents must insist on continence outside marriage and fidelity in marriage as the only true and secure education for the prevention of this contagious disease.[60]

Contemporary Catholic approaches

Since 1995, many Catholic dioceses have sent schools a booklet produced by St Brigid's National School in Greystones, Co. Wicklow.[61] This was written by the staff with the help of Angela MacNamara – one of the most senior and well-known figures in relationships and sexuality education. It was written with the co-operation of the Archbishop of Dublin's Education Secretariat. The booklet is designed for use in primary schools, and has been recommended by some bishops as the primary resource material to be used to teach the RSE programme. It concentrates on helping pupils to develop an understanding of themselves and to place this within the context of their family life and their relationships with others. The programme aims to develop children's understanding of themselves by helping them to appreciate their Catholic religion and the community, society and environment in which they live. The pedagogical strategy is based on giving pupils the appropriate language and terms to enable them to name, read and understand the world of relationships and sexuality in which they live. The booklet has a quote from the Irish Catholic Bishops' pastoral letter *Love is for Life* (1985) on the cover:

No young person should leave school without proper preparation for integrating his or her sexuality with Christian Faith and morality, with love, with respect for others and a sense of responsibility for other's welfare.

The aims of the programme are: to nurture Catholic values of love, marriage, parenthood and family life; to aid the development of Christian attitudes towards sex; to develop skills necessary to assess and cope with sexual stimuli in advertisements and the media; and to help children make appropriate decisions on sexual matters. Children's sexual understanding of themselves is not introduced until third class. The emphasis is on the naming of parts, with no mention of their function. In fourth class, it is suggested that the womb be described as the home for the baby during the nine months' gestation. The booklet recommends that if at this stage – about nine to ten years of age – an explanation of intercourse is sought it should be described in terms of 'the Daddy puts the seed in'.[62] In fifth and sixth class, it is suggested that intercourse is explained in more depth.

When a man and a woman love each other very much they sometimes hold one another very close. In making love, semen which carries seed is passed from the man into the woman. When the seed enters an egg in the woman's body a baby is conceived. God made the sexual act pleasurable and good. As a result of their love for one another the couple bring new life into the world.[63]

The pedagogical strategy of this programme is based on protecting innocence through not mentioning or discussing aspects of human sex and sexuality which may disturb the children. If anything is mentioned it is done obliquely and is couched within Catholic language and Church teaching. The children are introduced into an ethical system of care and understanding of the self in which sexual understanding is a small aspect. Little attention is given to the pupils' existing knowledge and understanding and the way they have learnt to read and understand their world. The implication is that what they have already learnt or understood is either incorrect or inadequate. There is no mention of encouraging children to discuss what they have learnt from the media or elsewhere. There is no attempt to discover what the children themselves would like to learn about sex. In her study of 13 schools in the mid-west area of Ireland in 1995, Walsh recorded 1,164 questions posed by 10–12 year olds. The majority of these had to do with menstruation, sexual intercourse and a wide variety of sexual activities including wet-dreams, masturbation, erections, kissing, dating and relationships with the opposite sex.[64]

But it is important to remember that within the specifically Catholic approach to sex education there are many different attitudes and approaches. For example, the language and approach of the Quinns' *How to talk to your child about sex,* which received an imprimatur from the Archbishop of Dublin in 1981, was far more direct. For example, sexual intercourse is explained as follows:

We also show our love when we hug and kiss and cuddle each other. (Do you like to see us doing that? What do you like to see us doing?). When this happens in bed we hold each other very close and Daddy places his penis in my vagina very close to my womb. In that way he gives part of himself (his seed or sperm) to me. Once a month I have an egg waiting in my womb and when Daddy's seed meets the egg, a new life starts. That's how you were made – God and Daddy and Mummy all working together to make a baby. Aren't you special![65]

As with many other teachings and recommendations of the Church, it would be wrong to think that Catholic parents, or indeed bishops, priests, nuns and brothers, adhere to the Pontifical Council's directions. Indeed there are many examples of educators who work from within a Catholic ethos, and who speak progressively about sexuality. Angela MacNamara, who helped write the St Brigid's booklet mentioned above, has produced her own sexuality education programme for primary schools. She recommends an early start to sexuality education and that children between first and third classes be given a simple, straight-forward description of sexual intercourse and conception. It is important, she argues, that children be given the freedom to ask whatever questions they want – about masturbation, sex before marriage, condoms, abortion, and that these are dealt with in an open and honest manner.[66] Carmel Coyle carried out a detailed evaluation of a wide range of programmes, books and audio-visual materials which are available as teaching resources to teaching Relationships and Sexuality Education in secondary schools.[67] She recommends Herron and McGinley's *So You Want to Know?* (*About Sex and Growing Up*) which she feels is an 'excellent book for the Irish market'. She notes that the 'advice is very direct' and that it 'pulls no punches'. On the other hand, the book is based on 'strong Christian values'.[68] Since Heron and McGinley deal directly with a controversial topic like masturbation, it is worth noting what they say.

Handling the private parts for pleasure is called *masturbation*. It was once thought that masturbation could be harmful, whether orgasm was achieved or not. This is simply *not* so and sadly many people suffered seriously from worry because of this misunderstanding. Masturbation does not cause physical harm. Many boys and girls and adults masturbate from time to time. This does not affect a person's ability to have a sexual relationship or have children later in life.[69]

There are, then, elements within a Catholic way of writing and talking about sexuality which, instead of corresponding to a traditional perspective, begin to merge gradually with a progressive discourse. In this respect, they come closer to a broadly Protestant perspective. Of course, within the Protestant tradition there are, however, different perspectives which are too numerous to deal with here.

The Church of Ireland perspective

In dealing with the moral and ethical issues in relationships and sexuality education, Canon Kenneth Kearon is anxious to draw attention to how a Church of Ireland perspective on sexuality would differ from other Christian viewpoints – particularly, presumably, that of the Catholic Church.[70] He points out that the *Book of Common Prayer* clearly indicates that sexual activity is an important part of marriage and fulfils three purposes: having children, expressing love, and demonstrating mutual dependence. Within Anglicanism, he argues, it is accepted that the purpose of expressing love can be separated from having children. This means that contraception is permissible. The emphasis on the relational aspect of marriage also suggests, as Kearon recognises, that while sex is best expressed within marriage, it does not necessarily have to be confined to it.[71]

Kearon goes on to point out that within the Church of Ireland there are different views about divorce and homosexuality. Those in favour of divorce point out that 'using the language of relationship in understanding marriage implies acceptance of the fact that in certain situations such a relationship may die, and so divorce, on the grounds of irretrievable breakdown, though always regrettable, has to be accepted as a reality'.[72] When he comes to discussing homosexuality, his views could be seen not just as progressive, but very liberal.

We have seen above that many Christians today believe that the proper context for sexual activity should be within a long-term committed relationship, where the function of sex includes the support and building up of that relationship. If that relationship is a homosexual relationship, why should sexual activity within it be condemned?[73]

Although Kearon does not deal specifically with what would be contained within an Anglican RSE programme, it is evident that the Church of Ireland would encourage debate about what could be taught. Its views are certainly, in comparison with the teaching of the Catholic Church, less absolutist.

Conclusion

In this chapter I have argued that Irish sexuality has been dominated throughout this century by a traditional discourse created and maintained by the Catholic Church. Common knowledge, understanding and communication about sex, as a physical and biological activity, and sexuality – particularly sexual feelings, desires and pleasures – have been confined to an ethos based on the Catholic Church's moral teachings. Sex was seen as a danger, the most significant threat to the health and well-being of the individual and society. It had to be controlled through strategies of modesty and chastity. In this regard, innocence was bliss. The less that was known about sex the better. It was the greatest of all sins, and so to mention, talk or write about, or dwell on it in any way, was to enter an occasion of sin. The strategy of parents, teachers and priests was to instil modesty and purity, innocence and ignorance.

However, even within the Catholic Church, the traditional discourse about sexuality and the traditional approach to teaching children about sexuality, are beginning to recede and fragment. There has been a gradual move, particularly among those involved directly in relationships and sexuality education, towards a more progressive perspective. There are, however, strong residues of a traditional perspective to be found both in the institutional teaching of the Church and in the attitudes and values of many Irish Catholics, particularly those brought up within a traditional perspective. Many of these Catholics are now teachers in primary and secondary schools and, if they are to become involved in teaching RSE, will have to learn to take a more progressive attitude to teaching children about sexuality. There is still a considerable gap between the traditional perspective of the Catholic Church on sexuality and the progressive perspective of the state. This gap is at the centre of many of the contradictions concerning the implementation of relationships and sexuality education in Ireland.

3
Learning to be Independent and Responsible

A progressive view of sexuality education emphasises politics rather than ethics: it emphasises helping children and young people to adapt to the way the world is, rather than teaching them about the way it should be. It focuses on empowering them to operate in the world in which they find themselves. The intention is to enable children and young people to understand themselves, their bodies, feelings, emotions, to reflect critically about their lives, their family and friends, and to learn to adapt and change their personal behaviour to the circumstances in which they find themselves. Although progressive educators incorporate many traditional values, they tend, as Carlson argues, to be 'less condemning and more therapeutic' in their approach to the 'problem' of sexuality.[1] A progressive discourse sees sexuality education more as a question of pragmatics than ethical absolutes. Issues such as premarital sex, masturbation, contraceptives and abortion are phrased less in terms of moral teachings and more in terms of what works in the fight against sexually transmitted diseases, unwanted pregnancies, infanticide and the abandonment of newborn babies. It tends to be based on a secular, rational, pragmatic perspective concerned with finding the best remedies to existing social problems. In other words, the move from a traditional to a progressive discourse in sexuality education represents a move from teaching children and young people the way the world should be and the way they should behave, to teaching them about the way the world is and about being mature, responsible, active participants in that world. It is, in effect, a move from ethical to political education.

In the move from teaching ethics to politics, the organisation and control of relationships and sexuality education gradually began to shift from the Catholic Church to the state. Changes had been taking place in moral attitudes to sexuality since the 1960s, particularly through the media. The state began to accommodate to these changes through, for example, easing the laws on censorship. Further changes took place in the 1970s and 1980s, particularly in relation to contraception. But although the state was gradually moving away from the Church's perception and understanding of sexuality, it was slow to enter the field of sex education. That was because the Church still exerts considerable control in the field of education. In 1993, all but ten of the 3,235 ordinary national schools were denominational schools – 93 per cent of which were under the patronage of the Catholic Church. At second level, the picture is more complicated, with the existence of vocational schools and community colleges, community schools and a number of non-Catholic denominational schools. Since the 1990s, most second level schools are run by boards of management, and so Church influence over and control of schools is no longer clear. In 1982, 85 per cent of the secondary schools were Catholic, but the influence of the Church has declined since then. The rapid fall in the number of priests, nuns and brothers has forced the Church to amalgamate its schools with existing community and vocational schools. But, as Lynch and Drudy point out, even though the Church's direct ownership and control of second level schools is declining, it is still well represented on the boards of management of formally non-Catholic schools.[2] For the state, then, to enter the field of relationships and sexuality education meant an encroachment into two areas – education and sexuality – over which the Church traditionally held a monopoly. The Relationships and Sexuality Education programme represented not just another stage in the separation of Church and state in Ireland, but a diminution of the Church's influence in a wide number of social fields including health, social welfare and education.[3]

The state has always recognised and accepted the right of parents to raise their children in accordance with their own beliefs and values and, according to their religion, the rights of priests and ministers to assist them in this task. However, from the beginning of the 1990s, the state began to insist that it also had rights and obligations to ensure that young people received adequate social, personal and health education to enable them to become responsible citizens. The task of the state, then, centred on trying to develop a programme which, while recognising and incorporating the rights and wishes of the majority – as represented by the Church – tried to respect and accommodate the wishes of minorities.

The problem in Ireland, however, is identifying the majority. One might think that this would be easy given that over nine in ten of the population formally identify themselves as Roman Catholics, and the majority of Catholics send their children to schools owned and run by the Church. The problem faced by the state was that while the majority of Catholics send their children to a Catholic school, there are many who disagree not just with specific Church teachings, but its general approach to sexuality. For example, many Irish Catholics disregard their Church's teaching on contraception and sex outside marriage. But it is not just members of the laity who speak with a different voice about sexuality; so too do representatives of the Church. This turned out to be a major problem for the state in the implementation of the RSE programme.

From the outset of the debate, the Catholic Church said that it was in favour of a programme of sex education being introduced in schools. It indicated that it had certain reservations about when, where and how such a programme might be introduced. Various bishops argued that sex education should be incorporated within existing religion classes. Representatives of the Catholic Church, including the Catholic Primary Schools Managers' Association, took part in the organisation, design and implementation of the RSE programme. However, shortly before the programme was to be introduced in September 1997, Catholic bishops began to distance themselves from it, indicating that the existing materials used in religious education classes in primary schools were adequate resources for dealing with the issues raised in the RSE programme. In other words, as the Church had argued from the outset, RSE should and could be integrated into existing religion classes.[4]

But not only has the state had to respond to the institutional Church and its representatives, it has also had to deal with a number of antagonistic interest groups, mostly representing a traditional Catholic perspective, who have lobbied persistently against RSE. Much of this lobbying, as we shall see in chapter 6, is done at local level, during parent information meetings held in schools. But it also takes place through the media.

The Relationships and Sexuality Education programme is not so much about telling children and young people what they should think, say and do sexually, as enabling them to read, understand and respond responsibly to the sexual world in which they live. The programme is based on each school developing policies, programmes, resources and materials which help children and young people adapt and respond to their sexual interests, needs, concerns and worries. Control of the programme and what children and young people are to be taught about sexuality is left to each school and, in particular, to the parents, teachers and managers who come together to devise the school policy. The policy committee elected for each school decides what topics will be covered in the various classes, and what teaching resource materials will be used. However, much of what is actually taught and the way it is taught is left to the teachers. Devolution of policy control to the school and to the individual teacher may be seen as the Irish state's solution to an Irish Catholic problem. It certainly helped avoid a major clash between Church and state. It was a strategy which had been first used in the Stay Safe programme. To understand the response to the state's RSE programme, it is helpful to describe and analyse what happened to its Stay Safe programme.

The Stay Safe programme

The first real challenge by the state to the veto which the Catholic Church exercised over sexual and moral education came with the Stay Safe programme. The programme emerged as a result of people working in the Eastern Health Board expressing concern about the increased level of child sexual abuse. Confirmed cases of child sexual abuse in the various Health Board Regions had risen from 37 in 1983, to 568 in 1989.[5] An educational programme was devised for use in primary schools. This was tested in the Eastern Health Board area in 1989 as a joint initiative with the Department of Education. It was formally introduced on a nationwide basis in 1991. By the end of 1994, it was operating in about half of the primary schools in the country. One of the reasons for the slow implementation of the programme was the opposition organised at local level by members of lay Catholic groups. They lobbied the local media, newspapers and radio stations, and attended meetings held in schools to discuss implementing the programme. The main thrust of the opposition was that the programme was an unnecessary intrusion of the state into the private life of the family. They argued that the programme was based on a secular humanist philosophy which, among other things, encouraged children to be the final arbiters of what was right and wrong.

The aim of the programme was to teach children personal safety skills, particularly in relation to feeling afraid, getting lost, being bullied, dealing with strangers and inappropriate touches.[6] There was no direct reference to sex or sexuality in the programme. However, it is clear from the *Users' Handbook* that the primary aim of the programme was to reduce the incidence of child sexual abuse. Consequently, while the programme did not refer to sex directly, there were regular references to the body, touches and feelings. In many respects these oblique references to sex correspond with the traditional approach to sexuality education. But despite the attempt to respect the innocence of some children and, at the same time, help them recognise and deal with abuse, the programme was seen to be at variance with Catholic Church teaching.

The most remarkable characteristic of the Stay Safe programme is the way in which it nominates individuals – in this particular case children – as arbiters of what is right and wrong. This raises fundamental issues about the formation and exercise of individual moral responsibility which, of course, has relevance to adherence to Catholic Church teaching. The programme begins by getting children to identify and describe things which make them feel safe. This leads to a discussion about things which make them feel unsafe, uncomfortable or angry. These are identified as 'no feelings'. Children are told that if something happens to them which they don't like, it is a 'no feeling'. A particular 'no feeling' may emerge in relation to someone touching the 'private parts' of their body.

Other parts of your body are private and don't get touched so much, except if you're sick or at the doctor. The parts of your body which are covered by your swimsuit are private and special, and no one has the right to touch you there.[7]

In other words, it is the individual child who has the initial say in who has the right to touch him or her. If they have a 'no feeling', they are told to tell an adult who will tell them whether it is right or wrong. But the hidden message is that there are people – inappropriate people – who may wish to touch their private parts. This not only introduces children to sex and sexuality but, in the absence of other knowledge and information, introduces it as a problem. There are other messages within this text. Certain parts of the body are designated as being special with little or no explanation. They are mysteriously special. More important is that children are told that they have ownership and control of their own bodies and that other people, including their fathers and mothers, do not have a right to touch them unless they want them to. Instilling a sense of ownership and control of their bodies, and encouraging critical reflection about feelings, helps create and develop not just a sense of sexuality, but of individual moral responsibility.

An analysis of the video accompanying the Stay Safe programme reveals some of the key presuppositions which underlie the approach of the programme. These have important consequences for children learning about themselves, society and what is right and wrong. The most revealing aspect of the Stay Safe programme video is not so much what is present, as what is absent. In a video made within a traditional perspective one would have expected to have a recognised figure of authority, for example, a priest, doctor, teacher or parent, telling children what are right and wrong things to do, good and bad thoughts and feelings and, consequently, what is acceptable and unacceptable behaviour. In the original video there is no strong, traditional figure of authority. Instead, the 'person' who facilitates the discussion among the children and gives them advice is a puppet called Pago. In other words, the traditional male, authoritarian figure of the past becomes transformed into a tall, imposing, but cuddly, human-like teddy bear. More important, whatever lesson is to be learnt is seen to emerge not from Pago, but from the children themselves as members of an encounter group discussing the different issues affecting them. The message is that what is good and bad, right and wrong, emerges from an open democratic forum. Knowledge and understanding is achieved through open communication leading to consensus. The children announce their world to themselves through a discussion of their feelings. This is shared and critically reflected upon, and leads to a new collective understanding of their individual experiences. This approach is derived from American humanistic psychology, and is in line with contemporary approaches to learning within many adult education programmes.

In the next sequence of the video, the discussion moves on to 'private parts'. The children are asked to imagine someone coming up and touching their private parts. If it gives them a 'no feeling' they are told to tell the other person to stop, to get away from them and to go and tell someone they trust, for example their teacher, their mummy or daddy. Children are only told what to do when it is a 'no feeling'. It could be argued that what is therefore suggested is that if someone touches their private parts and it produces a 'yes feeling', then it is all right for them to continue. The determination of what is right or wrong moves not just from an authority to be obeyed – that is a representative of the Catholic Church —but to feelings and bodily sensations which are morally assessed through engaging in discussion and critical reflection with one's peers. There is no external, objective, absolute morality. Right or wrong is not defined by parents or teachers. More important perhaps in the context of Irish morality, it is not defined by the Church, whether by priests, bishops, or other interpreters of the Natural Law.

The Stay Safe programme represented the first competitive struggle between the state and the Church in relation to the identification and teaching of what is morally right and wrong when it comes to sex and sexuality. The Catholic Church and priests, for so long the arbiters of sexual morality, are ostensibly written out of the programme and replaced by a process of dialogue and decision-making based on secular humanist philosophy and psychology. Exposure to the programme, Gogan has argued, does not so much help protect children from bullying and abuse, as 'move many of those exposed to it some further steps down the road to a liberal permissive lifestyle.'[8]

This was at the heart of the argument of those who have opposed the Stay Safe programme. Dr William Coulson, an American psychologist, came to Ireland to lend his support to this opposition. He argued that the programme 'gives permission for children to order part of their lives around sexual themes'. He emphasised the existence of the latency period (roughly from the age of five or six years through to puberty) and claimed that it is taboo for adults to talk to children during this stage 'lest the children become corrupted'. Coulson argued that the main problem with the programme is that it leaves out any mention of right and wrong and reduces morality to 'yes' and 'no' feelings. He emphasised that the reason why nobody can touch beneath our swimsuit is not because it gives rise to a 'no feeling', but because it is sinful.[9] The implied message for the learner under the Stay Safe programme is, Coulson argues, that: 'It's my body. I have a right to say who touches me and how . . . I can share it with anyone who gives me a Yes feeling: the sequel, teenage pregnancy and abortion.'[10]

Participation in the Stay Safe programme, unlike the Relationships and Sexuality Education programme, is voluntary. Each primary school decides whether to implement the programme. The decision is made at a meeting of parents, teachers and the Board of Management. However, it is the Board of Management which calls the meeting and this gives it an effective veto since if no meeting is held, no decision can be made about implementation. Once the meeting is called, it is up to the parents and teachers to approve or reject the programme for use in the school.

People working for the Child Abuse Prevention Programme (CAPP) argued that the opposition voiced at these meetings is nationally organised, particularly through a group of parents who formed a group PASS (Parents Against Stay Safe). They claimed that prior to any meeting lobbyists against the programme write letters to the local papers and radio stations, circulate literature to schools, and appeal directly to members of the Board of Management of the school. They argued that lobbyists attending the meetings position themselves strategically around the hall, dominate question time, use misinformation and imply that the Stay Safe programme is part of an international conspiracy.[11] In addition, it was claimed that the manager of every Catholic primary school received a copy of Gogan's booklet.[12] In a response to these criticisms, Gogan argued that Irish parents had been the target of a well-organised public relations campaign through the press, radio and TV which had been devised by specially trained groups of teachers and social workers supporting the Stay Safe programme.[13]

In her study of the Sligo-Leitrim area, Gilmartin found that almost half (47 per cent) of the schools involved had not implemented the programme. Schools were less likely to implement the programme when staff and the Board of Management were not positively disposed to it. This negative disposition, Gilmartin suggests, was linked to the prevailing ethos within the diocese, particularly the attitude of the local bishop. It was also linked to a general lack of interest in child abuse. For example, 47 per cent of school principals did not know if child abuse was a problem in their area, while 39 per cent were adamant that it was not. It is clear from Gilmartin's study that when the Principal, the staff and the Board of Management were not positively disposed to the programme, it was likely that neither would a meeting with parents be called, nor the Programme implemented.[14]

Lobbying against the Stay Safe programme continued through to 1998. In March, Mary Kennedy of The Irish Family League wrote to the papers calling for support in the struggle against the programme:

> It is consoling to know that there are teachers who are concerned about the children in their classes, and who refuse to teach the Stay Safe programme. The fact that there is child sexual abuse in the news frightens some parents who are led to believe that this programme will save their children from abuse.
>
> There is much evidence elsewhere to show that this is not so. Stay Safe is 'sold' to the public as a health programme, but it carries no recommendations by leading figures, academic or professional, in the child care world.
>
> A distinguished psychotherapist, Dr W. Coulson, has made a study of child abuse prevention programmes including Stay Safe. He claims that this programme does great harm. It gives permission for children to order part of their lives around sexual themes. Children in the latency period 6 to 12 should not be introduced to sexual issues.
>
> Under the authority of the teacher a once unmentionable subject is indulged in. Sex between adults and children must be thought of or talked about lest children be corrupted. Yet this programme asks teachers to do just that. Stay Safe does not mention right or wrong. A lesson deals with unwanted touch and Yes or No feelings. But a seducer could very well be able to produce Yes feelings in a child while the parent or teacher could well produce No feelings when correcting a child.
>
> The best safeguard against child abuse is to teach children about modesty, as was done in the past. Stay Safe intrudes into family relationships. It can make children distrustful of parents, whom they could resist or reject if they give them no feelings. Feelings cannot be used to say what is right or wrong, good or bad. An objective judgement is called for.[15]

Regardless of the strategies and tactics used by those in favour or against the Stay Safe programme, both interest groups seemed to recognise and accept how central debate and discussion in the media is to the acceptance or rejection of the programme.[16] Control of the curriculum has moved out from behind closed doors into the public domain. What is remarkable in this process is the general unwillingness of Church leaders, particularly bishops, to oppose the programme openly and to participate in public debate.[17]

The Relationships and Sexuality Education (RSE) programme

The Expert Advisory Group appointed by the Minister for Education concluded that Relationships and Sexuality Education should be a required part of the curriculum of each primary and post-primary school. It was envisaged that relationships and sexuality education would be a module within a broader programme dealing with Social, Personal and Health Education, and that SPHE would be allocated one timetable period per week. The part dealing with relationships and sexuality would take up five to six of these periods each year. However, the Expert Group felt that this broad SPHE programme would take some time to design and implement. In the meantime, they said that there was an urgent need to implement a relationships and sexuality education programme.[18]

The aim of the RSE programme is, according to the policy guidelines, to help children 'acquire a knowledge and understanding of human relationships and sexuality through processes which will enable them to form values and establish behaviours within a moral, spiritual and social framework.'[19] The Expert Advisory Group had suggested that there were numerous reasons why such a programme was now necessary in Ireland. They pointed to earlier physical maturation of children, and young people reaching puberty before their teenage years. Another reason was the increasing evidence of earlier sexuality activity among young people. The context of sexuality in Ireland had, they argued, changed, particularly in relation to the messages about sexuality emanating from teenage magazines and the media in general. They also pointed to the health risks for sexually active young people in an era of AIDS and HIV. Finally, they argued that increased travel, communications and information technology meant that children were regularly being exposed to alternative value systems. In this context, it was necessary for children to learn more formally how to know and understand themselves, how to express themselves, and how to relate to others socially as well as sexually.[20]

It is important to recognise that, as with the Stay Safe programme, the emphasis in RSE is on developing individual moral responsibility. This takes place within the moral ethos of the school. But the difference with a traditional approach is that the moral and spiritual framework is not given first. Indeed, as we shall see, the proposed curriculum guidelines make little or no mention of the moral and spiritual framework. The reason for this is that it is recognised that the moral and spiritual framework will vary depending on the family and school, even when they are both ostensibly Catholic. There can, in effect, no longer be an orthodox moral and spiritual framework based on absolute truths which are accepted without contention.

The second, more important, point is that it is suggested that the RSE programme is a neutral form of knowledge and understanding which simply fits in with the existing moral framework. However, it could be argued that the whole programme is, in effect, an ethical programme which gives precise guidelines as to what is right and wrong, acceptable and unacceptable behaviour. In itself it is a secular programme which provides a way of seeing and understanding oneself and relating to others which is independent of Church teaching. If implemented in schools, it could be a direct challenge to the monopoly which the Catholic Church has held over morality in Ireland.

The procedures to which schools are expected to adhere in developing their own RSE policy are quite specific. Whatever programme is adopted has to be the result of a partnership between parents, teachers and school authorities. Each school is required to set up a committee. The exact composition of the Committee is not specified in the Policy guidelines, but in practice it is generally composed of: two people from the school management; two teachers; and two nominated parents. The composition of the Committee is an important issue. Although the RSE programme recognises parents as the first teacher of children in handing on values and attitudes and that it is the function of the school to work with them on this, management and teachers can often out-number parents on the committee.

Once formed, the first task of the committee is to study the relevant documents – particularly the curriculum and guidelines produced by the National Council for Curriculum and Assessment (NCCA) – and to engage in consultation with the wider body of parents, teachers and school authorities. It is also expected to carry out a detailed review of whatever kind of social and personal health education and relationships and sexuality education are already in existence in the school. Once this work is completed, the committee draws up a draft policy statement which is submitted to the school authorities for approval and dissemination to all parents and teachers.

There seems to be a hidden form of veto here. It is not clear what happens if the school authorities disapprove of the draft policy statement. Nevertheless, it is anticipated that, at this stage, the committee engages in further consultation not just with the parents and teachers, but also perhaps with the pupils. Once the process of consultation is completed, the amended draft policy statement is presented to the school authorities 'for discussion and approval'. Again, there appears to be a veto here, and it is not clear from the policy guidelines what happens if the school authorities disapprove of the final policy statement, or to what extent they can amend it. This statement becomes the school's Relationships and Sexuality Education Policy and is circulated to parents and teachers. The booklet notes that in the pre-test phase, most schools completed the policy development process in two or three meetings over a two-month period.

One of the purposes of the school developing its own RSE policy is that it protects teachers from being challenged by parents or pupils about subject matters that have been dealt with in class. If anything emerges within a particular class which is difficult or controversial, the teacher and the pupils can decide if it conforms to the school's policy statement. For example, if pupils wish to discuss abortion, the teacher may be able to say that this is not permissible since it is not contained within the school's policy. On the other hand, if it is contained in the policy and it is discussed in class, then the teacher is protected if some parents are critical.

It must be remembered that sexual morality is a contentious issue in Irish society and, particularly, in Irish education. Requiring each school to decide what it should include and exclude may be seen as an exercise in local democracy in which schools are able to tailor the programme to meet special needs and interests. On the other hand, it could be argued that it is an unwillingness of the state to take difficult decisions, and that it will lead to some children and young people not getting as good an education in relationships and sexuality as others. But there are flaws within the approach. Firstly, as indicated, it is not clear to what extent the school authorities have a final veto on what is taught in the schools. Secondly, the mechanisms for changing the policy are not clearly specified. Finally, the approach does not see the pupils as one of the groups, along with parents, teachers and the school authorities, who should be included in drafting the policy. The pupils are consulted, but do not have an equal say in identifying the issues of relationships and sexuality about which they would like to learn. This is an important issue, particularly for those teenagers who are sexually active. It hinders the possibility of establishing a free and equal dialogue between the teacher and the pupils. There is a mechanism of power – that is agenda setting – which results in decisions being made, regardless of the interests and concerns of the pupils, on what they should learn about sexuality.

RSE curriculum and guidelines

In 1997 the NCCA produced curriculum guidelines for RSE in primary and post-primary schools. An analysis of the content of the guidelines shows that the emphasis is clearly on relationships rather than sexuality education. In primary school the RSE is orientated towards helping children develop a concept of themselves as individuals and to enhance their self-esteem and self-confidence. Given that the ethos of Catholic social teaching has, in the past, emphasised the importance of self-denial, this programme represents a radical rupture with the way children used to be taught to see and understand themselves and the world in which they live. Children are taught to understand their relationships with family and friends from an established base of self-confidence and self-esteem. The emphasis is on learning to share, co-operate, express feelings and emotions, make decisions, communicate, maintain group loyalty and resolve conflict. Pupils are taught about personal hygiene, assessing risks and keeping themselves safe and healthy. The aim is to help children acquire important social and personal skills. In relation to sexuality, the objective is to demystify some of the 'acquired assumptions around sexuality' and to help children develop a language which enables them to 'communicate confidently about themselves, their sexuality and their relationships'.[21]

In the earlier classes children are taught about the different parts of the body, how babies grow in their mother's womb, and are born and nurtured. In fifth and sixth class it is proposed that children be taught about the changes which take place during puberty, about sexual intercourse, and sexually transmitted diseases, particularly AIDS. The objectives of the curriculum are: to place sexual intercourse within the context of a stable, committed, loving relationship; and to make children aware of the ethical issues, consequences and responsibilities involved in sexual intercourse.[22] The curriculum notes that the resource materials used to teach the lessons, such as booklets, videos and so forth, as well as any class discussion, will be informed by the religious ethos and teaching of the school. For example, it notes that a school may wish 'to place an emphasis on the commitment that a man and a woman make to each other in marriage'. But this is to imply, if not condone, sex taking place outside marriage. There is, in other words, a strong liberal dimension to the curriculum. No definite rights and wrongs are announced. Rather children are encouraged to feel comfortable with their sexuality and 'are provided with language through which they may seek clarification, ask questions and discuss all aspects of their growth and development'. Part of this involves an examination of the various people and institutions who determine their understanding of sexuality, that is, family, friends, churches, the state, media and sports personalities.[23] This element of critical reflection – of enabling children to ask themselves who it is who speaks to them about sex, and who it is that speaks the truth – marks a radical departure from previous approaches. However, facilitating such a discussion demands special skills since it could raise questions about the power of the teacher, not just in relation to sexuality education, but in relation to the rest of the curriculum and the management and control of the school. But it may not have been the intention of the producers of the guidelines to provoke such debate and critical reflection. Indeed, there is no proposal for a discussion about the nature of power and the truth about sexuality in the guidelines for the post-primary curriculum where it may have been more appropriate. Instead it is suggested that there should be an exploration of the range of attitudes, values and beliefs regarding sexual behaviour in modern society.[24]

It is stated clearly at the outset that the aim of the programme is to set RSE 'firmly within a moral, spiritual and social framework'.[25] There is a reluctance – which may be a residue of the Church's monopoly over sexual morality – to name and discuss controversial issues such as masturbation, oral sex, abortion, contraception and gay and lesbian sexuality. This could be seen as a public deference to the Catholic Church, and when it comes to actually implementing the programme, it may not be reflected in the school policy nor, indeed, in what takes place in the classroom. Nevertheless, it is significant that there is no specific lesson devoted to methods of contraception. Instead it is suggested that children 'develop a deeper awareness and understanding of male and female fertility' which leads on, naturally, to learning about the different methods of family planning. Although is suggested that there is a specific lesson on sexually transmitted diseases, there is no specific mention of pre-marital sexual practices, teenage pregnancies, abortion or other controversial issues. But this is not to preclude debate and discussion on these topics.

Debate and discussion is encouraged, since the radical adult learning approach – introduced at primary school – is developed significantly at the post-primary level. In particular, there is an emphasis on experiential learning through art, narrative expression, role playing and group discussion.[26] This is very different from a traditional discourse in which learning about sex is directed by a teacher who, acting with the authority of the Church, is definitive about what are good and bad, right and wrong, sexual attitudes and practices. In the proposed programme, much depends on the teacher's ability to act less as an instructor and more as an engaged and sympathetic facilitator. The successful implementation of the programme will require teachers being trained to use participatory and experimental learning methods and in the delicate and skilful handling of questions and answers.[27] In part, this requires teachers to be able to surrender traditional roles and practices associated with their position and facilitate frank, open and honest dialogue about the sexual interests of their pupils. In fact, many people experience unease and embarrassment when discussing feelings, emotions and bodily functions. This may be due in part to an inadequacy of language or the negative associations acquired over time about these issues.[28]

Given the absence of such a dialogue in their own upbringing and, perhaps, in their own relationships, it may well be that many teachers require more than a few days training. Indeed some might need to go through a whole programme of sexuality education.

It is in this regard that there is an absence within the proposed curriculum. While there is mention of sexual orientation, this is placed within the context of 'information on and sensitivity to sexual orientation'.[29] This could be an important opportunity to discuss the nature of sexual desire and pleasure: what it is to be turned on and sexually excited; the difference between male and female desire, pornography, combining sex with alcohol and drugs. This could also lead to important discussions about how to communicate these feelings and, most important of all perhaps, how to negotiate safe sex. The skill of the teacher will be in helping pupils direct the dialogue in such a way that they learn to learn rather than perform in front of each other.

A more progressive discourse

In their *Resources Guide to Relationships and Sexuality Education*, the Marino Institute of Education examined a wide variety of resources including background material for teachers, books for students, classroom programmes, audio-visual material, and so forth. One of the programmes included in Guide is *Sex Education (Junior)* which was produced in 1990 by the BBC for use in Great Britain. The programme includes a video pack with a booklet. It is orientated to children in junior schools who are preparing to enter secondary school. The Institute concluded that BBC material had been 'thoroughly researched, and it is obvious that a lot of thought and effort has gone into presenting the material in a way which would be appealing and informative to young children and young adolescents.'[30] Since the BBC programme is an example of a more progressive type of sexuality education than that produced in the RSE programme, I will describe what may be considered the more controversial content in some detail.

The video begins with the presenter, a mother, talking about caring for young children and the need to wash them properly. This includes, they are told, their penis and their vagina. These, it is announced, are their private parts; part of their reproductive system which will enable them to become parents one day. We are then told that boy and girls change as they grow up. This is called puberty. The second part of the video commences with two women, both late into their pregnancies, going through an ante-natal examination. We see the doctor examining the women and a film clip shows a baby growing in the womb from 4 to 38 weeks. The women are interviewed in their homes with their partners and their other children. The most dramatic moment is the detailed film of the birth. This part of the video ends with the mother back at home breastfeeding her new baby boy.

The third part of the video deals with the way life begins. It is explained that the new baby we saw being born was created by a tiny bit of her mother and a tiny bit of her father. We are told that the changes which take place during puberty enable men and women to have children. Men and women produce hormones which make women's breasts and men's testicles grow. Hormones produce the ovum and the sperm. When they link up the sperm fertilises the ovum. If sperm does not meet the egg, the woman has her period. For the sperm to meet the ovum, it has to get all the way from the man's testicles into the woman's womb. This happens when a man and a woman have sexual intercourse. The next section of the video is accompanied by cartoon images of a man and a woman in bed.

Many people call it making love because it is something that happens when two people love each other very much. It often happens in bed because that is a warm comfortable place to relax. Most people begin to make love by kissing. They stroke each other all over and tell each other how much they love each other. They want to be as close as possible. The woman's clitoris becomes very sensitive and enjoys being stroked. As the man and woman make love, the man's penis becomes stiffer and longer. Inside the woman, her vagina leading up to her womb becomes bigger and slippery so that the vagina and penis can fit together like pieces of a jigsaw puzzle. (The cartoon image at this point shows the woman lying on top of the man with his penis inside her). When they get together the feeling is very nice. And the man and woman move their hips to make the feeling even better. In the end the feeling is so good that the woman has a wonderful experience called an orgasm in her clitoris and vagina which makes her feel good all over. The man's orgasm is in his penis and all the sperm rush out and up his penis and into the vagina. He feels good all over too. (The video now turns to a film showing sperm travelling up to the womb.) But when the sperm get inside the vagina they have to find the egg. So working as a team, millions of sperm race together up the woman's vagina. They swim all the way to the womb. And if the egg isn't there, they split the search; some going into one fallopian tube and some into the other. A lot of sperm don't make it, but some finally meet the egg. Still working as a team they circle the egg. Then one sperm manages to join the egg; that's called fertilisation. Together the egg and the sperm now have a complete set of coded plans to build a baby. The fertilised egg finds a place to settle in the soft coating of the womb and the new baby has begun.

The final part of this video is the Teacher's Programme. The aim is to provide some guidance for teachers about showing the video and responding to questions they may be asked. This shows a teacher sitting on a table on which the video is running, stopping it and talking to a class of, what appears to be, fifth or sixth class primary-school children. The teacher says he likes to raise contentious issues first by saying, for example, that he is happy to talk about periods, or masturbation. The booklet which accompanies the video says that this approach prompts questions which deepen the exploration of thoughts, feelings and actions and extend language skills. The booklet advises that:

It may help if teachers examine their feelings about the boundaries of taste in advance, so that it becomes easy to give a straight 'I don't know' or 'Perhaps

I can find you someone else to talk to about that'. One teacher confessed that she had been unaware of having any boundaries until a ten-year-old girl said: 'I understand what condoms are for, but why are they sometimes strawberry flavoured?'[31]

Later, we see the teacher watching a segment of the video which has the following sequence. 'A boy's penis is very sensitive to touch. Sometimes as he grows older he may want to touch it and massage it. That's called masturbation and it's quite natural.' The teacher stops the video and turns to the children. He says:

Now maybe we will just talk a little about masturbation, because some people find it's something to giggle at. Pretty much all men you see out in the streets, and outside, will have done it at one time or another. So it's something that everyone does. It's not something you should do in public.

It is emphasised in the teacher's programme that sex should be described as a positive experience. This, it is stated, will help a child decide whether sex in certain situations is right or wrong for them. If a teacher is teaching that sex is positive then, it is claimed, a child who is suffering sexual abuse may recognise that negative experiences of sex are wrong and seek help.

Up until now sex education has been about birth education. We have talked about sexual intercourse in order to talk about birth and how life goes on. We now need to talk about sexual pleasure. Teachers will need to talk about non-penetrative sex so that young people can understand that to protect themselves from the virus (HIV), and to enjoy themselves sexually, it is going to be non-penetrative sex or sex with condoms.

The video and booklet which the BBC produced for use in post-primary schools concentrates on older teenagers. The video revolves around young people sitting in a circle talking about their attitudes to, and experiences of, sexual relations and sexuality. The video begins by dealing with the contradiction between sex being something which is private and generally takes place behind closed doors and, at the same time, being highly public, openly displayed, promoted and advertised in magazines, film and television. It discusses gay and lesbian issues. There is a very detailed section on contraception with a discussion of what to do in the case of an unwanted pregnancy, and the pros and cons of having and keeping the baby, having it adopted, or having an abortion. The final part of the video deals with sexually transmitted diseases and includes footage of a teenage girl going to a clinic for an examination. As with the programme for junior schools, perhaps the most progressive aspect is the part that deals with masturbation.

Getting to know yourself through masturbation is often the first experience of sex that you have. It is important to feel safe about where you masturbate and that others should respect your right to privacy. For some people it is just not right either for religious or personal reasons. If you wish to masturbate, exploring your body and getting to know how you like to be touched, can be a positive and natural way of giving yourself sexual pleasure.

This section of the video is accompanied by a film which alternates between a man and a woman, each lying naked on a bed with a sheet up to the waist, but both ostensibly masturbating underneath it.

Conclusion

It is important to realise that as there are different ways of talking about sexuality within an overall traditional discourse, there are also differences among those who speak and write within a generally progressive discourse. Most people who take a progressive stance on relationships and sexuality education would probably agree there is a need to provide a knowledge of sex and sexual relations which would help young people develop sexually responsible and enjoyable relationships and, at the same time, avoid abuse, disease, undesired experiences and unwanted pregnancies. However, while some would stress the need for young people to learn about condoms, contraceptives and safe sex practices, others would emphasise the importance of teaching young people that sexual relations are something which should be confined to within marriage.

As with many other issues relating to sexuality, the implementation of the RSE programme has been an Irish solution to an Irish problem. The strategy of the state was to avoid a major confrontation with the Catholic Church. This was done through incorporation of Catholic representatives in the decision-making process and through ongoing discussions. The solution to devising a progressive programme for use in a variety of Catholic and non-Catholic schools was to abandon any attempt to make sexuality education compulsory, or to developing a national curriculum. In other words, as happened with the Stay Safe programme, a national issue was resolved by turning it into a local issue. Effectively, this meant that what was proposed as a progressive discourse could, in some schools, be turned back into a traditional discourse through (*a*) the teaching materials and resources adopted, (*b*) the language, concepts and terms employed to talk about sexuality, and (*c*) the teaching methods used. Judging by some of the responses of Catholic bishops to the RSE programme, which we shall examine in chapter 6, it may be assumed that this is what in effect is happening.

4
Being Encouraged to be Sexual

From a liberal perspective, the main issue in Irish sexuality is how people can have sexually rewarding lives which produce pleasure rather than abuse, frustration, distress or disease. It centres on freeing sexuality from religious, political or social utilitarian purposes. It champions individuals' sexual rights and 'proudly celebrates sexuality and sexual diversity in defiance of established mores'.[1] When it comes to sex, each individual is deemed to be the ultimate judge of his or her own behaviour, and it is expected that individuals recognise and accept that what is right or wrong for them, may not be right or wrong for others.

A liberal perspective centres on experiencing, exploring and understanding sexuality. It is based on an interest in knowing and appreciating sexuality, sexual relations, responsibilities and responses. Carlson considers that the libertarian discourse came of age with the work of Alfred Kinsey in America in the 1940s and 1950s. It promoted an interest and fascination in knowing the sexual proclivities and activities of others. Understanding other people's sexuality became a means of reflecting on one's own beliefs, attitudes and practices. Carlson argues that Masters's and Johnson's research in the 1960s had a further liberating effect on American sexuality, particularly that of women. Their research showed that women were able to achieve multiple orgasms, stay sexually aroused longer, and enjoy an infinite variety of sexual responses.[2] A libertarian outlook emphasises that people should learn to let go, release themselves from the constraints of the past which they have inherited. It is about creating the conditions for sexual freedom and emancipation. It is about trying to remove feelings of fear, shame and guilt about everything to do with sex and helping people feel good, confident, and positive about themselves and their relations, especially their sexual relations, with others. A liberal approach to sexuality focuses on discovering and announcing to yourself and others what you like and dislike, and what it is that gives you pleasure. It is about being able to fulfil these pleasures and desires through open, honest communication and negotiation and, consequently, being able to form a sexual relationship which is healthy, egalitarian and mutually satisfying.

Carlson argues that this discourse, this way of thinking about sexuality, is dominant in textbooks used in liberal arts colleges in the United States where students take a wide range of courses. But the same type of educational programmes are not found in Irish third-level colleges. The main outlets for this type of learning would be marriage counselling courses, self-help groups, and a variety of sexual therapy counselling services, books, tapes and videos. One of the main sources of liberal sexual discourse are books such as Alex Comfort's *The Joy of Sex*. As Comfort says bluntly in the introduction, 'the aim of the book is pleasure'.[3] He goes on to define two main rules for sex '(1) Don't do anything dangerous or that is not enjoyable. (2) Find out what are your partner's needs and satisfy them if you can.'[4] As Seidman points out, a liberal discourse revolves around two fundamental changes: the sexualisation of love and the eroticisation of sex.[5] The eroticisation of sex demands that people be adventurous and experimental in their sex lives. Manuals encourage all types of behaviour and positions, from dirty talking to voyeuristic, fetishistic and even sado-masochistic sexual behaviour. Sex is deemed to be moral and legitimate as long as it is 'consensual, reciprocal in its pleasures, and involves mutual respect and shared responsiblity'.[6] Readers of *The Joy of Sex* are advised that in a consensual, safe and respectful interpersonal setting, there is no compelling reason for good friends or total strangers not to make love.[7]

It must be remembered that there is a difference between having a positive attitude to sexuality and thereby entertaining and liking the idea of making love with strangers, and actually doing so. The gap between people's attitudes – or more so between what they say they will do and what they actually do – is well established in social research.[8] An essential element of a liberal attitude is that human sexuality is good. It is good to be sexual, to feel and be sexy, and to have sex on offer. It is a positive stimulus; a source of life and energy. But just because sex is on offer does not mean that it is always taken up. This is where the control of passion and desire enters. A liberal sexual attitude emphasises the importance of discovering, announcing and fulfilling oneself sexually, but also stresses the importance of disciplining and controlling oneself, especially through internalised self-constraint. As the old Irish convent school adage said, 'You can get your appetite anywhere, but eat at home.' Indeed this advice seems to be followed by most married couples not just in Ireland, but in America and Britain. In an opinion poll in Ireland in 1993, 90 per cent of married people had remained faithful during the previous year. This compares with 91 per cent of married British people and 85 per cent of married Americans. Moreover, in Ireland, there is evidence that fidelity is frequently lifelong. Six in ten Irish people who had had sexual intercourse, had done so with only one person. Half of the respondents in the Irish survey thought that having sexual relations with someone other than their husband or wife was always wrong; a further 25 per cent thought that it was usually wrong. Two-thirds of the respondents said there was no likelihood of them having an affair, even if they were sure their husband or wife would never find out about it. Finally, nearly two-thirds (65 per cent) rated faithfulness as the most important factor for a successful marriage. In this respect, faithfulness was considered more important than, for example, shared religious views (3 per cent), or adequate income (11 per cent).[9]

In the same way that a liberal attitude creates a myth that people are having sex whenever, wherever and with whomever they please, it also creates a myth that people are having sex, or wanting to have sex, all the time. This myth is created and maintained through the media and the continual promotion, advertising, portrayal and talk about sex. Again the empirical evidence suggests otherwise. Survey data show that in most countries, including Ireland, people with sexual partners have sexual intercourse just two to three times a week.[10]

Display and promotion of sexuality in the media

So there is little evidence that Ireland has become a permissive, hedonistic society. This is not to say that there have not been dramatic changes in the way sex has been revealed, promoted and displayed. Sex is used to sell everything from cars to chocolate. In the beginning it was only women, but now men's bodies are used to sell perfume, soft drinks and jeans. Bodies are openly displayed. Breasts, chests and bums are revealed. But this is not any innocent or natural revelation as it might be, for example, in a nudist camp. It is an erotic display. Some women's dresses reveal more of the body than they conceal. They are an invitation to gaze, survey, appreciate, imagine, fantasise, and be excited. In films, videos and magazines, women and men pose and allow their bodies to be visually consumed. The pleasure of gazing at bodies, particularly women's, has long been an important ingredient in film. Although he was writing more than fifty years ago, John Gorey was well aware of the sexual stimulation and excitement in modern cinema and novels.

The cinema and the sex-novel of today insinuate into a boy's mind that the normal thing for him is to have a girlfriend. They propose as the natural relaxation and recreation for a boy, sentimental flirtations with all their usual accompaniment of sensuous fondlings and passionate love-making. Ninety per cent of the films you see and the novels you read have flirtation as their theme. They show you hero and heroine in love scenes reeking with sensuality – with sex appeal. Faces, attitudes, conduct, and even language, reflect sensuality open and unabashed.[11]

This reading of the content of films is still insightful. The only difference is that these images are constantly portrayed on television, and are viewed regularly by children of all ages. A content analysis of over fifty hours of American soap operas in 1987 showed that there was a high level of reference to, and depiction of, sexual behaviour.[12] The coding system the researchers used was a development of that used in previous studies. *Erotic touching* was defined as 'interpersonal touching that had clear sexual overtones, demonstrated or intended to demonstrate sexual love, or aroused or expressed sexual desire'. The researchers acknowledged that it was sometimes difficult to decide if the touching and kissing portrayed were sexual and erotic, or whether they were non-sexual 'peck' type kisses. Nevertheless they did report a high level of intercoder agreement. In other words, people asked to code the scenes tended to agree whether a kiss was sexual. *Heterosexual intercourse* was classified as 'verbal, implied, or physically depicted'. The verbal references included 'an affair', 'cheat on me', 'roll in the hay', 'make love'. Implied heterosexual intercourse was when two lovers were shown going to bed, actually in bed, or getting out of bed. Physical depiction was reserved for actual physical portrayals of intercourse. The researchers also noted references to prostitution, aggressive sexual conduct, homosexuality, incest, masturbation and so forth.

The researchers watched 52.5 hours of afternoon soap operas and found that there were 387 codeable instances of sexual behaviour, or an overall rate per hour of 7.4. The most frequent behaviour was erotic touching between unmarried couples. This was followed by verbal references to sexual intercourse. In analysing their findings, the authors concluded:

The transcending message on soap operas concerning sex is that it is primarily for unmarried partners. Yet, though contraception is seldom mentioned, pregnancy is rare. Even though life on most of the soap operas takes place in the sexually fast lane, no one ever catches a sexually transmitted disease.[13]

As part of the research for this book, I examined two television pro- grammes shown on Irish television. The episode of *Heartbreak High* which I analysed was shown on Thursday 13 November, 1997 at 7.00 p.m. It is an Australian serial about the lives of teachers and final-year pupils in a secondary school. The main theme in the first part of the episode revolved around the relationship between two pupils. Jodi has dropped out of school to go and play in a rock band in Melbourne. She phones her boyfriend Nick. They meet, kiss erotically and arrange to make up for lost time later that night. However, a member of Jodi's band, Louis, comes to town, and Jodi is seen hugging and kissing him. In the final scene of the first part of the episode, Nick confronts Jodi and asks her if she slept with him. Jodi admits that she did: 'Once at his house, once at mine. You know it wasn't like us. It wasn't terrible either. It was good.' Judging from what was said later in the episode, it appears that Nick hit Jodi at this stage. However, this part of the scene was not shown in the version I watched.

I examined the episode using the same coding system devised by the American researchers. For *erotic touching*, I coded three instances of sexual embracing, and two of prolonged heavy or French kissing. For *heterosexual intercourse*, I coded two instances of verbal references and four where sexual intercourse was implied. Excluding the censored scene, there was one instance of sexual aggression. This gave 11 instances of sexual behaviour over the hour which is 50 per cent more than the average for the study on American soap operas mentioned earlier. Nevertheless – and this was similar to the findings of the American study – all the instances of sexual behaviour in the episode I watched involved unmarried people.

One code not identified or used by the American researchers, but which figured prominently throughout the *Heartbreak High* episode was erotic looking or gazing. While erotic gazing at women has been a standard feature in film and television, it is only recently that writers and directors have included scenes where, acting as the eyes of female characters, the camera focuses erotically on men's bodies. This has been a particular feature of Diet Coke advertisements in recent years. In the episode of *Heartbreak High,* a new teacher, Phil North, arrives in the school and the beauty of his body is admired and talked about by the female pupils and teachers. There were two scenes where this erotic looking and talking were the central features.

The same evening, I watched *Beverley Hills 90210.* This serial revolves around the loves, trials and tribulations of rich young Californians in their late teens and early twenties. In the episode which I watched there was little mention of school, college or work. Most of the content centred on the personal relationships of the lead characters and their romantic and sexual liaisons. There were two instances of heavy or French kissing, two of erotic gazing, and three instances where sexual intercourse was implied. There was one reference to sexually transmitted diseases. Omitting the instances of erotic gazing, the number of instances of sexual behaviour is somewhat similar to the 1987 American study.

An unanswered question from this analysis is what effect these kinds of programmes have on young people. Does the portrayal of sex as enjoyable, worry free and without consequences influence young people's perception of sex and sexual practice? Or have soap operas and serials become a realm of entertainment which young people see through and are easily able to distinguish from real life? It may well be that the pleasure is in the fantasy and, just as much as they learnt that characters in children's comics such as *Beano* and *Dandy* are not real, so too do they learn that the social life and characters in soap operas and serials are essentially fantastic and entertaining. On the other hand, it could be argued that films, soaps and serials contain liberal moral messages which are received in various formats in the privacy of the home on a daily basis.

But it is not just on television that there has been an increasing portrayal and promotion of sexuality. It has become a regular feature in newspapers. I examined the contents of the *The Sunday Independent* for two separate six month periods – the first six months of 1963 and

1993. I devised three broad categories to analyse the content. *Explicit* material was where there was a specific story relating to scandals, prostitution or pornography, or where there was a photograph displaying a woman's breasts or legs. *Direct* material referred to stories and accounts of court cases relating to rape, abuse, harassment, and so forth. *Indirect* material referred to body length photographs of women and stories about the lives of actresses, pop-singers, models and so forth. My analysis indicated that over the thirty-year period, the number of *explicit* articles or photographs increased from 2 to 33; the number of *indirect* items about sex increased from 1 to 44; and the number of *direct* items increased from 11 to 76.[14]

Teenage magazines

Teenage magazines are another major source for liberal views on sexuality. These magazines promote, advertise and encourage young people to be sexually active, experienced and adventurous. At the same time, however, readers are encouraged to be critically reflective and responsible about their sexuality. Young people are encouraged to look good, feel good and be sexy. The magazines promote a type of romantic, self-discovery, self-realisation ethic which demands that they live to achieve the ideals of being slim, beautiful and healthy – like the advertising models and pop stars portrayed in the magazines. There is little or no mention of traditional Catholic ideals such as modesty and chastity. The focus is on the individual, struggling to achieve, to look good, and be recognised and accepted as good and 'cool'. Life is a series of ups and downs, rewards and punishments, of ongoing struggles with boyfriends, girlfriends, parents and teachers, from which there is no salvation. And so there is a series of pictures, stories, advertisements and advice columns which remind readers of the vagaries of life. To be recognised, to be accepted and to have status, it is deemed necessary to balance the demands of being educationally and occupationally successful with the social demands of having a good body, speaking the right language, being in the right places, eating the right food, avoiding the worst drugs, buying the latest fashions, wearing the best beauty-products, following the right bands, listening to the latest sounds, watching the recent films and videos and, of course, reading the right magazines. Teenage magazines represent the needs and interests, concerns and worries, passions and excitements of young people.

The question whether these magazines create or represent young people's needs and interests is relevant, but difficult to answer. Moreover, it is important to realise that the lifestyle represented and advocated in the magazines is not unethical. It is rather that they operate within and promote a secular ethical lifestyle – a way of life which although very different is still often as ethically demanding as trying to live up to the ideals of a Christian sexual ethic.[15]

An analysis of teenage magazines on sale in Ireland is difficult since there are many magazines which, while supposedly for teenagers, are bought and read by pre-teenage children. On the other hand, there are young people in their late teenage years who have moved on to reading adult magazines. There is also a gender difference. Most of the magazines dealing with sexuality, love and romance are directed towards, and are bought by, girls. The magazines directed towards and bought by boys are orientated more towards sports and popular music. However, although magazines may be directed towards girls, this does not mean that they are only read by girls. The proportion of boys who read girls' magazines, particularly the advice columns, may be significant. But this is conjecture. What is remarkable, however, is that given the content and readership of these magazines and the influence they have in the public sphere of youth affairs, that there is little information available in Ireland on their sales and readership.[16]

For this study, I looked at the contents of five of the more popular female teenage magazines. The magazines were chosen on the basis of distribution information received informally from a national distributor. The choice of the month was partly random and according to convenience, although I did delay the analysis until the *Relationships and Sexuality Education* programme had commenced, since I wanted to compare the viewpoints in the magazines with the perspective in the guidelines and curriculum.

The main cover story on the December 1997 issue of *Sugar* was 'Body Talk: all your scariest sex questions answered'. This was a '16-page sealed special'. The article began as follows:

It's easy to get confused about sex when you're hearing different things from different sources. People at school, TV, boys, friends – everyone's talking about sex, but some people get their information seriously wrong! That's why we've done this 16-page sex sense special (sealed for your privacy) – in order to untangle the facts from fiction and make sure you've got all the info you need to make your own decisions. Every piece of information has been approved by our very own *Sugar* doctors, so you can be sure that *we've* got our facts straight, at least!. And please remember, no matter what anyone says, it's illegal to have sex if you're not 16, and you should always wait until you're in a loving relationship and feel 100% ready. And that's a fact.

The special feature began with a 'crucial quiz'. The answers argued that: (*a*) 'condoms are the only method of contraception to protect against AIDS and other STDs, as well as pregnancy'; (*b*) 'masturbating alone is about the safest form of sex going'; and (*c*) that while the risk of becoming HIV is low, it is 'still always safer to use a condom during oral sex'. The next item was an autobiographical story about a 16-year-old girl who ran away with her Dad's best friend. The next section discussed the different forms of contraception available in terms of their effectiveness, their advantages and disadvantages, and their availability. The next four pages were given over to an A–Z of sex. Under G for Gay it said that '10 per cent of the population *are* attracted to the same sex and if you are gay or bisexual (attracted to both sexes), it's certainly nothing to be ashamed of, and you can still look forward to a fulfilling love life'. Within this A–Z section there was a page devoted to sexually transmitted diseases. There was a two-page autobiographical story about a girl who became a mum by mistake. Finally, within the *Sugar* doctor special section, there was a question from a 15-year-old girl about heavy petting. The response provided the following information and advice:

'Fingering' is when your partner inserts his finger into your vagina. By the time you feel ready to do this, you should be aroused enough to be naturally lubricated so you won't feel any discomfort, as long as your boyfriend's nails are short. But, it's important not to consent to anything unless you are certain, in which case you should be gentle and loving.

Besides the Special on Sex, the issue of *Sugar* I examined revolved around ten features on fashion and beauty, twelve articles on media celebrities (mainly from films, TV and music), and 'regular' features on love, embarrassment, pets, friendships and communication.

However, there were other important characteristics about the content of *Sugar*. Of the 155 pages, 76 are given over to advertising. The majority of these are for clothing and beauty products. The magazine is also dominated by photographs, mostly of young men and women. Of the 87 full-length body photographs of women, there is only one who could be regarded as overweight. Similarly, all the male photographs are of beautiful young men.

More is a fortnightly magazine orientated towards older girls. The content is similar to *Sugar*. In the issue I examined (no. 251, 18 November 1997), there were nine articles on fashion and beauty and six on celebrities. But again, the main content is glossy photographs and advertisements. The advice section contained a black and white photograph of a naked man and woman kissing and had a 'Position of the fortnight' which gave a detailed description of what a woman should do in order to enjoy sexual intercourse from behind. The overall message in the advice section was that sex is good for you. This was best reflected in the answer to the dilemma whether women need to have an orgasm to enjoy sex.

True, but that doesn't mean you should go on a no-orgasm diet – sexual pleasure is good for us. Experts say regular orgasms can alleviate symptoms of stress, such as insomnia, nervousness and irritability. Plus the vaginal and pelvic contractions or orgasm can soothe menstrual cramps and minor headaches.

The remaining features in the 'Excess' section were concerned with the way men talk about and treat women, and what women should do to attract men. The first of these was the main cover story – a taped interview with four men in a sauna engaging in a 'no-holds barred debate' about how they seduce women. The next article was a confession about a man who ended up sleeping with four women within 24 hours. The final feature in this section was based on 21 pieces of advice on the best way for women to seduce men.

The main cover story on the December 1997 issue of *Bliss* was 'Cosmic girl: how to be the star attraction'. Other cover stories were 'The sex scoreboard: how far should you go?' and 'Be a firecracker! Hot looks to light his fire'. However, *Bliss* is probably aimed at a younger market than *Sugar*. Certainly the advice about engaging in sex is more circumspect, if nevertheless direct. Again, the emphasis is on doing whatever young girls feel comfortable with and which gives them pleasure. The feature on 'how far should you go' contained a description of the different stages of having sex. Having gone through kissing, petting and frottage, the feature eventually discusses oral sex and full-blown sex. In comparison to *Sugar* the advice is quite cautious.

Make sure you never go further than you want just to prove a point. . . . It's up to you to decide if you want to get into anything as saucy as oral sex, but remember, it's best not to do anything like this with a lad unless you know he really cares and respects you. . . . If you really think you want to have sex, you need to ask yourself some serious questions. Am I 16? Can I cope with this emotionally? Do I understand about contraception? Does he respect me? Am I in control of my senses? Will I regret it afterwards?

Advice such as this can sometimes be best understood not so much in terms of what is present, but by what is absent. There is, for example, no recommendation in any of this advice to: (*a*) talk the matter over with a trusted friend; (*b*) discuss it with their parents, teachers or guardians; (*c*) raise it as a general issue during sexuality education classes; or (*d*) place it within the context of the religious or moral education which they have received.

The November (1997) issue of *Mizz* would also seem to be orientated towards the younger teenage years. It had no direct or explicit material about sex on the front cover. However, there was a special feature, 'The A-Z of Boys'. Much of this is light, inane, tabloid material. For example, 'B is for Breasts. What is it with lads and our boobs? They're obsessed with 'em'. And 'K is for kissing. Lads love snogging as much as we do.' Other items included: P is for Pamela Anderson, and N is for Naughty Magazines. While *Mizz* contained a similar proportion of advertisements and features on beauty and fashion, the difference was its emphasis on television programmes and stars. The Agony Aunt section contained a detailed question and answer section on the morning-after pill, and its availability and effectiveness. A letter from a reader asked:

I've been with my boyfriend for two years, and we really do love each other. But recently, when we tried to have sex for the first time, he said there was a sort of lump inside me. Is this because I'm a virgin or because I haven't started my periods yet?

There was no age given for this letter writer. However, in the three letters published where the ages were given, the writers were fourteen and fifteen.

Shout (7–20 Nov.) is also aimed at young teenage girls. It again contained a high proportion of advertisements and fashion and beauty features, mixed with short stories such as 'My Step-Dad is Having An Affair', and pictures and information about music and television per-sonalities. *Shout* contained six problem pages. There were letters from a ten and an eleven year old. Three of the letters were about difficulties the writers were having with periods. Other letters were about a girl being bullied, someone who thought they were fat, a girl who was not allowed shave her legs, a girl who had lost her friendship with another girl, and so forth. Only two of the letters had a sexual theme. One girl thought she was a lesbian – 'I dream about kissing all of the Spice Girls and pinching their boobs like they do to each other'. Another girl was anxious that her boyfriend's love bites would cause skin cancer.

There are no Irish equivalents to the British teenage magazines. Irish magazines which young people may read and which would be orientated towards a liberal sexual perspective are *Hot Press* and *In Dublin*. The November issue (No. 22) of *Hot Press* had no features about sex. However, the classified advertisements at the back of the magazine contained over two pages of sex phone call services. *In Dublin* (Vol. 22, No. 22) had four pages of 'fag 'n' dyke happenings'. But the only section which dealt overtly with sex were the ten pages of glossy advertisements for male and female escort services, massage parlours, saunas and sex telephone calls.

What is important to realise is that a liberal attitude to sexuality in which sex is displayed, revealed, questioned and analysed, has become an accepted part of Irish social life. It is no longer shocking to see 'page three girls' in tabloid newspapers, or semi-naked women dressed in 'almost or nearly there' clothes in broadsheet newspapers. Sex scenes have become standard fare in films and television serials. People may not engage in sexual intercourse any more frequently than in previous generations, but there is an ethos, particularly in the media but also in many areas of public life, for people – still mainly women – to be sexually attractive and behave in a sexually alluring manner. Sex has become public. Adults and children have become accustomed to confronting sexual messages and images. In many respects, the increase in the portrayal and display of sex symbols has become matched by the decline in the portrayal and display of traditional Catholic symbols. There is a now a different form of symbolic domination at work. Instead of young people's bedrooms being adorned with images of Our Lady, Christ and, perhaps, the Child of Prague, they are now more likely to be adorned with images of Boyzone and the Spice Girls.[17]

Most of the media messages about sexuality consumed by young people in Ireland are, thus, produced outside Ireland. Most of these messages encourage young people to be sexually active, attractive and desirable. Young people are represented as being most concerned about relationships with the opposite sex, being in love, having sex and being good lovers. Young people are seen to have a need and a right to express themselves, to be desirable, and to be sexually satisfied. The liberal educational message in teenage magazines generally and in their advice columns in particular is that it is right and appropriate to be sexually active. Being sexual is a pleasure to which young people have a right. However, this is balanced with the view that they also need to be fully and properly informed about issues such as what the law allows, appropriate forms of sexual activity, and the rights, duties and consequences of their sexual behaviour. The message, then, is to do sexually what feels good, always to honour, respect and never hurt or violate the body, feelings or emotions of one's partner, and always to practise safe sex. For the younger age group, mainly those under sixteen, it is recommended that sexual activity be confined to non-penetrative forms of sex – that is, masturbation, petting, or oral sex. For the older age group, penetrative sex is acceptable as long as it is always with a condom – unless, of course, couples have been engaged in a stable, long-term, monogamous relationship such as marriage.

Liberal approaches to sex education

If Ireland is exceptional in being so late into the field of sex education, Sweden was exceptional in being so early. Sex education was recommended for secondary school pupils in 1921. It became a voluntary part of the State school curriculum in 1942. In 1956, sex education became compulsory and, in 1964, a Government Commission recommended that sex education commence at the pre-school level. National guidelines for sex education were first produced in 1945. These were revised in 1956 (240 pages) and were updated regularly. The 1977 *Instruction Concerning Interpersonal Relations* (300 pages) was probably the most detailed curriculum guidelines ever produced in the field of sexuality education.[18] While there were many factors which made the Swedish attitude to sex and sexuality unique, the success of the sex education programme was gauged by the reversal of increases in adolescent pregnancies, abortions and STDs in the 1970s.

However, the liberal Swedish philosophy of the 1970s – that sexuality was a positive force for pleasure, self-expression and intimacy – resulted in many legal constraints on sexual behaviour being removed. The result was a huge upsurge in pornography and the social depravity which liberal policy makers had hoped would have been avoided. This led to a revision of the curriculum guide and a greater emphasis placed on the significance of personal relationships.

One of the principal characteristics of the Swedish 1977 curriculum was to make young people aware that any education about sexuality is necessarily based on certain values. In this regard, the curriculum stated clearly that it was founded on democratic principles of tolerance, partnership and equality of rights; on respect for truth, justice, personal privacy; on the inviolability of human life and the dignity of the human being. In the classroom, it was recommended that the teacher *either* stated clearly with conviction what behaviour he or she believed to be right, *or* subjected all basic values to free and open scrutiny. For example, the teacher was expected to endorse sexual fidelity within a regular relationship as a fundamental Swedish value. However, the curriculum required that this be revealed as an area of differing values with some saying that it is ordained by God, others that is socially or psychologically desirable, and others that it is unnecessary and unrealistic. There was an emphasis on teachers creating a secure environment in the school so that adults and pupils would feel free to express their feelings, thoughts and opinions.

Within this overall framework, pupils between 10 and 12 years were introduced to issues such as homosexuality (including their own possible feelings about being homosexual), contraception and abortion. The curriculum was compulsory and much of the handbook was given over to defending this approach in opposition to the beliefs and interests of religious, ethnic and cultural minorities. This was justified on the grounds that young people would be exposed to a variety of competing images of Swedish society through the media. It was argued that a school education which did not provide a factual and moral basis for judgement could lead to confusion and misunderstandings in social relations, which could be harmful to both the individual young person and to other members of society. In other words, it was argued that compulsory sex education, albeit from a liberal democratic perspective, was necessary for upholding the common good over the rights of individuals and minorities.

The Danish state took a similar perspective in a case brought by Christian parents before the European Commission on Human Rights in 1971. The parents argued that compulsory sex education violated their rights to hold the beliefs they had as Christian parents. The Commission found in favour of the Danish state.[19]

In a paper given at a HIV/AIDS seminar in Ireland, Doortje Braeken, youth consultant with the International Planned Parenthood Federation, argued that if educators wished to communicate with young people about sexually transmitted diseases, they needed to understand how sexuality fits into the lives of young people. From the results of a worldwide survey of 600 young people from 52 different countries, she concluded that 'sexual enjoyment was an essential part of their sexual lives' and that 'love was a pre-requisite for a sexual relationship'. More important, perhaps, was that 'almost all the young people who were interviewed said that they needed more information on all aspects of their sexual and reproductive health, including ways to enjoy sex'.[20] She argued that the absence in relationships and sexuality education programmes of any mention of sexual pleasure, sexual fantasies and sexual techniques, suggested that health educators were 'uninspired lovers with no creativity'. She maintained that educators will not be able to change sexual behaviour until they can initiate comfortable discussions with young people about love and their sexuality and the place it has in the context of their entire lives. She stressed the importance of peer-led education, arguing that young people should be involved at policy making and decision-making levels.[21]

Peer educators can be effective because they use the same language and arguments, and are therefore more credible and can help in value development and offer more applicable solutions for problems in a personal situation. They can educate in a more informal day-to-day safe environment.[22]

Certain characteristics of a liberal approach to sexuality education can be now identified:

(*a*) It tends to be positive rather than negative about sex and sexuality. The overall message about human sexuality is that it is a beautiful pleasure, rather than a sordid, unmentionable, problem.

(*b*) It tends to be non-judgmental. There are no ethical absolutes. What is right and wrong, good and bad about sex depends on the individual, their partner and the particular situation. There may be golden rules about sex, but there are few rigid regulations.

(c) The task of the individual is to balance the pleasure of sex with other pleasures, and to do so within an overall system of ethical care and commitment to others by recognising certain rights, duties and responsibilities.

(d) The task of the teacher is to help young people read, understand and operate in the culture and society within which they live, and to normalise sex by removing the guilt, shame, awkwardness and embarrassment which has surrounded it in the past.

Irish approaches to liberal relationships and sexuality education

Although the liberal point of view is a minority one in Ireland, there are some examples of liberal RSE education in this country. The Health Promotion Unit of the Department of Health has been actively engaged in promoting safe sex for a number of years. In 1990, it introduced an AIDS programme for use in post-primary schools. The Unit organised seminars about the programme which were attended by over 1,500 teachers. In the beginning, the Unit ran into opposition about advocating the use of condoms. However, in 1993, it devised a series of six television advertisements which were broadcast after 9.00 pm. The advertisements were also broadcast on radio. The advertisements featured six different people, some of them media personalities, speaking straight to camera, advocating that people should protect themselves by using condoms. The messages were stark. In one advertisement Pat O'Mahony, a television presenter, says: 'So whatever your previous sexual history, if you're having sex, make sure you or your partner wear a condom.' In another advertisement, Mary McCarthy – a mother of a person with AIDS says: 'I urge all mothers to talk to their children about safer sex, and I ask them to please, please tell your children to use a condom if they are having sex.'

In 1995, The Irish YouthWork Centre and the National Youth Federation produced an analysis of the issues in the policy and practice of sex education. They argued that a critical approach to sex education – which corresponds to what I have identified as a liberal approach – is the most empowering for young people. This approach challenges the notion that there is an objective, value-free approach to teaching young people about sex and sexuality. 'Sex education is not and cannot be value free, but youth workers can be aware of their own values and the chances of imposing these on the young people with whom they work.'[23] They note that the goal of youth work is to foster 'the responsible exercise of freedom, as opposed to manipulating, conditioning or training young people'. It attempts to do this by raising consciousness through encouraging young people to challenge the values of society. However, they argue that youth workers must continually engage in a process of critical self-reflection, examining their personal motives for being involved in sex education, and what they hope to achieve. In this approach, the youth worker becomes a facilitator more than a teacher. There is no set curriculum, no hidden agenda. There is an emphasis on peer education and on young people learning to educate each other. This is important, given that many surveys indicate that young people learn, and prefer to learn, from people of their own generation.

A sex education course is devised through the discussions with a group of young people about their learning needs in relation to sexuality. Where possible young people are involved in organising the course, i.e., sourcing materials, organising inputs on specific subjects, contacting speakers, etc. Learning starts by acknowledging what skills and knowledge participants do have. There is an emphasis on learning from peers. Workers enable young people to examine and understand their life experiences in terms of the broader societal context, becoming aware of how structures impact on their lives.[24]

Much of what is recommended within this youth work approach corresponds to teaching methods used in adult education. The teacher surrenders a didactic approach of telling young people the way of the world of sexuality and what they should and should not do, for a dialogic approach in which his or her own knowledge is not predicated as necessarily more profound. This is regarded as particularly important in a situation where young people feel that they are more knowledgeable and experienced about sex and sexuality than their teachers or parents. It is argued that if the teacher gives a description and analysis of sex and sexuality which does not correspond to the experiences, needs and interests of the young people, there is a danger of adding to any existing feelings of distance, alienation and oppression. The task of the teacher in a liberal approach is to be able to sympathise with young people and the stress they experience in dealing with different messages about sexuality – many of them contradictory – which they receive from different sources in their daily life. The task in a liberal approach is not so much to teach as help young people read, understand and relate to the sexual world in which they live. The teacher becomes a skilled facilitator who helps young people learn from each other. In this learning environment, it is not that the teacher necessarily knows the world of sex and sexuality any better, but just in a different way. The teacher learns from young people as much as they learn from him or her. In other words, in a liberal approach, it is recognised that there is no truth about sex and sexuality other than that told by those in power. And so the task of the educator is to help reveal the structures and discourses of power and, when they feel it is desirable and necessary, to resist and challenge them.[25] This, for example, is particularly important in relation to the gendered construction of knowledge about sexuality. Sex education, as Lees points out, 'needs to be approached with reference to the powerful and taken-for-granted assumptions about sexuality which, rather than being naturally or biologically given, are social and reflect and reinforce the subordinate position of girls and women in our society.'[26] In a liberal approach, teaching young people about sex and sexuality is not like teaching them any other subject. It is about helping them to know, understand, and be able to reflect critically about themselves, others and the culture, community and society in which they live. In other words, in a critical, intersubjective, facilitative approach, young people are enabled to reveal and evaluate the psycho-cultural assumptions which constrain the way they see themselves and their relationships.[27] We can summarise the distinction between a didactic pedagogical approach to teaching sexuality and adult educational or andragogical approach (table 6).

Conclusion

A liberal perspective on relationships and sexuality education sees sexuality and being sexual as healthy, life-enhancing and pleasurable. However, it is argued, just as young people should learn to see and understand sexuality in a positive light – rather than as a sin or a threat – they also have to learn to become responsible, caring, critically self-reflective sexual actors. Within traditional and progressive perspectives, references are absent to the pleasures of being sexual and of the skills and responsibilities in being a good lover. The main source of a liberal perspective on sexuality comes from within the media. Within films,

Table 6. A Comparison of a Pedagogical and Andragogical
(or Liberal Adult Education) Approach to Sexuality
Education – following Jarvis and Knowles.[28]

	Pedagogical Approach	*Andragogical Approach*
The Learner	Dependent	Moves towards independence and self-directed learning.
	Teacher directs what, when, and how sexuality is learned.	Teacher encourages and nurtures this movement.
The Learner's Experience	Of little worth. Hence teaching methods are didactic.	A rich resource for learning. Hence teaching methods include discussion, problem, solving, etc.
Readiness to Learn	Young people learn what society expects them to, so that the curriculum is standardised	Young people learn what they need to know, so that learning programmes are organised around life application.
Orientation to Learning	Acquisition of subject matter. Curriculum organised by topics and subjects.	Learning experience should be based around problems, since young people are performance centred in the learning.

television soaps and serials, young people are encouraged, either directly or by implication, not to be afraid to become sexually active. In teenage magazines, they are encouraged to discover themselves through the consumption of a wide range of beauty and fashion products. Indeed teenage girls' magazines are little different from women's magazines, many of which use stories and features about sex to sell more copies.

A liberal perspective on relationships and sexuality education emphasises that there are no absolute truths about sex. Consequently, children and young people have to learn to recognise the different agendas of the institutions, organisations and groups which produce the different messages, and then to decode them within the context of the family, group, community and society in which they live. In other words, learning about relationships and sexuality is about learning to be a skilled social actor who is knowledgeable, responsible, caring and critically self-reflective. Liberal RSE often corresponds closely to the philosophy and methods of adult education. The main example of such an approach in Ireland comes from the programme developed by the Irish YouthWork Centre and the National Youth Federation.

5
Radical Sexuality

There is a fragrance in your kiss
that I have not found yet
in the kisses of women
or in the honey of their bodies.
(Pádraig Pearse, *Little Lad of the Tricks*, 1914)[1]

Beyond liberal attitudes to sexuality, and still more incompatible with traditional views, lies a discourse of radical sexuality. Its proponents call for radical changes in the way we see and understand sex and the way we relate to each other sexually. The argument is that if we changed the way we relate to each other sexually, we would create new and better ways for people to fulfil themselves as individuals. They would be more in tune with each other and with nature. This would help develop better social relations and, consequently, a new and better way of regulating society.

Radical sexual attitudes were popularised during the sexual liberation movement in the 1960s. The conception of sexuality portrayed within this cultural movement was linked to dropping out from the existing economic and political system, and its constant demand to perform, produce and consume. The emphasis was on discovering the simple pleasures of mind and body. In Freudian terms, it was giving primary importance to the pleasure principle – that is, abandoning the demands of participation in the real world and surrendering more to the pleasures, experiences and excitements of life.[2] It was founded on a profound disenchantment with the reality of Western society. The pursuit of a well-ordered, civilised society was seen to be shallow in the face of war and nuclear annihilation – particularly following the Cuban crisis. The counter-culture movement questioned the taken-for-granted, so-called objective reality of capitalism, mass media, male power and the mastery and domination of nature. It resisted and challenged this reality through creating alternative forms of relationships between men and women based on pleasure and fantasy. Making love meant abandoning inherited conceptions of oneself and learning to see and appreciate others, particularly those with whom one made love, not as a love object to be owned and possessed, but as a source of beauty, understanding and self-realisation.[3] It meant questioning social institutions such as marriage and the family and abandoning existing possessions and, along with them, the conceptions of who one was and what one did with one's life. It meant resisting and challenging the traditional way of thinking about men and women, marriage and family within which existing gender relationships were constituted. Having sex was seen as the culmination of a political process of making love and abandoning the constructed image of oneself. Dropping out involved an attempt to develop a new language, a new way of reading and interpreting the world. Surrender of the self was enhanced through a communal, highly ritualised practice of taking drugs. The counter-culture movement in Western society in the 1960s may have reached its political peak in the formation of alternative forms of community life, but its legacy is still found in the attempts within, for example, New Age or other radical religious movements, to resist and challenge the dominance of patriarchy, capitalism, science and technology.

A radical perspective on sexuality suggests that the problem for every one of us is that as part of having a well-ordered, efficient, productive, civilised society, sex has been repressed both in the individual and in society. This, it is argued, is not healthy, either for the individual or for society as a whole. If being sexual is the primary drive, then confining sexual activity to procreative, genital-focused acts within marriage, is at the heart of the malaise of modernity. Instead of being able to lounge in each other's company with open, passionate bodies, instead of being able to explore ourselves physically in the relaxed, uninhibited way which primates do – and which we did as infants – we have become obsessed with breasts, vaginas and penises. The reason why sex has become reduced to a fixation with genital sex is because it has been repressed in order that we produce more. Producing more necessitates consuming more and, it is argued, we end up in a never-ending, ever more alienated form of existence. Partially revealed bodies, tantalising invitations and suggestive signs of being highly sexed, have become a mechanism for creating and maintaining highly efficient, productive, but fundamentally inauthentic, human relations. Proponents of radical sexual attitudes hold that our salvation, and the salvation of society in general, is dependent on developing alternative forms of work, leisure and gender relations. While certain individuals may be able to lead unrepressed sexual lives, there will be no fundamental changes in society until the underlying structure of gender relations, family and the way we work are changed. These changes have to begin with breaking the artificial divide between body and soul. It involves challenging and abandoning the existing ways in which we have become sexed. It demands the discovery of new ways of being sexual. It is only by being sexual in a radically alternative way that the disease of capitalism and the malaise of modernity can be stemmed and, consequently, the human soul saved. What is crucial then, in this radical programme for change, is how we teach and prepare our children for a new way of life.

Lessons from the Frankfurt School

Radical attitudes on sexuality are associated with the writings of Eric Fromm, Herbert Marcuse and Wilhelm Reich. They were a group of German intellectuals who moved to the United States during the 1930s. They incorporated a Freudian understanding of sexuality within a Marxian explanation of alienation in capitalist society. Freud had argued that sexual love gave the 'strongest experiences of satisfaction' and was 'the prototype of all happiness'.[4] However, the reality of rejection, unfaithfulness or the death of a loved one leads people to be realistic about pursuing sexual pleasures. Consequently, civilised human beings learned to quell the sexual impulse and replace it with a more general, platonic type of love. Nevertheless, at bottom, the love we have for other people is displaced sexual love. As Fromm claimed, from a Freudian perspective, 'man is driven by a limitless desire for the sexual conquest of all women, and that only the pressure of society prevented man from acting on his desires.'[5] The problem, however, is that Freud was working within the then dominant ideas of Darwinism and capitalism and, consequently, over-emphasised biological and social competition. He also failed to recognise the influence of social relations in the way sexuality was lived out.

One of the arguments of the Frankfurt School was that economic and political oppression within capitalism was linked to sexual repression and that human liberation necessarily involved an overthrow of conventional beliefs, attitudes and practices regarding sex. Radical social transformation required changing the foundations of modern society. Oppression and alienation are founded in the nature of social relations in capitalism. The family maintains patriarchal domination from one generation to the next; the class structure which reproduces the domination of the bourgeoisie and the cycle of production and consumption prevents any change. Radical social transformation requires alternative forms of personal relationships and families. It involves new ways of understanding sexuality, and engaging in sexual relationships. Marcuse suggested that Freud never in fact argued that civilisation depended on a subordination of the pleasure principle to the reality principle. He agreed that while some degree of sublimation and repression of pleasure was initially necessary, advanced civilised societies, as existed in the West, could gradually reduce and abolish such repression. His aim was to create an alternative social structure that would lead to a 'resurgence of pregenital polymorphous sexuality' in which the body 'would become an object of cathexis, a thing to be enjoyed – an instrument of pleasure'.[6]

Reich argued that the oppression of the working class by the ruling class was founded on sexual repression. Achieving the necessary discipline, order and control essential for production and profits centred on the repression of working class sexuality. Radical change involved abandoning the traditional nuclear family in which relations of domination and subordination are learnt and accepted as normal.[7] For Reich being sexually expressive and unfettered is the main source of human happiness and people who are free and able to express their sexuality do not have a desire for power. He sought to introduce into Germany the type of radical sex education programme he had witnessed in the Soviet Union in the 1920s.

In Soviet schools adolescents were informed openly about procreation, birth, contraception, and venereal disease. Abortions were available and encouraged, and prostitution was largely eliminated. Women were depicted as equals of men in the household and the economy, traditional patriarchal practices were criticized, and permissive or self-regulating patterns of child-rearing were encouraged. The official Soviet position on homosexuality was also 'modern' and rather tolerant, at least in the beginning under Lenin.[8]

Reich argued that sexual repression becomes so inculcated into the mind and body that release is not possible through the self-realisation techniques of psychotherapy. Repression became built into the tissues and muscles and the whole way the body was presented. Release depended on programmes of relaxation, initially through massage, but ultimately through orgasm.[9]

Contemporary radical discourses

The type of radical Freudian discourse espoused by Marcuse and Reich is not much evidenced in contemporary Western society, let alone in Ireland. However, there is often a thin line not just between liberal and radical discourses, but between radical and traditional discourses. An article in *Playboy* magazine which espoused the virtues of chastity and modesty as a form of sexual fulfilment would blur the lines between traditional and radical discourses. Likewise, as we shall see in chapter 7, there are authors who, although writing for example as Catholic priests, espouse ideas which represent a radical departure from what is normally written within the Catholic tradition.

Nevertheless, most radical discourses about sexuality in Ireland are found in alternative magazines and newsletters which cater for minority or specific interest groups. In recent years, the Internet – especially some of the discussion groups – has become the major source for such viewpoints. Occasionally articles in pornographic magazines will cross the verge from being extremely liberal to being vaguely radical. Indeed the argument for pornography can be radical. For example, in the film *The People v Larry Flint,* there is a part where Flint is shown on stage addressing a Convention of Americans for a Free Press.

I have a thought for you. Murder is illegal. You take a picture of someone committing the act of murder and they will put you on the cover of *Newsweek.* It might even win you a Pulitzer prize. And yet sex is legal; everybody is doing it, or wants to be doing it. Yet you take a picture of two people in the act of sex, or just take a picture of a woman's naked body, and they will put you in jail. Now I have a message for all you good moral Christian people who are complaining that breasts and vaginas are obscene. Hey, don't complain to me. Complain to the manufacturer.
Okay, although Jesus told us not to judge, I know you are going to judge anyway, so judge sanely. Judge with your eyes open. What do you consider to be obscene? Is this obscene to you; or perhaps this, or maybe this is obscene to you. [*While he is speaking images of naked women are shown on the screen behind him, interspersed with images of violence, murder and war*]

You know politicians and demagogues like to say that sexually explicit material corrupts the youth of our country and yet they lie, cheat and start unholy wars. They call themselves men, but they are sheep in a herd. I think the real obscenity comes from raising our youth to believe that sex is bad and ugly and dirty and yet it is heroic to go and spill guts and blood in a most ghastly manner in the name of humanity. With all the taboos attributed to sex, it is no wonder we have the problems we have. It is no wonder we are angry and violent and genocidal. But ask yourself the question: what is more obscene, sex or war?[10]

Radical feminism

While there are few contemporary examples of a radical Frankfurt School attitude to sexuality, there are many feminists who call for a reconceptualisation of sexuality and sexual relations. Some radical feminists argue that engaging in heterosexual relations with men is to engage in the maintenance of women's inequality. Lesbian separatist theory claims that the structure of patriarchal society means that the family, and the domestic sphere in general, become the main site for generating the beliefs and practices through which women's inequality is reproduced. The way women think and act sexually, their desires and erotic feelings, are socially and culturally constituted to the extent that they impose restrictions on themselves, for example, in public places; where and how they chose to sit, and how they avoid and engage in eye contact.[11] The extreme of this is what Bartky refers to as feminine masochism which, for example, is manifested when women become erotically excited by male pornographic images of other women in submissive positions.[12] Adrienne Rich has argued that being hetero-sexual is a political stumbling block for women, as not only are women physically, economically, emotionally and psychologically coerced into heterosexuality, but engaging in heterosexual relations reproduces the social structures, such as marriage and the family, which dominate and oppress women.[13] Through heterosexuality, women become implicated in long-term domestic relations in which men's interests, needs and desires are fulfilled through their paid and unpaid labour.[14] Lesbian feminists call for greater sexual freedom, diversity and pleasure for women. They argue that the way sexuality is understood and practised coerces women into types of sexual relations which serve the interest of men and, con-sequently and necessarily, maintain patriarchy. It is not simply that women are depicted, understood and treated as men's passive sexual servants. Nor is it that women tend to see themselves this way. The biggest problem is that at the level of erotic pleasure and desire women are sexually turned on by how men see and treat them.[15]

As Bartky points out, how women experience, dress and display themselves has been inscribed in their bodies.

Feminine movement, gesture, and posture must exhibit not only constriction, but grace as well, and a certain eroticism restrained by modesty: all three. Here is the field for the operation of a whole new training: A woman must stand with stomach pulled in, shoulders thrown slightly back, and chest out, this to display her bosom to maximum advantage. While she must walk in the confined fashion appropriate to women, her movements must, at the same time, be combined with a subtle but provocative hip-roll. But too much display is taboo: Women in short, low-cut dresses are told to avoid bending over at all, but if they must, great care must be taken to avoid an unseemly display of breast or rump.[16]

The task in a radical feminist programme of relationships and sexuality education would be to deconstruct and dismantle this automatic disposition of women, according to which they see themselves as sexual objects to be possessed and penetrated by men. The aim would be to deconstruct the belief that the primary sexual fulfilment for women comes from giving men pleasure.[17] However, as with the Frankfurt School critique of capitalism, male domination of women is not confined to sex and, for many feminists, to dismantle men's domination of women and women's oppressed understanding of themselves, it is necessary to dismantle the many other ways in which gender domination is enacted in the home, at work and in social life.[18] Yet, if nothing changes until everything about patriarchal domination changes, then the question is where does the struggle begin, and what is the ideal form of sexual relationships for radical feminists to engage in? This is particularly important within radical feminist theory which advocates not just that the personal is political, but that personal radical action can change social structures.

Radical sexuality education

In a radical approach to learning about sexuality, young people would be encouraged not just to question and challenge existing philosophies and perspectives about sexuality, but the structures of power within which they are created and maintained. Young people would learn through dialogue, debate and discussion how these structures of power and ways of thinking and speaking operated in their lives, and how to engage in practices which successfully resisted them. Learning would revolve around discovering new ways of relating to bodies and pleasures beyond the understanding and practices constructed through the beliefs and attitudes developed by the Catholic Church, the state, and the media.[19]

A radical discourse about sexuality is absent from Irish society. However, given the historical context and dominance of traditional attitudes about sexuality, gay and lesbian writers and organisations can be seen to be promoting a radical perspective. It is only since the 1970s, but particularly in recent years, that the views and interests of gays and lesbians have been articulated in the media and the public sphere generally.[20] Although much of the debate which revolves around gay and lesbian issues centres on political rights, the arguments put forward in favour of gay and lesbian recognition, acceptance and symbolic legitimisation can be seen as radical, since they challenge existing conceptions of gender, sexuality and the family. They are often at the forefront of the argument that the truth about sex is not only socially and culturally constituted, but that it is political. It has been the power of the Catholic Church – and the doctors, teachers, politicians and civil servants who were its allies – which created and maintained a traditionalist viewpoint within which legislation and policies were enacted which silenced gay men and lesbian women, marginalised and ostracised them, kept them out of public life and, ultimately, confined them to the home, or the asylum.

In the November 1997 issue (No. 87) of *Women's News: The Irish Feminist Monthly*, Emma Donoghue describes the ambiguity of being a lesbian and a Catholic in Ireland.

I haven't called myself a Catholic since 1989 when an Archbishop called homosexuality 'an affliction'. But it'll always be one ingredient in my stew; I'm culturally Catholic, if not religiously. It colours my spirituality, my ethics, my language, my humour, the delicious guilt without which no sexual fantasy would be complete for me.

A feature article on Mary Dorcey in the same issue confronted bisexuality among women. Dorcey argues that most women are probably bisexual and are trained and moulded by society into heterosexual beings. She says:

There are people, very definitely, who can fall in love with both sexes – and do – and I think we should be able to recognise that and ultimately that is what we want as feminists. That is what I would want as a feminist, that people's sexuality is flexible and truly emancipated.

Diva is an English magazine for lesbians which is only available in specialised outlets in Ireland. However, the October/November 1997 issue gives an impression of the ongoing struggle for lesbian rights in Britain and other countries. Many of the feature articles are about politicians and pop stars coming out. There are some articles which deal more specifically with relationships and sexuality issues. One feature article 'Let's Stay Together' discusses lesbian bonding.

Lesbians question long-term monogamous relationships for good reason. Marriage hasn't historically been a happy place for women. And in both straight and gay relationships, long-term monogamy can be stifling, unimaginative and oppressive. Exploring the other options – non-monogamy, casual sex, dating and so on – has been an important aspect of lesbian culture.

Irish gay men do not appear to engage in the same political soul searching as lesbians. Nor is there – in comparison with Irish lesbians – an established genre of authors writing about love, relationships and sexuality. But there is a radical sexual counter-culture of gay men, swingers, sadomasochists, autoeroticists, who through their attitudes and practice resist and challenge established norms and values about sexuality. A central belief in this counter-culture is that it is inhibiting and restrictive to confine sex to intimate expressions within exclusive long-term relations. Because of its radical nature, this attitude is necessarily pushed underground and is rarely encountered, except through the Internet, gay clubs and adult bookshops.

Separating love and sex

It would be wrong to think that a radical attitude to sexuality is confined to a gay and lesbian subculture. There is within Western society a process in which love is becoming sexualised and, at the same time, sex is being eroticised.[21] A dimension of this process, according to Cas Wouters, is that love and sex can become rationally differentiated from each other. In other words, sex for the sake of sex moves from being regarded as degrading to being seen as acceptable. This allows 'more women and men to experiment with sex cheerfully and outside the boundaries of love and law'.[22] It may well be that as women become economically more independent, they free themselves from the image they have of themselves as constructed by men. In this process they overcome the way they have been symbolically and politically dominated. As they become more assertive in controlling their fertility, and the way sex takes place, they develop a new balance between lust (or sex for the sake of sex) and love. For example, Wouters quotes one Dutch woman:

For years and years I did not want any emotional commitment with men . . . What I did do regularly at the time, though, was pick up a one-night stand. In fact, that suited me well.. Because I was not emotionally committed to those men, I was able to take care of my sexual needs very well . . . It also gave me a feeling of power. I did just as I pleased, took the initiative myself and was very active.[23]

While women have undoubtedly become more assertive in sexual relations, it is not directly linked to a move towards less love and more lust. In fact, there is evidence that the balance has shifted more towards love in the 1990s. However, what has happened is that the art of being intimate, and the art of being sexual have, in some spheres of social life, become separated. In social situations in which some men and, increasingly, women are seeking sex – rather than intimacy and love – communication can be difficult. In such situations, being distant rather than intimate may be associated with issues such as sexual harassment, date-rape, prostitution and pornography.[24]

Conclusion

Radical sexual philosophies recognise that there will always be other philosophies which claim to announce the truth about sex and which necessarily constrain, restrict and repress the way people behave sexually. A radical attitude is one which challenges and resists these philosophies. A radical attitude to sexuality is not, then, based on a utopian dream in which sexual repression will be ended and we all become sexually liberated. Women who demand to be sexually satisfied and to be socially accepted when they want sex for the sake of sex, can be seen as part of this resistance.[25] A radical attitude to sexuality challenges the dominant definition of what is sexually normal and acceptable. This is what has made gay and lesbian discourse and practice radical. It is through the radical practice of sex that people can continually rediscover sexual pleasure and alternative erotic, passionate and loving relationships with each other.[26] In this regard, perhaps the most radical discourse of all is that which argues that the present obsession with sex on the part both of men and women can never lead to liberation. What is needed, it is argued, is a radical desexualisation of society. This cannot be attained by men who have promoted the cult of sexual satisfaction. Nor can it be attained by women who become enmeshed in the cult. It can only be attained through women surrendering physical interest in sex – which Freud argued they never had – and attaining a symbolic domination over men by continually seducing them but never physically satisfying them. Desire becomes dissolved in a game of illusion and play-acting.[27]

6
Shaping Young People's Sexuality

The types of beliefs, attitudes and opinions which have been identified in previous chapters provide a framework for examining the way Irish people think, talk, write about, and embody sexuality. As mentioned in chapter 1, it is useful to think of the different beliefs and attitudes about sexuality as 'discourses'. Such discourses are produced and recorded in books, reports, newspapers, films, television and radio programmes, plays, art and so forth. Although they have an important oral dimension, particularly in relation to everyday life, it is useful to consider discourses as having some kind of material existence, and being capable of being catalogued and stored in libraries, museums and archives. My argument, so far, has been that a description and analysis of what has been written, said and recorded about sexuality in Ireland in this century suggests four main discourses: traditional, progressive, liberal and radical. The task of this chapter is to examine how these discourses become part of the everyday lives of young people, and are reflected in what they do and say. In other words, how do these discourses shape the sexual beliefs, attitudes and practices of young people? How are they passed down and received within homes, schools, playgrounds, churches, cafes, discos and pubs? What is the link between what is written and said about sexuality within the Catholic Church, the state and the media, and the sexual beliefs and lifestyle of young people? How do young people filter and adapt the different messages which they receive from parents, teachers, priests, friends, radio, television, films, magazines, media gurus, agony aunts, and many others? In other words, we need to go beyond formal discourses produced within powerful institutions such as the Catholic

Church, the state and the media, and discover the way young people read, understand and operate in the sexual world in which they live.[1]

It is important to realise that young people receive various different messages about sexuality from numerous sources. Television, radio, magazines, schools and homes are the main providers of these messages. Young people receive these messages directly, and indirectly as they are filtered through sisters, brothers and friends. Through this process, young people develop an understanding of themselves as sexual human beings and, at the same time, develop an ongoing orientation or disposition towards sexuality. This understanding and orientation is based on a distillation of the attitudes, beliefs, values and practices they encounter. It provides a lasting, adjustable basis by which young people can read, interpret and know what is happening sexually in social situations and, consequently, enables them to operate more or less successfully within them. It gives them a practical sense of what to do and say, of what is appropriate and inappropriate, at home, in school, among friends, at discos, in cafes and restaurants. While fairly permanent in that this understanding and orientation does not change significantly over time, it is flexible for use in different social contexts. In other words, young people develop a habitus which enables them to encounter various different situations, to be able to read and understand what is happening, and to be able to say and do appropriate things.[2] This shared disposition frames their understanding, outlook, actions and reactions to their everyday relationships and encounters with sexuality. It also gives them a sort of intuitive knowledge which enables them to know the rules and regulations of the game of sex as it is played in their social life with adults or other young people. They have a feel for the game, of what can and cannot be said and done with whom, when and where.[3] The sexual habitus of young people varies between different societies and periods of history.

Young people who are good readers, interpreters and actors in the field of sexuality – who develop a good knowledge, understanding and interpretation of the sexual habitus in which they operate – develop a certain honour, respect and status. They are, so to speak, good players. They develop a kind of sexual capital. When sexual attitudes and opinions were heavily influenced and controlled by the Catholic church, sexual capital was conflated with religious capital. In other words, as we saw in chapter 2, when it came to sex, good young people were chaste, modest and by and large asexual. In the present era, in which sexuality has become differentiated from religion, being sexual revolves around being fit, healthy, attractive, engaging, enticing and flirtatious. Sexual capital, once accumulated, can be traded for other forms of capital, for example, economic, political and social.[4] In other words, by being a skilful player in the game of sex – which depending on the context may involve being chaste and modest or sexy and attractive – young people can accumulate sexual capital which can then be traded for economic, political and social rewards and benefits.

The knowledge, understanding and attitudes young people have about sex and sexuality, and the way they play the game of sex, may be seen as a subculture adapted from the general discourses identified and described in previous chapters. We need now to examine how these various discourses – sets of beliefs and attitudes – interact with each other and then how they trickle down and shape the sexual habitus of young people.

The field of Irish sexuality

To understand the relationship between institutional structures, their discourses and people – that is between what is formally said and written about sexuality and what people actually do and say in everyday life – it is necessary to place sex and sexuality within the wider context of social life. In this regard, it is useful to think of the area of sexuality, what is said, written and done, as a social field. In the sexual field, there are experts – people who become skilled at writing and speaking about sexuality. There are also ordinary people who, in their daily lives, engage in sexual behaviour. They talk about sex, look at it in public life, listen to it on the radio, see it on television, and read about it in newspapers. Within any social field, the task is to identify the relationship between what the experts say, whether they be priests, doctors, psychologists, sociologists, therapists, and so forth, and what ordinary people do and say.[5]

There are of course hundreds of different social fields in which people operate in everyday life. Some of the more important ones are economics, politics, education and religion. Much of what we know about economics comes from what is written and said by economic commentators or analysts. We can call these expert, or formal institutional, discourses. We live in a capitalist economy and much of what is written and said about economics comes from what may be termed a traditional perspective. These experts argue the virtues of a free market economy. But there are other discourses or perspectives, for example, liberal-democratic, socialist, communist and, more lately, green.

Related to, but separate from, these discourses is the way people in their everyday life, read, understand and interpret economic behaviour. The way people behave economically is shaped by the policies and programmes which are devised and implemented by the economic experts who advise those in power. But people are inventive. They rarely follow the letter of the law. They adapt rules and regulations to suit their needs and interests. They are not dependent on what expert commentators write and say. They are, for example, influenced by non-economic discourses, such as their religious beliefs. Consequently, instead of trying to maximise profit, a shopkeeper may behave charitably and give something away to a poor customer. Similarly, in the field of sexuality, behaviour is shaped by the individual's circumstances and beliefs.

By identifying different formal institutional discourses in previous chapters, I was able to classify and categorise what has been written and said about sexuality in Ireland. I argued that the Catholic Church was the main proponent of a traditional perspective on sexuality. It would be convenient if then, for example, everything that was written and said by the Catholic Church was within a traditional perspective. But, of course, social life is much more complex than this. There is in fact a variety of attitudes and opinions about sexuality within the Catholic Church. There are many Catholics, including clergy and religious, who speak about sexuality from a progressive or, indeed, liberal perspective. On the other hand, there are gay and lesbians who have a traditional attitude to sexuality, especially perhaps those who are priests, brothers or nuns. Secondly, at the level of the individual, people's sexual attitudes, values and practices do not neatly fit into any one of the discourses identified. People may be liberal and progressive on some issues and quite traditionalist on others. Thirdly, what people say and do, and to a certain extent what they believe and value, depends on the context – where they are, and whom they are with. What people say, and how they behave sexually in, for example, a pub or night-club, will often be quite different from what they say and do at home or in school. Indeed one of the key things which young people have to learn about sexuality is that context is of primary importance. In other words, they have to learn that what they say to each other is different from what they say to priests, teachers and parents.

Let us take, for example, a sixteen-year-old boy attending Catholic secondary school. Let us say that he is sexually active in that he has had a steady girlfriend for the past year with whom he has had close sexual encounters, including deep kissing, fondling, petting and perhaps a couple of attempts at sexual intercourse. Say he masturbates a couple of times a week. How he thinks and talks about sex is neither obvious nor straightforward. If, in class, he is asked by a teacher about his attitude to pre-marital sex, he may gave a quite traditional response, saying that sex outside marriage is not a good thing. What makes social life and sexuality difficult to understand is that when he announces this, he may actually believe it. He may at least like the sound of what he says. Learning, after all, is about being able to think about, transfer and apply what is seen and heard in the classroom to other contexts.

At home, however, if the same topic emerges, he may come forward with a more progressive perspective. Much will depend on the context – who is present (parents alone or perhaps brothers and sisters), how the subject arose, the place (the dinner table or his bedroom). Now he may say that sex before marriage is perfectly okay as long as you and your girlfriend are in love and practise safe sex. Then again, when he is out with his friends, he may take up a much more liberal position saying that as long as it is consensual, people can have any type of sex whenever, with whomever they please.

Just because a young man speaks differently about sex in different contexts, does not mean that he is inconsistent, a liar, or hypocritical. Rather it is an indication that in many areas of social life, what we say and do depends on the social context in which we find ourselves. This is important, as it will have a bearing on what is said in the classroom when young people are learning about relationships and sexuality. What is read and accepted in magazines, or what is said and discussed in the playground, might not be even raised or referred to in a relationships and sexuality class, especially if the teacher is deemed to be a traditional conservative. Given young people's exposure to different views of sexuality, it is important to recognise and accept the different and often inconsistent ways in which they think, talk about and understand sex.

But it is not just young people. What teachers and parents think and say about sex in, for example, the privacy of their own bedroom could be very different from what they say at a public meeting in the children's school. Moreover, speaking about sex, sexuality and relationships is very different from speaking about English or history. No matter how well we try to protect ourselves, there is necessarily an element of self-revelation and disclosure in speaking, or indeed writing, about sex. And, no matter how good the attempt to overcome it, there is always a political context to what is said in a classroom. Teachers and pupils know each other. Pupils have records. The memories and legacies of previous encounters are not easily dissipated. The political context might be changed dramatically if the teacher and the pupils were anonymous to each other. Even so, a guarantee of anonymity and confidentiality does not mean that people will speak freely. For example, although the confessional is constituted on being confidential and anonymous, how a person speaks to the priest about sex may be very different to how they speak, for example, to a psychoanalyst.

So there are within the field of Irish sexuality numerous experts who have made significant contributions to shaping the way people see, think and understand sexuality. In the past, it was popes, bishops, priests and theologians who shaped our understanding. In the last thirty years they have faced increased opposition, first from the media and, more lately, from the state. What is written and said by these experts may not dictate, but has had a considerable influence on what people think, say and do sexually. It is also important to realise that while what is said and written by experts contributes to our common knowledge and understanding of sexuality, these contributions emerge through a competitive struggle between different interest groups to have their views heard and adopted as policy either by the school or the state. Much of this struggle takes place through debate, discussion and argument, some of it at public meetings, some of it through the media. In the past, when the Catholic Church dominated the field of sexuality in Ireland, it was difficult for artists and intellectuals – or those working in films, television, radio and newspapers – to have liberal or radical ideas about sex recognised and accepted. It was even more difficult for teachers, doctors, nurses, politicians and civil servants. When informal self-censorship did not work, the Church had recourse to formal censorship. The Church's view of sexuality was willingly enacted and enforced by the state.[6] But changes began to take place. New ideas and beliefs began to be debated and discussed which were eventually to filter through and have a profound effect on shaping Irish sexuality.

The struggle for control of sexuality

The dominance of the Catholic Church's view and understanding not just of sexuality, but of desire, pleasure, sense of self and relationships, first came under threat from the media, at first through film and, later, through television. The ideas, images and lifestyles presented on television were not significantly different from those presented in film; it was just that they appeared more regularly and had direct entry to people's homes. At the same time, the women's movement began to grow and, later, a number of reform movements emerged to campaign for an end to sexual discrimination, abuse, rape and violence. Part of this campaign included women's right to limit and control their fertility. Alongside the media and these movements were an increasing number of artists, writers and intellectuals who produced ideas about sexuality which were at variance with, or contrary to, the perspective and teaching of the Catholic Church.

The state was slow to challenge the Church's monopoly. There were a series of small, but important changes such as the easing of the censorship laws in the 1960s, the gradual admission of artificial contraceptives from the late 1970s, and the decriminalisation of homosexuality in 1990s. However, the most significant challenge to the Catholic Church's monopoly over the field of Irish sexuality began with the Stay Safe Programme and reached a peak with the proposed Social, Personal and Health Education programme of which Relationships and Sexuality Education has been the first component to be launched. For the first time, the experts who decided what children and young people – most attending Catholic schools – needed to know and understand about sexuality, were not bishops or priests or, indeed, loyal followers of the Church.

The state's challenge to the Church's dominance in sexuality education did not come from the knowledge and understanding which the programmes produced about sex and sexuality. It had more to do with young people developing knowledge, understanding and appreciation of themselves as individuals with their own sense of self and, most significantly, their own sense of what is right and wrong.

Reaction to the RSE programme

The most negative reaction to the RSE programme has come from Catholic interest groups. In his critical analysis of the programme, Ger Casey claimed that the demand for it was created by the Irish Family Planning Association which is a member of the International Planned Parenthood Federation.[7] He argued that RSE is largely an ideological programme which, under the umbrella of popular psychology, liberal sociology and sexology, fosters self-esteem and gives children the opportunity to discuss and explore attitudes, values, beliefs and opinions.

The ideology at the root of RSE-1 is a closed individualism that places God at the outer fringe rather than the centre of life. The word 'God' doesn't appear once in RSE-1, but there's lots and lots of talk about 'self'. 'Self-esteem' and 'self-confidence' are mentioned about thirty times, not to mention self-awareness and self-worth as well.[8]

He was critical that topics such as conception and intercourse are dealt with in primary school, noting that the proposal to 'teach the intimate details of sexuality in class is a serious encroachment upon the authority, autonomy and privacy of parents'.[9]

Casey called for the RSE programme to be opposed at every possible opportunity. He regarded organised opposition within each school as a struggle by Catholics against an ever-expanding secular state.

Those who seek to assure Catholic parents that there is no need for alarm, and that we can trust the State and its interim curriculum and guidelines, give the appearance of being afraid of engaging in a dispute with the State. But this is to avoid facing the fact that there is a cultural war in progress in Ireland now between the secularist view and the Christian visions of the human person and human development. What is contained in RSE-1 is part of that cultural war.[10]

Casey gave a blueprint of the type of action which parents should take at local level. He urged them to find out exactly what was happening regarding RSE in their children's school. He suggested that they try to become members of the Steering Committee elected to implement the programme, and to keep a record of all meetings and conversations. He recommended that if parents could not prevent the introduction of an RSE-type programme in the school, they should consider withdrawing the child from the programme.

The spirit of the age is Statist and secularist. Sometimes we must make a stand to prevent the State from encroaching into areas in which it has no direct interest, especially when it is proselytising for a secularist sexual ideology. Nobody wants to engage in a long protracted struggle with the State and its agencies but parenthood has its duties as well as its privileges.[11]

There are at least three groups – Human Life International, Tuistí and Parents' Network – which are actively involved in opposing the introduction of RSE.

The reaction of the Catholic bishops was more careful and considered. They provided a detailed analysis of the programme and specific guidelines as to how it should be introduced in Catholic primary schools. They noted at the outset the imperative that the policy adopted by each school 'should reflect the core values and ethos of the school'. They insisted that

[T]he Catholic school, in the formulation of its policy, should reflect Catholic moral teaching on sexual matters. Even more fundamentally, it needs to be specific in excluding approaches which are inconsistent with the very foundation of Catholic moral thought.

Moral truth is not arrived at by consensus. It is not the product of feelings or instinct. It is not arrived at by simply weighing up the likely consequences of various lines of action. It is not some arbitrary or legalistic imposition. It is not just a matter of being sincere, so that what is right for one person may be wrong for another. All of these approaches can readily be identified in contemporary debates.[12]

It was clear, then, that in Catholic primary schools, when it came to teaching children about relationships and sexuality, they had to be told the truth as defined by the Church. The bishops decided that the truth about such issues was already contained within its own religious education programme *Children of God*. Consequently, the bishops produced a resource manual for teaching relationships and sexuality in Catholic schools. In the manual, each of the specific topics detailed in the National Council for Curriculum and Assessment (NCCA) guidelines for RSE in Primary Schools was noted, and specific references were given to readings and activities within the *Children of God* series which, it was claimed, covered the topic adequately for Catholic primary schools. In other words, the argument of the Church was that that there was really no need for the NCCA to produce its detailed curriculum guidelines, at least as regards Catholic primary schools. The Church's existing religious curriculum covered everything that children needed to learn about relationships and sexuality adequately. Teaching children about sexuality becomes reduced to teaching them about religion.

There are significant differences between the RSE curriculum and the *Children of God* religious education course. The RSE programme is secular. Unlike the *Children of God* programme, it does not have constant references to the Bible, the gospels and the teachings of the Church. Secondly, although the *Children of God* programme deals with relationships, there is not the same emphasis as in the RSE about developing self-awareness, self-confidence and self-esteem. Finally, in the *Children of God* programme, there are no references to sex or sexuality in the pupil's book. In the teacher's manual there is a section which deals with human life and how it begins, puberty, human love and how love creates life. This section is seen as optional. It is included 'to facilitate teachers who wish to include sex education as part of the programme. . . . It also provides a context for teaching children the Sixth and Ninth Commandments.'[13] This corresponds to what appears in the pupils' books where the reference to sex and sexuality appears, in both fifth and sixth class, is as follows:

Q. What is commanded by the Sixth and Ninth Commandments?

A. In the Sixth and Ninth Commandments we are commanded to be pure of heart and to be modest in our thoughts, words, looks and actions.

Q. What is forbidden by the Sixth and Ninth Commandments?

A. The Sixth and Ninth Commandments forbid adultery, and all immodesty in our thoughts, words and actions.[14]

So the Catholic Church was not opposed to the RSE programme. It was rather that they insisted that in Catholic schools the policy and programme adopted reflected the Catholic moral tradition. To ensure this, it was recommended that Catholic schools fulfil the requirement of introducing the programme, but that the content of the programme should be taken from its existing religious education programme. In other words, through osmosis of the *Children of God* series with the RSE curriculum guidelines, relationships and sexuality education became – as the bishops had argued from the outset – an integral part of existing religion classes.

Nevertheless, it must be remembered that Church personnel and the Catholic Primary School Managers Association had represented the Church in the process of forming the curriculum guidelines for the RSE programme. In other words, the Church could claim that, yes, it had been supportive of relationships and sexuality education and that it had participated in the formulation of the policy and curriculum. Part of the policy was that each school would decide what resources to use to implement the RSE curriculum and all the Church was saying was that the *Children of God* series was the best resource for Catholic schools.

The role of the media

The opponents to RSE see the programmes devised by the state as letting Protestantism creep in the back door. But, it could be argued, it is not so much how RSE deals with Catholic or Protestant perspectives which is important in young people's lives, but rather how RSE deals with the media. It is, after all, the media which now dominate the field of sexuality and which have most influence in shaping young people's attitudes and opinions.

Media dominance in the field of sexuality has occurred in two ways. Firstly, through the messages produced within soaps, serials, advertisements, the music industry, teenage magazines and so forth which advocate and legitimate the discovery of self and the pursuit of pleasure. Secondly, the media have become the clearing-house for ideas about sexuality. It is through chat shows, talk-radio, and discussion programmes that issues and ideas about sexuality are revealed and discussed. The media have developed a monopoly over setting the agenda for debate and discussion in the public sphere.[15] Thus, at the same time that the media promote liberal viewpoints, they also organise and preside over public debate among different interest groups and, as we shall see, judge and evaluate the ideas and policies they produce. The pursuit of public support, whether by the state, the Church or other interest groups now, by and large, takes place through the media. The ability to inform minds, raise consciousness, change opinions, develop support, and alter government programmes and policies which, in this instance, shape young people's sexuality, depends on the ability of interest groups to attract media attention.

Public debate about RSE

An interesting example of how the media fulfilled the role of influencing and controlling public debate and understanding about RSE was evident in a discussion which took place on *The Pat Kenny Show* on RTÉ Radio 1 on Thursday and Friday, 26 and 27 February, 1998. The debate followed a protest at a meeting in Trim, Co. Meath held to discuss the introduction of RSE in the local primary school. The first person interviewed was Sean Dempsey, the Principal of the school. He indicated that while the meeting was organised as an information session on RSE for parents, it was disrupted by 'strays from outside' who heckled and shouted at the proposed speakers before the meeting started. The chairperson of the meeting, he said, had been called a pervert and a paedophile. He described how a local member of Family Solidarity, Brendan Cleary, had taken over the microphone. The gardaí were called, and people eventually left without the meeting commencing.

Pat Kenny suggested that the names people were being called were 'the stuff of legal action'. He went on to claim that 'this is Hitler's blackshirt territory isn't it and disruption of meetings and all the rest of it?' Later, however, Kenny and Dempsey came to the conclusion that although the meeting was directed towards parents, it was, in effect, a public meeting which the protesters had every legal right to attend.

The next interview was with Meena Bean Uí Chribbín. She too invoked Nazi Germany, complaining that the RSE programme was not a matter of parents' choice, 'it is compulsory, it's worse than Hitler's regime'. She suggested that the anti-RSE movement had no platform to represent the huge number of parents and teachers who were against the programme. She claimed that the government had succumbed to a lobby which was marketing condoms and abortion. At this stage Kenny suggested that she was 'making a laughing stock' of herself. He went on to argue that the RSE programme was a substantial improvement on what most people, in his time, got in the school yard. He maintained that the purpose of RSE was not to corrupt children, but to give them information which would help them recognise child abuse. Bean Uí Chribbín claimed that teaching five and six year olds to identify and name parts of the body made them 'absolute fodder for the child abuser'. Pat Kenny asked her if she was one of those people who would prefer that a little girl didn't know that she had a vagina, or a little boy that he had a penis? Her response, deeply embedded in traditional attitudes, was full of indignation, complaining bitterly how the media had destroyed the innocence of Irish people.

The type of life that my people handed down to me was a life well above talking. But you shouldn't, as a man, be talking about those things anyway, and the life that I lived, men didn't talk about men's things. They weren't sissies . . . We lived a life on a very high level, believe you me, and we certainly didn't live a life where all these things – women's parts thrown around on the radio and on the television – we didn't live that.

The following morning, Pat Kenny talked to Anne McKenzie, a member of the National Parents Council. Before beginning the interview, he announced, 'I don't think any interview I've done on this programme in recent times caused more of an uproar, a reaction, than the one with Bean Uí Chribbín yesterday.'

Anne McKenzie had made a detailed study of the proposed curriculum for the RSE programme. She said that the keystone on which the RSE programme was based was 'values clarification'. However, she argued that what this really meant was that children will be taught that 'there is no objective right or wrong . . . that every situation is judged by how the child feels in a situation, how the peers feel and how the media feel and how the parents feel.' She felt that this was cheating children who, she said, needed strong formation now more than ever. She argued that as they become adults they can make up their own minds, but 'we must give them firm moral teaching'. She claimed that the word marriage was not mentioned in the curriculum, and that the word love was only used in inverted commas. It was time, she said, 'for some robust honesty on what we are going to teach our children as right and wrong'. She denied not wanting to give children sex education but said that 'we are questioning who gives it, where it is given, when it is given'. The Department of Education, she said, had never answered the question of how teachers would deal with RSE in a class with different age groups. It was because this type of fundamental question had not been answered and that the consultation meetings with parents were unhelpful, that there was the type of heckling which had occurred in Trim. She emphasised that the *Children of God* series was perfectly adequate for providing whatever knowledge and information children required about relationships and sexuality.

The most interesting exchange came when Anne McKenzie raised questions about what went on during the in-service days for teachers interested in teaching the programme. She said that with 'the sort of materials they were given you would question whether you want your child to be taught by people who have produced that sort of material'.

Pat Kenny: What sort of material?

Anne McKenzie: Well the sort of material that was produced to teachers on in-service days was very explicit and a lot of teachers were appalled, whole staff rooms walked out in Cork. We don't hear that in the evaluations that we have . . .

PK: But tell me. I don't know. These teachers are supposed to be of the world. They are supposed to understand things in the world so that they can protect their students. What type of material would shock a teacher?

AM: They would . . .

PK: I mean I'm really, unless you are talking about bizarre sexual practices, I mean they should not be shockable, or they should not be in that job.

AM: It was not that they were shocked, but that they were appalled and angry that they were being subjected in a setting of a training day to material that they considered to be totally inappropriate.

PK: But what, you can talk freely. This is an adult programme. The kids are in school. What exactly were they shocked about?

AM: Right. In one seminar, the staff were told all about what is meant by a blowjob and they were asked and they were told that they needed to know about this so that if it came up in a class they could discuss it in the class. The point they are trying to make is that that's not the type of thing to be discussed in class.

PK: But Anne, they are talking about this in the daily press with respect to Monica Lewinsky and President Clinton, come on.

AM: Exactly but what are they trying to teach . . .

PK: They are talking about it, fourteen year olds are talking about this in schools in Dublin. I don't know how it is in Tralee. We've had surveys of sex talk among kids. They have, they talk about things I don't understand.

Anne McKenzie argued that young people should be encourage to reserve sexual activity for marriage. She said that sex education had been going on for years in Britain. The stated aim 'was to reduce teenage pregnancies and abortions and the opposite has happened. They have spiralling rates.'

The final interview in this series was with Emer Egan, Senior Inspector of the Department of Education with responsibility for the RSE programme. She argued that while the education system sought to develop the whole child, there had been a gap in the past in teaching children about sexuality. The Expert Advisory Group had suggested that this gave the wrong message to children – that sexuality was something that teachers and adults could not, or did not want to talk to them about. It recommended that RSE should become an integral part of the work of schools. There was then a lengthy discussion about the justification and viability of leaving the content of the programme to be decided by a committee appointed in each school. Pat Kenny suggested that leaving it to the discretion of each school – what should and should not be taught – could lead to discrimination, with some children becoming well-informed and knowledgeable about sexuality, while children in other schools would remain ignorant and uninformed.

The discussion then moved to how the RSE programme would be implemented in two-teacher schools where there are different age groups in the same class and how teachers could be trained to implement the programme in just three days. In the final part of the interview Pat Kenny asked if it was desirable or appropriate to teach young children the proper names for parts of their body. Emer Egan argued that while it was quite acceptable for children to have pet names for their genitals, it was important that they learnt the correct names, 'because it enables them to communicate in a respectful way about their bodies and that is something that should be cultivated at all times'. The interview concluded with a discussion about how democratic the programme was. Emer Egan emphasised that while individual teachers and parents could opt out of the programme, individual schools could not. She said the Department would need to talk to those schools which did not want to introduce RSE. She concluded by stressing the collaborative nature of the programme.

Somebody has not just decided that this is what we are going to have. This has been developed by all the partners in education so you have the Catholic Primary School Managers Association, The Church of Ireland Board of Education, the INTO, all of the post-primary teacher unions, National Parents Council. It is the combined wisdom of all those groups that has brought us to the stage we are at.

In effect, the interview with Emer Egan was more a discussion of the technical difficulties of implementing the programme rather than a debate about the content of the programme. The issue of whether the content of the programme was suitable for Catholic children being taught in Catholic schools was avoided, particularly the issue of children being taught what was right and wrong.

There is much to be learnt about the way the debate and discussion about the RSE programme was brought into the public arena by the media. In the first instance, the issue came to light through a well-organised if not staged demonstration at a meeting in Trim. It was as if the media knew in advance that there was going to be a public protest. However, although the anti-RSE lobby gained the initial publicity, Pat Kenny showed a bias towards progressive and liberal attitudes. The interviews with the school principal and the Inspector of the Department were not as challenging as those with Meena Bean Uí Chribbín or Anne McKenzie. Pat Kenny did not suggest to Sean Dempsey or to Emer Egan, as he had done to Bean Uí Chribbín, that she could be 'making a laughing stock' of herself or, as he had suggested to Anne McKenzie, that she was living in an ivory tower. It is also noticeable that the former were official representatives while the latter were interviewed as individuals whose representativeness might be queried. Finally, it was noticeable that the first and final interviews, which opened and closed the debate, were with the official sources.

There has also been considerable debate in the newspapers. In the 'Education and Living' supplement of *The Irish Times* on 24 March 1998, Carmel Wynne wrote an article which was critical of anti-RSE lobbyists. She said that they misrepresented traditional moral values. There was a need, she said, to teach young people a form of chastity that was positive about loving, touch and sexual feelings. She argued that when sexual desire is thought of as sinful, repression is almost inevitable. When the anti-RSE lobby claimed that similar programmes in other countries had led to an increase in teenage pregnancies, abortion and rampant immorality, they failed to make clear that they were talking about value-free programmes.

Such programmes teach children how to manage their emerging sexuality through non-coital sex. This includes a range of behaviours, from intimate kissing to mutual masturbation to full body massage. Value-free programmes give young people positive messages about expressing sexuality – but fail to balance these with equally positive messages about not expressing sexuality. Programmes that give abstinence messages have been shown to be effective when they are introduced before young people become sexually active.

She maintained that the proposed RSE programme would not be value-free, but would put sex within a moral framework. She agreed that parents have a right and a duty to educate their children about sexuality, but said that many do not. But she claimed that the failure of parents to provide timely and accurate information led young people to turn elsewhere. 'The value-free information they receive from friends frequently leads to wrong sexual thinking and poor sexual decision-making.'

Carmel Wynne's article drew sharp criticism particularly from Nora Bennis, leader of the National Party and a well-known critic of the RSE programme. In a letter to *The Irish Times* she assured readers that 'there is conclusive evidence, world-wide, to prove that classroom sex education has horrendous effects on children. . . .'[16] She referred to one international expert who, she claimed, was 'adamant that classroom sex education leads children along the road to being cruel, dangerous and even psychopathic'. She maintained that the RSE programme was the brainchild of the Irish Family Planning Association and that the Vatican's *The Truth and Meaning of Human Sexuality* called on parents to reject all secularised, anti-natalist programmes such as developed by the IFPA.

The main purpose behind generating public debate through the media is to influence the policy and implementation of the RSE programme. This takes place at two levels. The first is at the level of the state devising and implementing its programmes. The second is at the level of the school developing its own specific policy. The RSE programme was formed by parents, teachers, policy-makers and representatives of different interest groups, including the Catholic Church, coming together to decide what young people should be taught about sexuality. There were two important absentees from this policy and programme formation process: the media and young people.

It could be argued that the media are too diverse and amorphous to have representatives making a contribution to policy formation. But while this may be true of television, film, radio, videos and records, it is less true of the owners and producers of teenage magazines, particularly the agony aunts who contribute to them. It is interesting, in this regard, that a report in *The Sunday Tribune* (5 April 1998) indicated that the British Health Minister, Tessa Jowell, had met with editors of girl teenage magazines to ask them if they would collaborate in promoting sex education. Secondly, it was remarkable that young people themselves were not included in the debate about what it is that they need to learn concerning relationships and sexuality. The absence of young people from the debate mirrors their minimal involvement in developing a policy and programme within the school.[17] As with any other subject, the government – particularly the National Council for Curriculum and Assessment (NCCA) – teachers and parents, deem themselves to know best what it is that young people need to know about relationships and sexuality. The problem is that RSE is not like any other subject since it is not about young people learning a specific field of knowledge with recognised experts, but about themselves, their relationships and their sexuality about which they, necessarily, have to have knowledge. If young people are not partners in deciding what it is that they want to learn about relationships and sexuality, if they do not have a sense that they can ask the questions and, with the teacher seek rather than be told answers, then there is a danger that the programme could become not just an empty exercise, but one which increases rather than decreases young people's sense of sexual alienation.

The continuing legacy of the Catholic Church

The Church's influence on young people's sexuality takes effect in three ways. The primary influence is, of course, through years of being brought up within the values, beliefs and practices of the Church. Young people's knowledge and understanding of themselves and their sexuality is shaped in the hours, days and weeks spent going to Mass, Holy Communion and Confession, on their knees praying, learning the teachings of the Church and behaving in a pious, modest and chaste manner. The influence of the Church is not just in defining what is right and wrong, but in providing an overall interpretive framework for determining moral behaviour. Morality comes down to young people as a series of rules and regulations – of 'do's and don'ts'. Sex and sexuality become classified, seen, understood and interpreted primarily as a series of sins. Years of being taught that certain acts – such as sexual intercourse outside marriage – are in their nature sinful, necessarily have an impact on people's sexuality. Young people spend years learning to see themselves as sinners, to feel shameful and guilty about sex, and to seek forgiveness. They also learn not to question the sin, for there is no questioning of the authority of the Church on these issues. Young people learn to see and interpret sexual behaviour in terms of living up to a series of demands and injunctions made on them. It is a classification system of rights and wrongs which is laid down and within which they operate. Whatever resistances or challenges they may make, they are still operating within a Catholic structure. This has two main consequences. First, since sexual behaviour among young people is morally unacceptable, young people will tend to be more covert and secretive about their sexual thoughts, feelings and behaviour. Second, young people will tend to see ethics of sexual behaviour in terms of their success or failure to live up to a series of rights and wrongs, rather than as part of an overall, integrated moral perspective which they have developed themselves.

The Church also shapes young people's sexuality through its ability to influence, if not control, what is taught, said and done in Irish Catholic schools. The influence is operated through the ethos, the subjects taught and the teachers employed. Religion permeates the whole curriculum of primary schools which, in Catholic schools, means the creation and maintenance of Church beliefs and rituals. Finally, children and young people's attitudes to sexuality are shaped by the values, beliefs, attitudes and practices of their teachers. In Catholic primary schools, teachers are expected to be practising Catholics, which is interpreted as, at least, attending Mass on Sundays. Teachers who do not have a lifestyle which is in keeping with Catholic Church teaching have, in the past, been dismissed. Generations of teachers have embodied a disposition which saw and understood sex and sexuality as issues about which as little as possible was said. Whatever was said in the classroom and in public was primarily in terms of sex being a source of sin and a threat to social and moral order. Generations of teachers grew up feeling awkward, embarrassed, shameful and perhaps guilty when it came to sexual issues. It is embodied in their immediate disposition and reaction to sex. In their days in the classroom, children and young people learn to read, decipher and respond to this disposition. Through interpreting body language and the coded messages of teachers, pupils learn to recognise and respond to any sense of unease, awkwardness or embarrassment they may have in talking about or dealing with sexuality. The years of silencing sex, of seeing it essentially as a sin and a problem, have been embodied in the minds and hearts of many teachers. It could take an intensive programme of re-education of teachers on their own attitudes to relationships and sexuality to dissolve the residues of such a traditional perspective.

The final way in which the Church shapes the sexuality of children and young people is through their parents. Sex and sexuality come under routine supervision and examination within the home. Children learn within the family what is appropriate and inappropriate to say about and do in relation to sex. The accepted forms of self-expression and self-assertion are learnt and instilled through parents, guardians, aunts, uncles and grandparents. Children learn through the guarded signals, through the terms used, through the oblique references and through the reactions of their parents that the body and sex are a primary problem. They are strictly private, the essential source of the self. Children recognise and embody concerns about chastity and modesty, what to say and do and, perhaps more importantly, what not to say and do. It becomes part of their automatic disposition, part of the skill of being able to read the game of Irish sexuality and to operate successfully within it. The Catholic discourse about sex and sexuality has been handed down and embodied in different shapes and forms through generations. Such learnt dispositions cannot be overturned in a few years. The RSE programme is an attempt to overcome this through developing self-awareness, self-esteem, self-confidence, self-expression and self-control. It is, so to speak, about the creation of a new form of self: people who feel good about themselves, who are confident about their body and their sexuality, and who understand the consequences of, and take responsibility for, their behaviour.

Filtering the influence of institutions

I have argued that the Catholic Church, the state and the media produce the expert discourses which have considerable influence in shaping people's attitudes and opinions about sex and sexuality and, consequently, the lifestyles and viewpoints of children and young people. However, it is important to remember that while messages from these institutional forces are received directly in church, at school and in the home, they are filtered through the attitudes and opinions of priests, teachers, parents and friends. Each young person is a member of a family, group and community which have, so to speak, their own resident experts. These expert opinion-makers could be a well-liked and respected priest, teacher, parent or friend. They can have a significant influence in shaping young people's sexuality (see Fig. 1).

But it is important to realise that teachers and parents are not perfect embodiments of traditional Catholic discourse. Their understanding of sex and sexuality, their sexual attitudes, beliefs and practices, have

Figure 1. The Field of Irish Sexuality: Shaping Young People's Sexuality

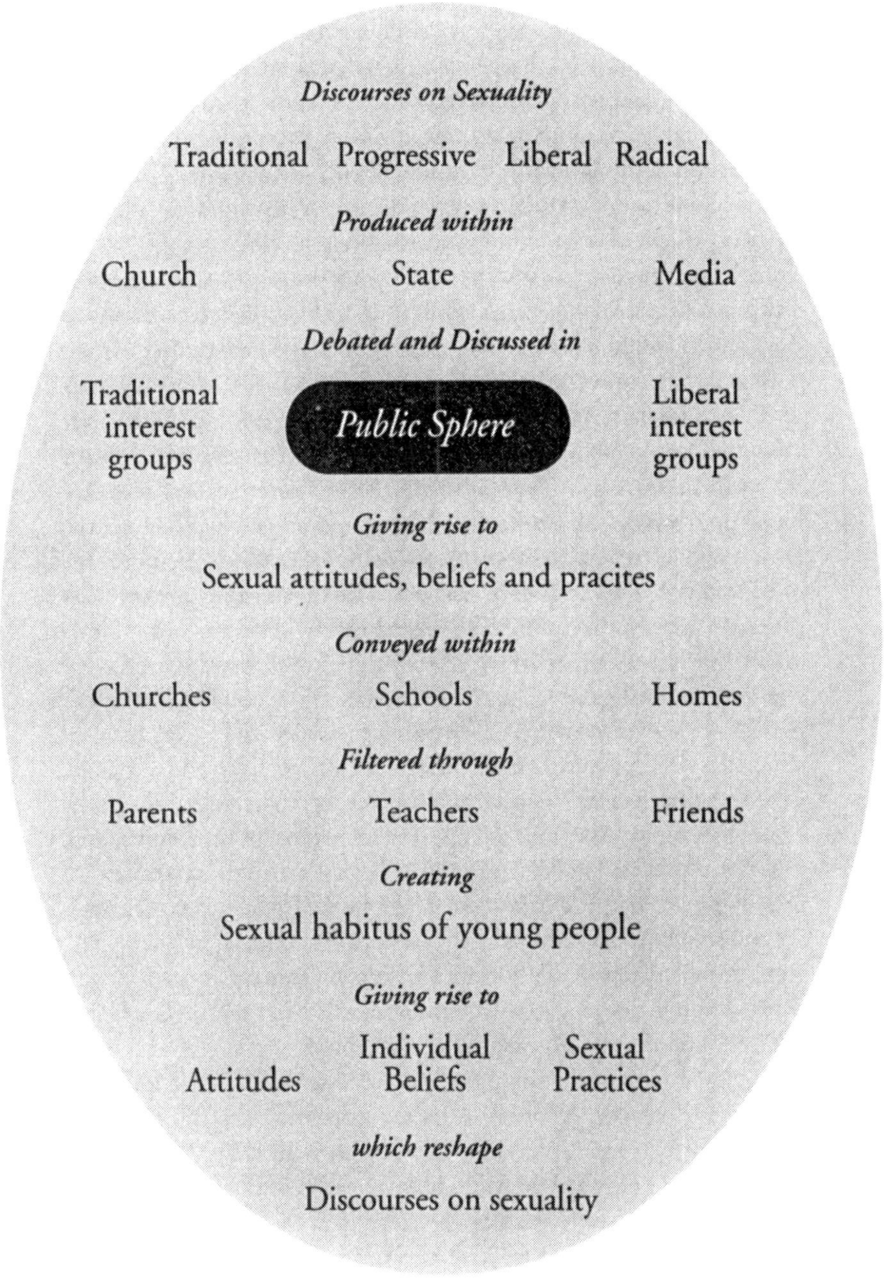

Discourses on Sexuality

Traditional Progressive Liberal Radical

Produced within

Church   State   Media

Debated and Discussed in

Traditional   Liberal
interest   **Public Sphere**   interest
groups   groups

Giving rise to

Sexual attitudes, beliefs and pracites

Conveyed within

Churches   Schools   Homes

Filtered through

Parents   Teachers   Friends

Creating

Sexual habitus of young people

Giving rise to

                  Individual   Sexual
Attitudes   Beliefs   Practices

which reshape

Discourses on sexuality

changed considerably over the last thirty years. They have become exposed and accustomed to sex in the media and everyday life. The way sex is announced, displayed, portrayed, written about and discussed is radically different from the 1960s. There has been a revolution in the nature and quantity of media items dealing with sex and sexuality.[18] Children and young people grow up in an environment which, in comparison with the 1960s, is saturated with sex. How they deal with and respond to this saturation depends, in the first instance, on their parents. Much of what children learn about sex and sexuality comes from living with their parents, seeing how they behave sexually, what their attitude is to sex, how they talk about it. If, for example, parents are – as the Church would recommend – extremely chaste and modest in their habits, if they conceal their bodies and their sexuality in the presence of their children, if they constantly monitor, supervise and censor what is said and done sexually in the home and what is received through the media, they may instil a traditional disposition to sex and sexuality based on strategies of inculcating shame, guilt and embarrassment. If, at the other extreme, parents and guardians are openly sexual in front of their children, if they watch pornographic movies and have sex with different people, they may instil an extremely liberal, if not radical, orientation to sex and sexuality.[19] However, between these two extremes, it is the relationship which parents have with their children, the open, hidden or guarded way they talk about sex, the way they react to incidents, the way they support, encourage or sanction talk and behaviour, which has the greatest, long-term influence. It is here that we begin to enter the realm of the unconscious, the formation of personality, and the crucial role the parents and guardians play in this process of sexual socialisation.[20] It is important to remember that the messages about sex and sexuality transmitted by the media are never read on their own, but within a matrix of relationships with parents, teachers and friends who, although they may not be present while the message is being received, preside, so to speak, in their absence.

The final filter in shaping young people's sexuality, is the group of friends to which they belong.[21] A lasting, automatic disposition to sex and sexuality – a feel for how the game of sex is played out locally – is established within the peer group. Here the rules of the game of sexual behaviour are laid down: what can be said and done by whom to whom, when, where and how. The peer group sets norms and standards as to what young people say and how they behave. These norms are filters, adaptations and resistances to what has been seen and heard from other sources, primarily through word-of-mouth, the media, parents, teachers and priests. The peer group becomes a major source of sexual information, myths and rhetoric. It is a microcosm of debate and discussion in the public sphere. It is the forum within which young people feel most comfortable telling their stories, discussing their concerns. However, there is evidence which suggests that practical assistance from peers in such matters as arranging contraception or encouraging safer sexual practice is rare. In other words, peer groups primarily operate as mechanisms for forming attitudes through taking on board, debating or resisting messages received from other sources and then setting norms, standards and procedures in relation to their own sexual behaviour. Again there is evidence which suggests that there is a link between young people's sexual attitudes and practices and the perceived attitudes of their peer group.[22] It is important, however, to realise that the influence is not necessarily towards sexual adventures and exploits. The influence, particularly among girls, can be just as much towards cautions and precautions.

Conclusion

The argument in this chapter has been that there has been a shift in the institutions responsible for creating the discourses which have shaped the knowledge and understanding children and young people have about relationships and sexuality. Up to the 1960s the Catholic Church dominated what was said and written about sex and sexuality. Since then, the media have become the dominant influence. This occurred in two ways: first through ending the silence about sexuality, and stimulating and developing public debate and discussion about all aspects of sexuality; second, through a process of displaying and promoting sexuality, providing knowledge and information about sexuality – making sex central to a path of self-discovery – and, finally, making it a source of entertainment and pleasure. In recent years, the state has entered the field with a new programme which, in effect, aims to bridge the gap between the discourse of the Church and the media. I have argued that the discourses produced by these institutions are filtered through agents such as parents, teachers and friends. It is important to realise that this is an analytical model for trying to simplify a complex environment. It has not taken into account important factors such as gender, biology, and homosexuality. The shaping of girls' sexuality in Ireland is a very different process to that of boys. This has not just to do with physiological and biological factors – it is girls who get pregnant – but also with cultural factors such as the double standard. Boys expect girls to be sexually attractive and active, yet if they do become active they can lose their reputation, honour and respect. What makes this more problematic is that boys and girls are reaching puberty earlier. Finally, regardless of whether the difference has its roots in biological or psychosocial factors, growing up as gay or lesbian obviously has enormous, if not primary, influence in shaping a person's sexuality.[23]

7
Views of Parents, Teachers and Pupils

To try and capture some contemporary Irish voices speaking about sexuality, particularly in relation to the RSE programme, I set out to listen to what parents, teachers and young people in one school had to say. I chose a co-educational community school in a small Irish town. No doubt if I had chosen a different type of school in a city or rural area, I would have obtained very different views. I also accept that if I had randomly selected two, three or thirty-three second-level schools and then taken a random sample from all the parents, teachers and pupils within the schools selected, I would have obtained a far more accurate picture of contemporary attitudes and practices. This is just a case study.

To capture the range of values, beliefs and attitudes about sexuality and young people, I used focus group interviews.[1] The idea was to bring together, in separate sessions, a number of parents, teachers and pupils, and to get them to discuss topics revolving around what young people needed to learn about sexuality.

After a preliminary explanatory meeting in the school, teachers were invited to participate in the focus group interview. Ten did so. Most were already involved in teaching RSE or Personal Development – the school's existing programme. Parents were contacted through the school. Nine agreed to participate, but only seven turned up – two men failing to arrive at the last minute. Four of the parents were in the Parents' Association. A preliminary meeting was also held with the pupils. They were in a Personal Development class in transition year. Most were 15 to 16 years old. They had been in PD class together since the beginning of the year. There were 19 in the class, 13 of whom participated in the focus group interview.

I conducted the interviews which were tape recorded by an assistant. The tapes were then transcribed and analysed. I make no claims about the representativeness of these voices. They are like photographs taken in a particular place at a particular point in time. They are accurately recorded, but I accept that the structure of a focus group has an influence on what is said. Because of the group dynamic, some things may have been dressed up or down a little. For example, I felt that the parents, especially at the beginning of the interview, wanted to present themselves to each other as traditional and conservative. The pupils, on the other hand, seemed to want to present a liberal image. But as with any posed photograph, there is always a certain level of presentation and, consequently, of distortion. But it is nevertheless an accurate record. I am confident that all the participants recognised and accepted that this was a serious research project. They also realised and accepted that what they said would be treated confidentially and anonymously and that, in expressing their attitudes and opinions, they endeavoured to be as open and honest as they could. The names used are fictitious.

The parents

The parents, most of them between 30 and 50 years old, all had teenage sons or daughters attending the school. At the beginning of the interview, the parents were asked to complete a short, pre-coded questionnaire. The main purpose of the questionnaire was to orientate them to some of the issues which might be covered during the interview. However, the pattern in the responses is revealing. Six parents agreed that most young people needed to learn to 'develop mature, responsible relations with each other'; 'be modest and chaste in their lives'; 'see sexuality as a part of a healthy personality and lifestyle'; 'understand the biological facts of life'; 'know about AIDS/HIV'; and 'know what it is to be gay or lesbian'. Five parents felt that young people needed to learn to see sexual practice as essentially part of married life; two were uncertain.

There was disagreement about other issues. Four of the seven parents agreed that young people needed to learn to 'practise safe sex'; 'respond to and express sexual feelings and emotions'; and 'talk openly about sexual attitudes'. But only three agreed that young people needed to learn to 'become sexually self-confident'. Only two parents agreed that when it came to learning about relationships and sexuality, young people needed to learn to 'live up to church/religious teaching'.

I began the interview by asking parents what influence, if any, teenage magazines had in shaping young people's attitudes to sexuality. The response was that they were 'shocking', 'very explicit', and 'very free'. As John said, 'the messages are direct and totally at variance to the message you would like to give them'. He claimed the magazines were sold over the counter to kids of any age, and were then passed around. The suggestion was that they were so 'out of sync', so 'over the top' that they were 'comical'. But, as Sarah noted, 'we think it's comical, but 13 year olds think it's normal'. And, as John and Sheila pointed out, it is not just the magazines, but sex is rampant in the films and television programmes which are deemed fit for 12 year olds.

The next question was whether the parents thought the sexual behaviour of young girls and boys was different from when they were young. Joan and Sarah said that they were more open. There was a greater public display of holding hands and kissing. Many of the liaisons seemed to be made at discos. There was a no-alcohol disco organised in the school which, Carol claimed, first-year pupils were allowed to attend. She did not agree with this and only let her two daughters go when they were 14 years old. Even then, she felt she had to tell them about the slow dancing, the French kissing and 'everything else'. Sheila gave a more detailed description.

When you go to the discos and see these slow dances and the tonsil tickling as I call it, it's terrible. That is very prevalent. You'd want to go and supervise a disco some night and you'd know then. And it's just acceptable. They're not going with a particular boy . . . Whatever about being asked for a quick dance, you won't be asked for a slow dance if you're not prepared to stand on the floor and smooch or shift or whatever the word is.

John felt that sex was endemic to the whole youth culture. He claimed that pupils in the school were smooching at lunchtime. He felt that things had changed dramatically since he was a lad.

To tell you the honest truth now, I'm not that old. But I think these lads start where I used to leave off. And that's a quick way of putting it. What's happening now is, from my perception anyhow, that where we'd be stopping, afraid of our lives that the ground would open up and we'd be gone straight to hell, they're just starting at that. And it's going all the way, as far as is let, or the opportunity is. There's no one barring them. And about the disco thing; it's comical what's going on in discos now. A lad won't ask a girl to dance. What he does is he asks his friend to go over and ask her. And he goes over and he points at him and says 'you dance with him or turn around and do a twirl and have a look at ya' and that's the kind of thing that's going on. I talked to some very young girls about this and they're mortified at discos. They're mortified. The pressure that's on girls now to perform and they do whatever the lads want. Young fellas have it made now compared to my era.

If this were the case, then the next question was how far did the parents think young people went in their sexual behaviour. Most of the parents felt that it did not go much beyond the deep French kissing or 'shifting' which took place at discos. I asked them if they thought this was the case among fifth and sixth years; what proportion of them did they think would be sexually active? Carol felt sure she knew what was happening.

I have a child in fifth year, and from her group of friends I would not think that they are sexually active. It's only a very small proportion. Having said that I have no doubt that this shifting goes on at discos. I have no doubt that that goes on, but I think that that would be as far as it goes.

When it came to the issue of what to teach young people about sexuality, there was a divergence of opinion. Carol, Sheila and Kate felt that despite the messages in the media and what went on in the discos and elsewhere, there was no need for them to be told about safe sex until they were about fifteen years old. As Carol said, 'I think if you give them too much information too young, you're encouraging them'. They emphasised that much depends on the questions parents are asked and how the questions are answered. But Sheila and Carol differed about the proposed RSE programme for primary schools.

Sheila: We were told the other day that in junior infants in this RSE . . . they're going to be told the names of the parts of their bodies and the proper names. That's all right, but does every junior infant – four and five year old have to be told in front of the class. It's all right mammy and daddy to tell them, and if they know it well and good. But what's wrong with the little names that they've had and learnt with until they get further up. I think that's really taking their innocence from them.

Carol: I wouldn't see anything wrong with names.

Sheila: It's not names, but they don't really know. Why give them something that they're not fully aware of, or fully understand either?

Carol: How much are they told?

Sheila: They're actually told that the girl has a vagina and the boy has a penis.

Carol: I don't see a problem with just that.

Sheila: Ah well it is for junior infants.

Carol: For a junior infant at four years and five years.

Sheila: Mother of God they're only babies.

Carol: But they're only names of the body.

There was general recognition that teaching RSE in the school was going to be a very difficult task. Carol felt that if you were going to teach sexuality, you would have to bring in safe sex and, 'you have to do the whole hog'. Sheila's fear was that teachers were not being educated enough in how to implement the programme. This led to a prolonged discussion about whether RSE should be kept separate from religious education. Kate felt that it might work since a lot of young people were coming back to Mass. However, Carol and Betty felt that the two should be kept separate. As Betty put it:

You can bring in your moral aspect all right in mentioning it. But I don't think you can sort of say about Catholic religion that you do not sleep with somebody before you're married. End of story. You do not use the pill. You do not use a condom. I don't think you can teach that.

Sheila supported this view. But again, much depended on the teacher. She was fearful that the teacher was 'not going to be equipped . . . and have the right approach to it'. She felt that they would put too much of their own stamp on the way they put something across.

John was a bit more philosophical. He felt that in the past people colluded with the Catholic Church to draw up laws to control their sexuality. But he didn't feel the Church was going to take on that role any more. He argued that if people feel that the sexual behaviour of young people is a threat to society, then society will have to come up with ways of controlling it. He was sceptical of the RSE programme. He felt that the designers of the programme had not figured out what exactly they were trying to do.

The sexuality thing. Could you sit down and teach me my sexuality? You couldn't, because it comes primarily from where you were reared; from the influence of your parents, and your family, and people directly associated with the family, and from an innate sort of being within yourself; because it will be affected by so many other different little things in life. I think teaching it is the wrong word. And if you're not trying to teach it, are you trying to uncover it? Are you trying to give the person the tools with which to uncover it themselves... .Just talking about it now I suppose really I was hoping for my child to get out of something like that would be the tools with which to develop it later on, or to unfold it, or to be aware that there is such a thing, and that it's there for them to do something with, but it's not something that you have to get out and work on and have it done for fourth year or third year.

Indeed John went on to suggest that if you were going to teach young people sexuality, then there was just as much need to teach parents. He wished there was a book on the facts of life for parents. He stressed that 'there's no point in the school working on one road and the parents either not working at all, or being ignorant of what's going on on the other side.'

There was, then, a sense of parents being caught in a rapidly changing culture, unable to say or do very much to help their children. They recognised that young people were inundated with messages from the media which encouraged sexual expression, experimentation and adventurism. They also recognised that young people had moved far more down that road than they themselves had when they were young. They did not feel confident that teachers or the RSE programme could do much to change the situation. They wanted sexuality education to be encompassed within a moral framework, but also felt that the Catholic Church no longer provided such a meaningful framework for young people. They also had a sense that they themselves could do little other than to lay down some kind of moral law and keep a supervisory eye on where their young people went, whom they were with, and what they did. There were constant references during the interview to the struggle to exert and maintain control.

Carol said that when it came to unsuitable programmes on television it was a question of saying 'no and that's it', and putting them out of the room, or turning it off. Sheila talked of nipping the desire to go to discos in the bud. Betty described the supervisory process in more detail.

I think they just know that you are there and you are going to insist on it. Where they're going? How are they getting home? Who's bringing them home? Who are they with? And you set a time. You set a limit, and if that's done from day one they will accept it. It's a bit more difficult if it hasn't been done at 12, 13, 14 (years), and suddenly they want to go out with their boyfriend or the girlfriend, and you start interfering with whatever, you might end up then antagonising them, but I do think if you start young.

But as Kate pointed out, the problem was when they went out in a mixed group and that if you told your child to be home at 10.00 and nobody else had the same restriction, then 'you're going to have some battle on your hands'. The parents claimed that one of the advantages of living in a small town was that mothers were able to work in unison. In this respect, while they may not know immediately who was going out with whom, they would soon find out. As Sheila said, 'I may not hear it today. I may not hear it tomorrow, but I will hear it.' Carol supported this. 'It is a small town and, somewhere, some mothers know.'

However, while there was this level of supervision and sense of knowing what was going on, direct communication was not very evident between parents and children about what they were doing. Joan said it was difficult.

I wouldn't ask them. I'd advise them. I wouldn't be afraid of the answer, but I'd be embarrassed to ask them now. . . . If my lad was going out I'd say to him 'respect that little girl'. That's the way I'd do it, but I wouldn't say 'did you have sex with her last night?' I would just advise him not to do it now.

In other words, a level of understanding existed between parents and their children – a tacit agreement about the type of questions that could be asked, that would be regarded as fair and that, consequently, demanded a fair answer. It is as if parents were constantly exploring the boundaries of the motto 'ask no questions and be told no lies'. If there was too much of an inquisition, the relationship and communication with their children could be badly damaged. It was as if parents and children were players in the game of sex and sexuality. Young people have an intuitive, often unstated, knowledge of what is acceptable and unacceptable. They all know the basic rules of the game. On the other hand, parents realise that they do not know the full story. They know that there are some transgressions. As Joan said, 'I don't think there's any parent that can say "well my lad or girl wouldn't do that", because you don't know what's going on behind your back'. But the task of the parent was defined as trying to read and evaluate how their children were surviving; how well, in other words, they were playing the game. This is the way John described it.

You're talking about the signals, asking them and warning them, 'and be responsible and be careful and don't do anything you shouldn't do' . . . as they're getting older we're allowing them a certain amount of leeway. But we don't want them to have intercourse. We want to get that message across. By degrees you can get up to it. But don't have intercourse, because that's when the damage occurs. That is really what we're saying. Because you take the moral and the teaching about no sex and all the rest, but regardless, we all grew and we all went in stage by stage – maybe some of us got to 35, but by degrees. You know what I mean, that there was a certain amount of things going on and that really the whole message is 'don't have intercourse' for various reasons.

The teachers

Ten teachers participated in the focus group discussion, one of whom, Matt, was the school chaplain. The school committee had already formulated its RSE policy and most of the teachers were engaged in implementing the programme. Most of the teachers had been involved previously in teaching personal development classes.

As with parents, I began the discussion by asking them what relevance the media, in particular teenage magazines, had in influencing young people's understanding of sexuality. The immediate reaction was that the magazines presented a distorted image of sex, and that they put pressure on young people to become sexually active. Alison felt that the magazines were part of a process in which children were 'being sexualised at an earlier age all the time . . . maybe at eight or nine'. She said that there was a hidden agenda in the magazines:

they are designed to kind of make you think about your own inadequacies. How to be a better lover, because the flip side of that is, well, you're not a good lover now. If you think you're not a good lover, go buy the magazines. And the message is 'if you're a good lover everybody will like you and you'll like it better'.

Judy agreed. She said she felt that many young people get practically all their information about sexuality from magazines and that they pushed a message that you could not possibly be a virgin at 14 or 15 years.

Barbara suggested that there were some positive aspects to the media's messages about sex. She was particularly supportive of some television soap operas like *Home and Away* which, she claimed, provided a valuable exploration of relationships. But Catherine felt that *Home and Away* was 'way more advanced than the stage of relationships that the majority of children would have here' and that, consequently, 'it leads to a lot of confusion'.

There was general agreement that the sexual world in which young people lived had changed dramatically since they were young, and that there was tacit acceptance of this by teachers and parents. As Barbara said,

I don't think as a group of adults that we tell the kids as dogmatically that sex before marriage is wrong for example which I would have been told very dogmatically in my generation. . . . And the fact that they go to discos very young . . . and they're put into a sexual arena.

Jane said that she had noticed a big difference in the Leaving Certificate pupils now, compared to when she came to the school first nine years ago. 'Kids are more sexually active now, and they're looking to be more sexually active if they're not.' Barbara agreed. She felt that the pupils were very sexually active.

By age seventeen, and this is guess, I would say seven out of ten of them are sexually active in terms of having intercourse with somebody that they're having a long-term relationship with. It seems from talking to the kids that they won't have sex with [tape unclear] . . . but the one-night stand thing would be very unacceptable, and some people do it. But I think that to have sex with your boyfriend is the norm, certainly by the time they get to Leaving Certificate.

Catherine linked this to the fact that many students have night-time and weekend jobs 'that gives the money into their pocket and they're very independent from home at a much earlier age'. Barbara agreed and said that by that age, they had an adult social life; 'they're drinking and they have money'. Moreover, she said,

what they seem to be doing now, they will take care of their sexual needs if you like, in a long-term, non-permanent relationship. . . . There is no question that somebody will stay celibate now until they get married.

But Matt, the school chaplain, argued strongly that 'what they're looking for is not just sex, but affection. You see it in the loneliness in their eyes and the pain in their eyes.' He told a story of a first-year pupil who was 'complimented by her peers for doing this great act . . . and she was being cheered on and supported big time by her fellow first years and none of them could see anything wrong, because it was totally acceptable.' Jane had a similar story to tell about peer pressure.

One of the teachers told me recently that she's counselling somebody who is going through absolute hell, because she's never had sex with somebody, and it's really difficult for the teacher to get through to her that not everybody's having sex, not everybody's sexually active. She believes she is the only one who hasn't got to this stage and is really suffering because of it.

Jim felt that parents were out of touch with all these changes. He suggested that parents did not know what their children were up to, where they were, or whom they were with. As Barbara said,

I guess the parents probably guess what their kids are doing, but hope they're not. And sometimes maybe the parents turn a blind eye, or whatever. But I think that in terms of education that we give the kids in school about sexuality, I think the parents would be delighted that we do that, because it's so hard for the parents themselves to do it. I don't think parents are fools . . . they see teenage pregnancies and I suppose the biggest fear for parents is that your daughter or son will become a parent. . . .

When it came to teaching RSE, there was disagreement whether it should be included in religion classes. Catherine was against it. She felt that putting the two together would narrow RSE too much. She said she spent weeks doing the self-esteem aspects of the programme and building up their self-confidence, and that this was not included in the religion syllabus. Barbara agreed. 'How many of us would say that sex outside of marriage is wrong and how many of us practise this in our own lives . . . the fact is that we don't agree with what the Church is teaching.' But Jane disagreed. She said that she taught the two subjects the same way, but always making a distinction between her teaching and the teaching of the Church. Matt, the school chaplain, asked:

Can we really separate any aspect of our sexuality? . . . can we put things in little boxes? . . . my general impression will be that it's an unbalanced, a very much secular RSE programme.

Susan thought that the tension between the Church teaching and the RSE programme was a healthy thing. 'I think it can be quite healthy in class that they can hear different points of view and they can be quite often quite surprised.'

There was also disagreement about whether the school should become involved in teaching safe sex and, if so, at what age. Olivia was in favour.

I find it hard to accept that these students are sexually active, but I think it's really important that we accept them; that they are. I might disapprove of people being sexually active, because they are very young, but I think it's my duty to cater for those who are from the age, that they can become pregnant, or impregnate somebody else.

Alison agreed and said there was a huge difference between innocence and ignorance. She said that in the previous school in which she taught, a girl had gone into labour in the classroom. 'She was pregnant and nobody knew she was pregnant. And again that was ignorance. . . . She was afraid, she couldn't tell anybody. That could have resulted in a tragedy really.'

Jane felt that giving a lecture on contraceptives did not take their innocence away. She said that in second class she would mention the different forms and she would say that if anyone wanted more information they should see her after class.

But I really think we should inform. I think it is promoting free will. I don't think we have the right to sit up and say 'I think it is wrong for you to do this'. If they ask you a question, you will give your personal opinion and you think that it would be better for them to do a certain thing, but I don't think you can say 'I think you were wrong if you do this'.

Barbara was adamant about the need to teach safe sex from third year up. She said that she grew up in an era when girls thought they could get pregnant if a boy put his hand on their waist. 'We were taught that you could get pregnant if you sat on a boy's lap and you should put a newspaper between yourself and him.' She would like to teach first and second years not so much about safe sex as about how girls can get pregnant. And, she said, 'I would be talking fairly explicitly about how they can get pregnant without full sexual intercourse . . . because in second and third year touching genitalia and that kind of thing and mutual masturbation would be what they might be doing.'

Ian was against teaching safe sex, especially to third years. He thought that teachers should help students 'make a new reality for themselves'. He would be in favour of teaching them how to say 'no' and to realise that it is okay to say 'no'. However, he admitted that he was going against the tide. But Susan agreed with him. She was emphatic that when it came to second and third years, 'I would say definitely "no" and I would be very clear in that. "No" you are too young.'

How I find in my class, my best way is to be honest and I don't approve of sex before marriage for the kids – at young ages anyway. I feel that if I go in and I just give them the facts that if they ask me my opinion, I will give them my opinion, and I think that it helps in the class that they can see that there's sincerity here, that she's not just pandering to our interests or needs or trying to make it interesting for us, that she actually thinks this is serious and this is her opinion.

Matt, the school chaplain, thought that teaching second years about safe sex was going too far.

Do we know what the needs of our second-year students are in this area? Is there a need for them to know. I would think not to know all about contraception in second year. I think you will find an exception, certainly yes. Unless I'm totally not with it any more. I would think the vast majority of second years are not having sexual intercourse.

Most of the teachers felt that the RSE was a good programme and, as Jane said, that 'it was well thought out'. Catherine, however, felt that it was reflection of middle-class families and concerns and that it did not take into account that many children come from broken homes. In her view the main benefit from RSE was that it built up students' self-esteem, especially in second and third year. She said it was crucial for students to learn that

if they feel insecure, or if this situation is not right for them, that they have the ability to say 'no' . . . and that's very hard to get into some kids' minds, because even from their home background . . . their opinion would never be valued, or whatever, and they would never be asked to voice it, or to show their own competence or whatever.

Perhaps the most important aspect, then, of the RSE programme for the teachers was that it concentrated on helping children and young people to develop a strong, independent sense of self which became the basis of forming good relationships. As Barbara put it:

I was chatting to the kids at lunchtime saying what do you think kids need as regards sexuality education, because I was trying to get my thoughts together. And they were saying things like, you need information, you need information about contraception, you need information about the facts of life. But they also said you need to learn the difference between love and abuse. And I thought that was really wise. And I think that the mechanics and the gymnastics of sex are taught in the magazines of the ten positions. But I think that for the kids the issue. . . . when they're growing up the whole sexual exploration, and the curiosity is very much a feature. But I also think their struggle is more with the relationships. When their relationships break up they really cry and are very sad, and if they can't make a relationship. And if they have a boyfriend. If they shift somebody, and it only lasts a day or two days or something, it's really bad for them. And I think in a sense where I think somebody would be a good lover is if they really love somebody. And I think that the issue is more about loving than about gymnastics, or about expertise.

The pupils

The pupils came from a transition year class in the school – that is pupils who spend a year out from examination courses to follow a more varied curriculum. Most of the pupils were aged 15 and 16 years. They had been together in the same Personal Development class since the beginning of the year, and would have attended similar classes in previous years. A meeting was held with the class to explain the purpose behind the interview, and the process by which it would take place. The pupils treated the interview seriously and were well versed in the art of speaking in turn, and not interrupting others when they were speaking. At the beginning of the interview, I reminded them that everything they said would be treated with strict confidentiality, and that they too had to treat anything that was said by other pupils with the strictest confidence. I emphasised that I did not want to hear about private, personal situations or practices, but rather about their understanding of relationships and sexuality education and the sexual attitudes, beliefs and practices of people their age in the town.

As with the parents and teachers, we began by discussing the influence of the media on young people's knowledge and understanding of sexuality. They were all familiar with *Sugar, Bliss* and *Just Seventeen*, but the girls saw them as more relevant and helpful than the boys. As Ann said, magazines are helpful '. . . if you're too embarrassed to talk to your parents . . . you can get the proper names and you can be told how to understand things better than you might off your friends.' Sarah supported this:

You're inclined to pay more attention when you read magazines because, like, you take your friends seriously, but you just kind of laugh it off when you're there with your friends. With magazines you sit down and read it, and you take it in, and you remember it.

When asked if the magazines were too advanced, or irrelevant to the needs and interests of young people, Ruth said that they were not advanced enough as far too many girls in the town were getting themselves pregnant by not having safe sex. The boys were more dismissive of the magazines. Peter said that he had learned nothing from them. Oliver found them 'funny all the time'.

There was general agreement that little was to be learnt from soaps and serials on television. Susan said that a serial like *Home and Away* was not like reality. 'It's just kissing and, like, most of them have a perfect relationship.' Paul felt that *This Life* was far more educational. It shows everything. Different relationships and how people, like, involve each other, and they talk about different things. It's good like. It's way better than *Neighbours* and *Eastenders*. It's much more serious. You actually look on the other side of them and the relationships between them and, like, what happens if somebody else has sex with someone, and what happens between them.

However, there was general agreement that young people learn more about sex and sexuality from their friends, brothers and sisters than from media, their parents or teachers. Some pupils, like Joe, said that they had learnt a lot from their parents. Sarah felt that being able to learn about sexuality from your parents depended on how close you were to them, and that this depended on how young the parents were. She thought that if they were older they would be too embarrassed to talk about sex. But Oliver disagreed. He said that age did not come into it and that it was the nature of relationship that was important.

There was also a general feeling that the older teachers were out of touch with reality and the needs and interests of the pupils. But the main problem for pupils was when they felt that teachers, regardless of their age, became awkward and embarrassed talking about sex. Susan felt that

children should be taught at a young age. But I think they should be taught in a balanced way. Because when there are people who are teaching them and they're embarrassed, that means the children will be embarrassed, and embarrassed about their sexuality, embarrassed to talk about these things.

Justin followed up on this. He felt that if children 'were taught at an early age . . . they wouldn't have the mentality to be embarrassed'. He argued that if children learnt to talk about sex and sexuality from the time they were able to talk that it would become a part of their lives. Nevertheless, the questions remained as to what they could learn about relationships and sexuality in school, and who should teach them. Most felt that what they learnt should be responsive to what was happening in their lives, like relationships, bad experiences, being drunk and having unprotected sex.

    In terms of who should teach whom, Paul was adamant that when it came 'to talking to first years about sex, like, and all of that, they should get a student from sixth year.' Ann and Stephen felt that it should be somebody young, but not from the town. 'Somebody', as Ann said, 'you don't have to see every day.' Moreover, she said,

It should be at a more personal level than educational. You'd feel more at ease, that's if there's something you want to ask. You don't mind as much. Somebody that's not going to be judging you every day in class.

On the other hand, Oliver said it was important that the pupils would feel comfortable with the teacher and that the classes would be confined to 'tight little groups' of five or six, which would keep together over the year. He felt that this would help overcome any embarrassment. Paul stressed that it was important that no teacher from the school would be present. Joe felt that if there was a teacher present, 'you'd be too embarrassed, like, to ask personal questions or anything'. He said it was important that pupils would know they would never see the teacher again. The problem, however, was to find a teacher who was young enough to be identified as the same generation as the pupils, who knew and understood the issues and problems they faced, who came from outside the town, and who was able to make the class relevant and meaningful. As Oliver put it:

If you're going to ask a person to come in, say, that would be your own age to talk about it like, it would be very hard to find a person with strong enough character like to keep the class in control because, like, you wouldn't take a person your own age seriously when it comes to teaching.

Whatever they thought about parents and teachers, the pupils considered priests and the Catholic Church to be completely irrelevant to what they needed to learn about sexuality. Oliver thought they were hypocrites. Susan said that they did not have the necessary experience. 'They don't have any problems, or anything like what we go through. So how would they know how to teach you?' Sarah had a particular story to tell.

A girl I know, she had sex with her boyfriend and she got worried about it. And she went to the priest, and the priest said 'everything is confidential here', but he went back and told her parents, and told her boyfriend's parents, and she was grounded and they had to break up. So they're not allowed see each other any more. That's not on. I mean priests just haven't really got a clue.

On the other hand, there was general support for the school chaplain whom Dave considered to 'be fairly sound'. Yet there was agreement that the problem with most priests was that all they would tell young people was to settle down and get married before having sex.

The question, then, was within what kind of sexual culture young people operated. As indicated by the parents and teachers, most young people learn to practise sex in the discos. The gap between dancing and 'getting off with' or 'shifting' a boy or girl – that is deep kissing – has narrowed. In fact, Joe suggested that when 'you get up with them, like to dance, then I suppose it's really like to shift'. Sarah described the practice where a friend goes up and asks the boy or girl concerned if they would like to shift their friend, pointing him or her out. The shifting then takes place without knowing each other's name. The first attraction is physical. And it is the same for both girls and boys. Joe described how shifting takes place

You just see someone and you ask them. And you arrange to meet next day or something and then you shift them again and then you get to know each other and then you get with each other.

Claire agreed that shifting is not emotional, 'it's just physical'. The shifting takes place anywhere that is quiet and dark. It would also seem that shifting becomes easier and more common with drinking. As Susan said 'you're not really afraid. You're more open.' There was agreement that drink made you less embarrassed and shy. Bill described a recent incident.

Like there, last Saturday, I was with this lad and we were going into town and like he didn't care and he just went straight up to a girl and he started talking to her and all. And he's the shyest lad I've ever met and since he had five Tequilas . . . (interrupted).

These stories become the myths and legends by which young people in the town read and interpret what is happening and struggle to find a place within it. They develop an ongoing knowledge and understanding of the scene, how to talk, behave and act. It is through these myths and legends, and the enacted scenarios, that young people come to know and understand themselves as individuals.

You'd be in the night club and a stranger would come up to you and hand you a condom. You wouldn't even know him and he would hand you a condom and say 'are you coming for a walk outside?' I remember one night we were in . . . and a friend got handed a condom with a little note on it: 'My name is . . .'. And where to meet her and all.

Bill seemed to support the notion that drink can make you do stupid things. After drink, 'you really start getting careless . . . you start doing that with a girl you don't even like. You just do it. That's why it's a piece of shit, like, you do it without a condom.' Susan agreed and said that the problem was that 'girls and lads, really like, only have sex when they're drunk'. But Sarah thought otherwise.

It all depends on the person you're with, how they treat you. I'm not going to say how drunk you are because it doesn't matter how drunk you are. You always know what you're doing. You know what he's doing. You know what she's doing. You know what you're both doing, and you know how far you're going. You can stop it if you want to, but most times you don't stop it because you want to like this person and you think they like you. Drink, no. It makes you less shy, but it doesn't matter.

Do these myths and legends lead to peer pressure to become sexually active? Bill, in a muddled way, answered this question:

It depends. Your friends, you see, could be doing it. And if you haven't done it, they're asking what's the story like. It's pressure. You get slagged in 'you're a virgin'. In the heat of the moment, you wouldn't know what to do.

Ruth had another story.

A teacher once told me that she caught these two first years on the dance floor and he had his hand on her breast, and they stopped that, and they went up to the office and they asked the guy why he did that. And he goes, 'well, I thought I had to, I thought since you kissed, I thought that's what I should do next'. They asked the girl why did she let him do that and she goes 'well I thought that's what happens after kissing'.

However, perhaps Oliver had the best insight into the dynamics of the way peer groups operate. He emphasised that when kids come to secondary school, it is important to be in a group. Young people do not want to be left out of anything. Peer pressure, he said, 'is all in your own mentality. . . . It's in your own head.'

The question, then, was that if young people want to be accepted, to be in with the group, and if at the same time they are drinking and shifting, does this lead to full sexual intercourse? If so, what proportion of young people of their age did the pupils think were having full sex. Of course, they were estimating, but the estimate was that four in ten had had sexual intercourse. This is in keeping with the survey results described in chapter 1 which showed that half of the 17–20 year olds had had sex before 16 years old.

As Sarah said, 'it depends on how aroused you get, that's just basically it. If you're in the mood for it you'll do it, if not you'll just go away.' What is striking is that this seems to be taking place outside long-term relationships. As Claire said, 'it's not really a relationship. It's just sex.' Susan said she only knew a couple of people who were in long-term relationships. 'Most girls would like to play the field. Try out.'

Given this scenario, did young people know enough about sex and sexuality to be so sexually active? The spontaneous and almost unanimous answer was 'no'. As Sarah said, 'younger people think it's okay, everybody else is doing it, why don't I? I know people as young as twelve having sex.' The next question was were these young people able and willing to practise safe sex. Ruth pointed to a basic lack of communication as the problem.

> One of the problems would be communication, because a lot of people don't have communication with the person that they're going to have sex with. They don't talk about safe sex, because they're too embarrassed maybe.

There was general agreement that it was not difficult to get condoms, either from a chemist or a pub. However, Joe did say he knew some boys who resented paying out £3 for a packet of condoms. Susan said that some girls can ask the doctor to go on the pill, and persuade him not to tell the parents or, if he does, that he says it is for bad periods.

When asked who they thought had responsibility for safe sex, the response was a mixture of 'both' and 'yourself'. However, Bill immediately said 'it's not equal because it's the woman who is going to have the baby'. Susan agreed that 'most women are left there with the children'.

Did young people see safe sex in relation to preventing pregnancy rather than sexually transmitted diseases, particular AIDS? The almost unanimous answer was yes, mainly because, as Ruth explained, 'there haven't been many diseases around . . . (the town). If they hit, then they would be more concerned about it.' The main fear for most young people was the girl becoming pregant.

Who, then, takes responsiblity for contraception? Here opinion was divided. If girls carried condoms, they were in danger of losing their reputation – among girls and boys. As Sarah put it, 'say a group of girls see a girl carrying a condom they would say, "oh my God what is she doing, she must be gagging for it the whole time"'. Joe agreed and said she would be called a 'slapper . . . people would say "you're getting around a lot"'. However, Oliver disagreed and said that he wouldn't think that about a girl 'if I found condoms on her'. He argued that both girls and boys should carry condoms. As Sarah said, 'you never know when you are going to end up having sex.' But Susan brought an air of political realism when she asked: 'What's the point of carrying around condoms like at our age? If our ma found them in our pockets, our parents would be shocked. My parents would kill me.'

Nevertheless the huge fear, particularly for girls, was that they would get pregnant. As Bill put it 'if they are the ones who get pregnant, it's on their head'. Susan agreed. 'I think most girls are afraid that if they get pregnant they are going to be the whole talk of the town. When she goes in the street they're saying, 'look, she's pregnant and she didn't know who it was'.

The second biggest fear for girls was gaining a reputation. As Paul put it: '. . . obviously you have to be careful. Like if you see a girl and you know that she's been around for a while, sleeping with other people, like, you wouldn't touch her.' Susan responded immediately by saying, 'I don't think girls feel that way about boys.' And so the classic double standard for girls and boys seemed to be alive and well. The girls may wish to play the field, but if they 'get around a lot', they will develop a reputation for being a 'slapper'. Worse still is that they may get pregnant. Nevertheless there was a sense that while avoiding pregnancy and a reputation was a girl's responsibility, girls ultimately had the final say as to what would and would not happen sexually.

It would be wrong to think that these young people were behaving immorally. That may be the case within the overall Catholic value system which permeates society, but there is a youth subculture which has its own vision as to what is right and wrong, acceptable and unacceptable behaviour. The game of sex is played out by different players. Boys and girls struggle to play the game, enjoy it, be a good player and, at the same time, not get offside by losing their reputation or, worse still, by getting or making someone pregnant. There was a distinct impression that despite drink, awkwardness and embarrassment, sex was a negotiated activity over which girls had ultimate control. There was no mention of aggression or violence. If girls say stop, boys stop – even though, as Ann said, 'they try again a few minutes later'.

Similarly, although there was a huge fear of girls getting pregnant, there was general negative feeling about abortion. Susan said it was terrible. Paul said he hated talking about it. Ruth said that they had talked about it during the case of a young traveller girl who was raped and became pregnant. There were mixed feelings then as to whether abortion was justified in such circumstances. Similarly, there was a general negative disposition about pornography. There did not appear to be much of it in the town and it was difficult to get. Many of the pupils in the group had not seen a pornographic film.

There was, however, a difference of opinion about homosexuality. The immediate reaction was one of disgust, particularly among the boys. Dave was 'totally against it. It would make you sick.' He was particularly against the notion of gays being able to adopt babies. Stephen and Oliver thought homosexuals were unnatural. Paul thought that they were funny. Bill said that 'you don't know how to feel around them, or how to react. You don't know. You look at them strange.' Ruth suggested that it was easier for boys to accept lesbians, but Claire maintained that this was because men were turned on by lesbians. Susan had a story to tell about a lesbian.

I know a girl. We didn't know that she was a lesbian and she tried it on with one of my friends in the toilet. She was a totally different culture from us, like. She's totally against lesbians. It's the way she was brought up and she went to start on the one who was a lesbian. And we all pulled her away and said 'look, it's not her fault, it's the way she is'.

The impression, however, was that the pupils did not have much contact or experience of gays and lesbians, and that this was at the root of their fears and prejudices. But once again, it seemed that it was the girls who were more open and less prejudiced. Sarah described a recent encounter.

. . . a few weeks ago I met for the first time a gay man. And he told me all about himself and I've nothing against it all. My father doesn't like coloured people or gay people. For a while I was prejudiced, when I was younger in primary school, until I managed to figure out in my own head that there was nothing wrong with these people and that the person I was talking to in the pub, he was so nice.

Conclusion

It must be remembered that these voices are like snapshots, taken in what I believe to be a school in a middle-of-the-range town in Ireland in 1998. There may have been some posing – the parents as a group tended to dress things down and were anxious to present a traditional conservative perspective while the pupils tended to dress things up and present a progressive, liberal perspective. But regardless of the overall presentation, these voices indicate a substantial amount of misunderstanding and miscommunication between parents, teachers and pupils about young people and what they want and need to learn about their relationships and sexuality.

The overall impression of the parents is that they are extremely anxious over the rapidly changing context in which the game of sex is being played. They are fully aware of the dangers as well as the pleasures. They would like to think that they have their finger on the pulse of what was happening and their children under control, but towards the end of the interview there was an acceptance that this was not the case. They did whatever they could to keep things under control. They gave instructions and offered whatever advice they thought necessary, and then hoped for the best. There was not any sense of frank, open and honest dialogue between parents and their children. Parents did not have the willingness or competence to develop and engage in open discussion with their children about relationships and sexuality. There was an acceptance that the school and teachers had an important role to play.

The teachers appeared to be more in tune with what was going on and to the needs and interests of the young people. They were certainly more progressive in their willingness to respond positively to their situation and problems. However, they seemed caught in a dilemma, between giving too much information too early – thereby possibly condoning or indeed encouraging sexual activity – and, on the other hand, giving too little too late. It was also obvious that most teachers felt that there was a need to place relationships and sexuality education within a moral framework. This varied between encouraging pupils to say 'no' to sex before marriage and, on the other hand, helping them learn to have good, but safe sex.

The pupils may be far more experienced and adventurous in their sexual attitudes and practices than either the teachers or the parents believe. Sex has become a part of their lives. It is a central aspect of their everyday relations, but particularly when they meet socially, either in cafes, discos, pubs, nightclubs, each other's houses and so forth. Engaging in sex – not necessarily sexual intercourse – is a central feature of teenage life. It is seen as a positive, pleasurable thing to do. There is the freedom and the confidence to be sexually expressive. It is something that girls and boys like to do. There is a sexual self-confidence. There is no longer the same shyness, embarrassment, guilt and shame about being sexual. There is not the same sense of fear that used to be a characteristic of Catholic Ireland. Sin and damnation seem to be a thing of the past. Being sexually active is the norm. What fear there is now may centre on not being accepted, being left out, and not doing what everyone else is doing. Once young people become sexually active, most fear centres on losing control, unwanted pregnancy (which is significantly reduced through practising safe sex), not being loved and, associated with this, a loss of respect.

Although there is a certain amount of sexual experimentation and adventure taking place, it would be wrong to read what these young people were saying as an indication that they are promiscuous. They operate within a different ethical system of who can do what, with whom, when and were. In the absence of reliable social surveys, we do not know the numbers involved or the type of sexual activities. But there is increasing evidence to suggest that a significant proportion of young people still at school are sexually active and that a significant proportion of these have had, and are having, sexual intercourse. Given the level of sexual activity and the difficulty in engaging in safe sex, the number of crisis pregnancies may not in fact be as high as might be expected. It is obvious from what they said that pupils are anxious to talk, listen and learn about sexuality. The question is to what extent parents and teachers can help young people read, understand and critically reflect on their lives and the ethical system within which they operate and, at the same time, help them operate successfully within it.

8
Putting Contradictions into Context

When it comes to relationships and sexuality, there have been major changes over the last thirty years in our conception of what is right and wrong, good and bad behaviour. The monopoly which the Catholic Church once held over sexual morality has fragmented. In the heyday of the Catholic Church in Ireland, if priests, doctors, teachers, politicians, civil servants, journalists and mothers did say anything about sex, they said much the same things. Alternative voices were silenced or driven underground. Today there are, as we have seen, very different discourses and voices. Young people, especially, speak quite differently about sex.

The debate about sex in Ireland and, specifically, about relationships and sexuality education, is central to the creation and maintenance of a mature democratic society. The different discourses about sexuality are part of the competing perspectives which emerge in civil society about the way we live and communicate, the different beliefs and values we have, and the ideal type of society we struggle to create and maintain.[1] The proponents of the different perspectives I have examined produce arguments, research and policy documents so that their view of sexuality and relationships and sexuality education are first accepted as legitimate, then gain credence and, finally, become part of government policy and social legislation. It is this struggle to be heard, to achieve acceptance and legitimacy and to change existing legislation about sexuality which makes the present era very different from when the Catholic Church held a monopoly over morality. Much of the struggle by the different interest groups in civil society to influence the state and other institutions and organisations takes place through private meetings, submissions, letters and personal contacts. However, the struggle also takes place, as we saw in chapter 6, through debate and discussion in the public sphere. This can be at local and national meetings, seminars and conferences. But most public debate now takes place within the media through news reports, feature articles, documentaries, panel discussions and talk radio.[2] Instead of silence, or oblique and heavily coded references to sexuality, children and young people are now regularly confronted with a large number of stories and reports which range across the different discourses. Media messages about sexuality are numerous, complex and contradictory. One moment a child might hear a nun talking about the beauty of living a contemplative, celibate life. The next, a gay man declaring that not only does he love sex, but that he particularly likes hairy men. It is in the nature of a well-developed public sphere to have a plurality of often opposing viewpoints on issues such as sexuality.

Cultural contradictions

Besides the different viewpoints and arguments within the field of Irish sexuality, there can be more fundamental differences. When we examine what is written and said about sexuality, we can see that some differences of opinion and belief are rooted in logically contradictory positions. The greater the number and the deeper the nature of these contradictions, the more unsettling and turbulent it can be for people involved, particularly children and young people learning about relationships and sexuality. Swidler argues that during a period of rapid social trans-formation – which Ireland has experienced since the 1960s – culture moves from *common sense* to *tradition* to *ideology*. The *common sense* understanding of sexuality in the 1960s was based on a 'set of assumptions so unselfconscious as to seem a natural, transparent, undeniable part of the structure of the world'.[3] As Irish society changed, the Catholic ethos became a *tradition*, which although taken for granted, had increasingly to be articulated in order to be protected. The final stage, in which we now live, is a period of *contested ideologies* in which there are regular, open challenges to Catholic tradition and common sense. These challenges are strongly felt and highly articulated. They come from people developing new understanding of themselves, and new styles of living, relationships, co-operation and authority. At the same time, many traditionalists are forced into developing highly articulated defences of their values, beliefs and practices. Such a highly charged atmosphere leads to what Swidler calls 'unsettled lives'. In such a period, symbols, rituals, rhetoric and body language, whether of traditional Catholic life or liberal individual sexuality, become 'fraught with significance'. Consequently, as we saw in previous chapters, for some traditionalists, the very mention of the words 'penis' and 'vagina' on the airwaves signals another attack on everything that is sacred and pure about Irish society. On the other hand, for some liberals, mention of the words 'modesty' and 'chastity' is a signal for a wish to keep sex in the realm of sin, shame and guilt.

In a similar manner, Archer has argued that the competition between different interest groups and different ways of understanding sexuality, have led to what she has termed 'constraining cultural contradictions'.[4] She argues that when certain beliefs and values within a culture are logically inconsistent, this leads to oppositions and conflicts in the lives of individuals. In other words, competition between fundamentally opposed ideas and beliefs about life leads to conflict, not just in the public sphere, but in the private sphere of the family, and the intimate sphere in which individuals try to discover and develop self-meaning and identity. In some respects, the most fundamental contradiction in the current debate about sexuality education is the persistence of traditional Catholic beliefs and practices within a modern, or indeed post-modern, secular society based on liberal individualism.

My argument is that the teachings of the Catholic Church and liberal individualism are two logically contradictory belief systems about morality and politics. The competition between these two belief systems is witnessed in debates and discussions every day on radio and television, and in newspapers and magazines. The opposing belief systems have been particularly evident in debates in the public sphere over the last twenty years on contraception, abortion, divorce and homosexuality. The problem for parents, teachers and young people is how to deal with the logical contradiction between conservative Catholic teaching on the one hand, and secular liberal individualism on the other. But before analysing this most fundamental contradiction, it is useful to examine some other contradictions which have emerged in the present ideological struggle.

The most glaring contradiction which emerges in terms of the different discourses I have examined is obviously between, at one end of the continuum, the traditional conservative attitude of the Catholic Church and, at the other end, a radical discourse on sexuality and the lifestyle and practices which emerge, for example, in gay and lesbian culture. However, although a radical discourse on sexuality is growing, the numbers ideologically committed to it are relatively small. This is not to deny that conflict or difficulties could arise in a traditional Catholic school if there was an attempt to discuss gay and lesbian issues or, more significantly, if gay and lesbian pupils sought to have their difference recognised and accepted. Such difficulties arose, for instance, in St Patrick's College, Maynooth in 1994 when the Governing Body refused to recognise the Gay and Lesbian Society.[5]

But a more immediate and obvious contradiction is between the secular, liberal discourse of the media and that of the Catholic Church. There is a logical contradiction between the way in which women are imagined, idealised, portrayed and described in the media compared with the images, portrayals, myths and beliefs about women in the tradition of the Catholic Church. It is the contradiction between the attitude, disposition and sexual lifestyle advocated by someone like Madonna and the image of Our Lady represented by the Catholic Church. It may well be that a characteristic of our open, democratic, pluralist society is that children are expected to be able to reconcile these contradictory images and, on a Sunday morning, move from watching Madonna on MTV, to praying in church to images of Our Lady.

Historical context

In previous generations, sexuality and desire were wrapped in words like fornication, concupiscence, adultery, modesty and impurity whose meaning was, perhaps deliberately, kept vague. The legacy of Catholic delicacy was reflected in the Report of the Expert Advisory Group on Relationships and Sexuality Education. When it came to outlining the possible content for a module on Relationships and Sexuality Education there was no mention of issues such as 'masturbation', 'petting', 'homosexuality', 'prostitution', 'pornography' 'contraception', 'abortion', or 'sterilisation'. The cultural legacy of the symbolic domination of the Catholic Church in the fields of sexuality and morality was reflected in the language and terms used in the report. The strategy of the state, in taking control of relationships and sexuality education, was not to challenge the symbolic position of the Church by attempting to name the world of sex outside the accepted language used by the Catholic Church. The words and terms excluded from the Expert Advisory Group report, and the practices associated with them, have historically been unmentionable in Irish Catholic society, and are still deemed immoral by the Church. In other words, in the same way that young people learn that what can and cannot be said and done depends on context, so too did the members of the Expert Advisory Group realise that what could be said and done within an RSE programme had to be within the context of the Catholic Church's symbolic power in Irish society as a whole and, in particular, its political power in the field of education. Ultimately, then, in the absence of people learning to reflect critically upon, challenge and resist existing terms and interpretations, it is power which defines how sex and sexuality will be read and understood. The Expert Advisory Group, its report, and the content and method of the RSE programme reflect the strategies and tactics employed by the state in its attempt to attain dominance within the fields of education and sexuality.

The contradiction between the progressive discourse of the state on sexuality and the traditional views of the Catholic Church is rooted in a broader, more fundamental contradiction. In many respects the Republic of Ireland is still a profoundly Catholic society. Over 90 per cent of the population still identify themselves in the Census of Population as Roman Catholics, and at least two-thirds of these go to Mass once a week. Most Catholics are born, marry and die with the sacraments of the Church. Most important of all, the majority of Catholics are born and raised in Catholic homes and are educated in Catholic schools.

The conception Irish Catholics have of sin, pleasure and sexuality is, however, changing. Many Catholics are distancing themselves from the moral teachings of the Church. Even though the Catholic Church still has considerable influence in schools and homes, gaps and contradictions are growing between what the Church teaches and, for example, how Catholics view contraception, homosexuality and sex outside marriage. The Church no longer holds a monopoly over what Irish Catholics consider to be morally right and wrong behaviour, what it is to be a good person, and what it is to lead a good life. An opinion poll in 1996 found that when it came to serious moral problems, 78 per cent of Catholics followed their own conscience rather than the teaching of the Church.[6] In other words, many Catholics may still be going to Mass, receiving the sacraments and bringing up their children as Catholics and sending them to Catholic schools, but there is a growing gap between, on the one hand, a ritual and symbolic allegiance to the Church as a source of spiritual meaning and identity, and on the other hand an adherence to its moral teachings.[7] However, as long as the Catholic Church has influence and control within the field of education, this contradiction will continue to surface in Irish schools and, in particular, in the implementation of the RSE programme.

The contradictory position of the RSE programme in many Catholic schools can, therefore, be linked to the gradual process over the last thirty years by which the state has sought to distance and separate itself from the Catholic Church.[8] By introducing RSE, albeit in a slow, piecemeal fashion, the state has made a direct intervention in the fields of education, morality and sexuality, three fields over which the Catholic Church used to have a monopoly.

The separation of sex and religion

To understand the origins of the separation of the Irish state from the Catholic Church and the growing contradictory position of the Church in Irish society, we need to examine three interrelated, long-term, social processes. The first relates to the growth in the complexity and rationality of Western society. There has been an increase in the number of social fields, for example, economics, politics, health, education, social welfare and the media. These social fields have developed their own specialised knowledges, theories, experts and personnel. They have become rationally differentiated from each other. More importantly, they have become independent of the overarching control of religion and, specifically, churches and priests. As part of this process of rationalisation, the inter-est and fulfilment of sexual interests gradually became separated from religion.[9] For hundreds of years, particularly within Christianity, sexuality was subsumed within religion. For most people, most of the time, their interest in being sexual was in contradiction with their interest in being saved.[10] This provides an insight into the antipathy between the Catholic Church and sexuality. With the rise of Western rationalism, sexuality began to attain its independence, and develop into a specialised social field with its own discourse, concepts and experts. From the eighteenth century on, ideas about sex began to be generated outside the religious field, not just within medicine and biology, but within psychology, psychiatry, sociology and education. The control of the discourse and practice of sex began to move away from priests and preachers into the jurisdiction of scientists, doctors, psychologists, sociologists, social welfare officers, counsellors and educators.

Secularisation of society

Another long-term social process, which helps explain the background to why the Irish state decided to enter the field of Catholic education and sexual morality, is the growth in secularisation. This centres on the way in which a supernatural, spiritual orientation to life gradually gives way to a rational, material, scientific and technological orientation.[11] Secularisation in Ireland is taking place at four different levels. The first is, as we have seen, where the Catholic Church loses the control it once had over social life and, in particular, areas such as health, education and social welfare. The second level of secularisation has taken place in the decline in personal involvement in religion. This is reflected, for example, in a gradual decline in the level of Mass attendance and attendance at Confession. The third level is the decline in the institutional strength of the Church. In the 1960s, more than 1500 boys and girls used to enter religious life every year as priests, nuns or brothers. Thirty years later the number of vocations has declined to just over 100. The fourth level of secularisation has to do with the fragmentation of the unified, coherent interpretation of life propagated by the Church. The sacred Catholic canopy, which used to hang over every aspect of Irish social life, has disappeared and with it the deference and respect previously given to priests, nuns and brothers. The united front of the Church has, in particular, been shattered through ongoing scandals about homosexual, paedophile and promiscuous priests and brothers, and nuns who were abusive to children in their care. The legacy of Fr Brendan Smyth is of the priest as pervert.[12] Ten years ago, the idea of a priest being left to talk to children about sexual morality would have been an unquestioned orthodoxy among most Catholics. Today, it would increasingly be seen as problematic, even unacceptable.

The rise of individual moral responsibility

The third long-term social process relates to changes within ethics and, in particular, in the move away from formal prescriptions, rules and regulations by religious institutions as to what is right and wrong, towards individuals taking responsibility for their own moral choices and, then, being able to defend their choices rationally. The differentiation of the fields of sexuality and religion is linked to the increased differentiation of morality from religion. This, in turn, is associated with the rise of individual moral responsibility and the demise of priests and preachers as the arbiters of right and wrong. The rationalisation of religious beliefs and values, particularly the development of an ethic of individual moral responsibility, has played a crucial role in the development of capitalism and the rise of Western modernity.[13] Ethics are no longer understood in substantive terms. The result is that 'the morally evaluating and acting individual is forced to choose his own moral fate.'[14]

The rise of individual moral responsibility and, in association with this, a move towards a more secular, liberal, and pluralist society, has been of major significance in Ireland; what makes Ireland peculiar in this respect is that this ethic of individual moral responsibility is increasingly in contradiction with a universal natural law ethic defined by the teaching of a Catholic Church still unusually powerful in international terms. Irish people who are good Catholics now move in a cultural reality polarised between, on the one hand, people making their own, individually legitimated and justified, moral decisions for which they alone are responsible and, on the other, loyally adhering to Church teachings.

This contradiction links into a debate within political science between two different models of democracy.[15] The first – the civil, republican view – emphasises the common good over the rights of individuals. Where there is a conflict of interest, the civil republican tradition holds that the primacy of the common good must hold sway, even if it infringes on what are deemed to be the rights of the individual. The second model, the liberal individualist perspective, emphasises the importance of continually securing and maintaining the freedom and rights of individuals against the state. It holds that whenever possible the rights of the individual should be incorporated into the definition of the common good.

The debate about sexuality education, and about sexual issues and the rights of individuals in general, can be located within this debate.

Arguments from the civil, republican position are often articulated from within a conservative Catholic tradition which maintains that there is an objective moral law – God's law – which is interpreted by the Church, and which provides ethical absolutes from which individuals and states cannot escape. On the other hand, the liberal-individual viewpoint holds that when it comes to matters like sexuality, there are no definitive moral rights and wrongs. It is up to individuals to work out their own position and to pursue whatever ends they desire, as long as in doing so no harm is caused to others. A liberal-individual perspective of democracy tends to separate ethics from politics and religion, and holds that what is regarded as right and wrong is not dependent on sacred religious law, but on the personal convictions of individuals. Part of the rationalisation of an ethic of principled conviction is an increased expectation and demand for consistency, an ability to defend rationally one's convictions and, at the same time, within the resulting pluralist society, to accept other people's convictions.

This contradiction can be seen within Catholic Church teaching, particularly since Vatican II, between positions upholding 'the objective moral law' and others emphasising the 'free human conscience of the individual'. The situation was clarified in Pope John Paul II's encyclical *Veritatis Splendor* when he stated that 'the Catholic Church is by the will of Christ the teacher of truth' and that 'freedom of conscience is never freedom "from" the truth'.[16] The Encyclical recognised that intentions and consequences can influence the morality of an act, but stated that there are specific kinds of behaviour that are always wrong to choose because they are intrinsically evil.[17] Consequently, without denying the influence of morality exercised by circumstances and especially by intentions, the Church teaches that 'there exist acts which *per se* and in themselves, independently of circumstances, are always seriously wrong by reason of their object'.[18]

Even when something is not intrinsically evil or contrary to infallible teaching, there is still an issue of when a Catholic can follow his or her own conscience. Hannon summarises the interpretation which has been put forward by what he terms 'the most authoritative writers':

[A]lthough it must be regarded as highly exceptional, it is in principle licit to differ with a doctrine which does not purport to be an instance of infallible teaching. But a dissenting view would have to be grounded in good argument and would presuppose that the holder was expert in theology, a requirement normally met only by an adequate theological education. It was emphasised that dissent should remain private so as to obviate disturbance in the Church. Scholars might communicate their difficulties among themselves, but not in a journal or other forum which was likely to be 'popularly' influential.[19]

Contradictions within the state

As described in chapter 3, the fear of an AIDS epidemic led the Health Promotion Unit in the Department of Health to broadcast a series of advertisements on radio and television which promoted safe sex through the use of condoms.[20] The approach of the Department of Health is, then, significantly different from that adopted by the Department of Education in relation to the development of RSE. The difference in approaches is rooted in a more fundamental contradiction. The state vacillates between a liberal, individual view of democracy and a civil republican view. On the one hand, the state promotes an economic liberalism which emphasises the free market, individual choice, pluralism and diversity and, on the other hand, it emphasises the importance of the nuclear family and the spiritual and moral guidance and responsibility of parents.[21] This contradiction is reflected in the liberal attitude of the Department of Health and its media campaigns promoting the use of condoms, and the conservative approach of the Department of Education which has been anxious not to offend the Catholic ethos of most Irish schools.[22] The difference is that the state's health education promotion campaign is directed at what young people are doing, whereas the Catholic sexuality education is directed more at what they should be doing.

Back to the future

While an understanding of long-term processes such as secularisation, the growth of individual moral responsibility, and liberal individualism are key ingredients in an explanation of current contradictions between the Catholic Church and the state in relation to sexuality education, they do not explain why sexuality has become so significant in contemporary Western societies. What transformation has taken place in these societies, and more recently in Irish society, that now results in the demand that children have a specific, detailed, practical knowledge about their bodies, their sexuality and how they form personal relationships? Indeed, quite apart from anything that has changed in the state, why is it that forty years after declaring that sex education was not only unnecessary but undesirable, has the Catholic Church now reversed its position? To understand this transformation we need, again, to take a long-term, historical view.

The first part of the explanation comes from an archaeological analysis – in Michel Foucault's sense of 'archaeology' – of the shift in the way we know and understand the world.[23] We have moved from the classical era in the sixteenth century in which God was at the centre of the universe and the individual was constituted within a religious moral discourse, to a modern era in which man has become the centre of the universe especially within scientific and literary discourse. What is happening in the present era is that the individual and his or her sexual erotic interests are no longer constituted within a religious framework, but within an ethical system centred on a general art of living. There is an emphasis on discovering, expressing and caring for the self. One of the aims of sex therapy and counselling programmes is to enable people, through critical reflection, to discover themselves and their sexual desires, pleasures, preferences, orientations and fantasies, thereby freeing themselves from the restrictive view of sexuality into which they were socialised.[24]

Thus, to use Foucault's terms, within the competing regimes of truth and discourses of power about sex perpetuated by priests, teachers, doctors, counsellors and psychiatrists, there has been a longer, wider rupture within the history of the West. In the ancient world, sexuality was a pleasure to be balanced among other pleasures and responsibilities. In the Christian era, the system of ethics moves from pleasures and responsibilities to a detailed classification of sins. In some respects, we have moved in the present era away from a pessimistic, sinful view of sex which sees it as a threat to social order, the common good and the personal well-being of the individual, to a more ancient world view in which sex is seen as a healthy pleasure which has to be placed within the overall task each individual has of living a good, well-balanced life.

The need for sexuality education is also related to the eruption of sexuality in Western society, particularly in the latter part of this century. This eruption can be seen as part of the growth of individualism, increased sexual freedom and the fulfilment of previously repressed sexual interests. The fulfilment of sexual and erotic interests has not only become separated from marriage, it is also becoming separated from affection, love and romance.[25] The regulation of sexuality has moved from external forms of constraint on the individual supervised and controlled by priests, nuns, teachers, doctors, censors and mothers, to internalised forms of constraint enacted by self-reflecting, responsible individuals.[26]

The notion of competing perspectives and ideas about sex provides an understanding of how power operates within this process. What appears to be an inevitable, linear, universal process of rational differentiation of social fields in which the ideas and understanding of sexuality become separated from ethical salvationary religion is, in effect, the result of a series of historical struggles between competing interest groups. Thus Foucault claims that what we see as a process of rationalisation is more an ongoing process in which discourses or regimes of truth are continually constructed and dismantled. It is not that we now speak with a better truth about sexuality, but that we speak within a different regime of truth, a different discourse of power. In the present era, there is a resistance against the 'truth' about sexuality pronounced by the Catholic Church.[27] In a post-modern world, people become sceptical of absolute truth. In such a world, young people have to learn to sift through and critically interpret all that they read, hear and see about sex.

The exploration and critical reflection about self and sexuality may be seen as part of an emancipatory struggle not just to realise an alternative self, but to help create a less repressive, more open, democratic society.[28] Sex education, then, becomes part of learning how to transform the self; of being able to see and read the world differently and to change set behaviour.[29]

Being able to learn to change means that people are able to analyse critically and evaluate not only what they know about the sexual world in which they live, but also about the knowledge they have acquired about sex – who told them, the way they were told, and what they were not told. One of the bases of emancipatory education is an ability to reflect about the taken-for-granted understanding one has about sex. Learning to be different, to be free, demands that young people critically reflect about themselves as sexual human beings. In effect, this becomes central to them developing an individual moral responsibility about sex.

Emancipatory sexuality education

Emancipatory sexuality education involves a number of teaching methods which have been developed within adult education. There is for example an emphasis on dialogue and raising consciousness, and of engaging in collaborative and self-directed learning rather than didactic teaching. It involves enabling young people to reflect on why they have certain beliefs and attitudes to sex, how they behave sexually, how they understand themselves as sexual human beings, how they relate to members of the opposite sex, how they talk about and communicate their love, feelings, fears, anxieties and misunderstandings. This type of learning is premised on the belief that without being able to reflect about themselves as sexual human beings, and about the way in which they fulfil their sexual erotic interests, they will be less able to develop mature, responsible human sexual relations which are suited to the culture and society in which they live.

This type of approach involves students identifying their own needs in relation to sexuality. They become involved in deciding what issues need to be addressed and how their programme of learning should be organised.[30] There is an emphasis on learning from each other. As Magee and Bissett describe it, the teacher becomes a facilitator who helps young people 'to examine and understand their life experiences in terms of the broader societal context becoming aware of how structures impact on their lives'.[31] But, as we have seen, the language – the words and terms – which young people use to examine and understand the sexual world in which the live can be very different from that of bishops, priests and teachers. Although dated, and a bit extreme, the following is an indication of how big the difference can be. *How to Talk to Your Child about Sex* (published with the imprimatur of the Archbishop of Dublin in 1981) suggests that explanations along the following lines be given to adolescents about masturbation and homosexuals:

Masturbation means handling the sexual parts to the extent where relief is had from sexual tension. It encourages one to seek fulfilment within oneself rather than through service to others and so it is an incomplete use of sex. Should the habit last into adult life, it could be an escape from real life either because of insecurity or immaturity or because of some disturbance.

A Homosexual (man) or a Lesbian (woman) is someone who has a need to relate to another person of the same sex in a genital way, rather than to someone of the opposite sex. These are a minority group and many of them regret that they seem unable to enjoy marriage and family life.[32]

This is a standard explanation within the traditional teaching of the Catholic Church. The language is distant and authoritative, pronouncing the truth about masturbation and homosexuality. The choice of words and the way they are put together means that there are many messages within what is said. The term 'handling' is usually used in relation to goods. This fits in with the use of 'parts', as if the body was something external to the self. The use of 'one' rather than 'you' is necessary to confirm that it is not something that 'you' would do. The use of terms 'incomplete', 'escape', 'insecurity', 'immaturity' all lead into the final pronouncement that masturbation is a 'disturbance'. Again, it has to be realised that 'disturbance' has often been used in the context of 'mentally disturbed'. In other words, the coded message is that if you masturbate you may go mad. The message fits in within the overall context of a traditional discourse which refers to sexuality primarily in terms of a moral or health disorder.

The coded message about homosexuals and lesbians follows the same path. The message here is that homosexuals and lesbians cannot relate to others in any way other than through their genitals. The implication is that they are dominated by sex; that they cannot think about anything else except each other's genitals. Any form of communication or affection is a means of fulfilling an uncontrollable sex drive. Homosexuality is made out to be an affliction or disease. It is certainly not a matter of individual choice. The message is that homosexuals are diseased sexual deviants who cannot do the normal thing of getting married and having children. They are outsiders who look at normal people and live an unhappy and remorseful life.

There are, of course, other hidden messages. Most important is the absence of young people. They may have asked a question, but the impression is that they are not allowed to speak. They are simply to be told the answer. When power speaks, it speaks authoritatively without engaging in dialogue. There is no encouragement to find out why the question might have been asked, what other issues or concerns they may have and, most important of all, what their own view might be. In other words, the message is that when it comes to understanding sexuality, your beliefs and attitudes do not count. It reinforces an ethos which denies self-expression.

In this respect, the approach in *How to Talk to Your Child about Sex* stands in stark contrast to the approach used in teenage magazines. Here the coded message is that young people can ask whatever questions they like, in whatever manner they like. The implication is that they set the agenda by announcing their concerns and worries. They are permitted to read the sexual world in which they live in their own language. Take, for example, this girl who wrote to *Just Seventeen* seeking advice about sexual intercourse.

Can you tell me if my boyf [*sic*] is lying to me? He knows a lot about sex and has much more experience than me. He says that if he does oral sex on me after we've gone all the way, this will kill all the sperm and stop me from getting pregnant. Is this really true? We haven't done it yet so please help.[33]

Of course, there are as many hidden messages within this text. There is the suggestion that boys lie to girls in order to have sex, and that because they are knowledgeable they are more in control of what happens. This is reinforced by the notion that sex is something which is done to girls and that somehow boys are mythical figures who save girls from pregnancy rather than make them pregnant. But it would be wrong to think that the girl came to ask this question, suddenly out of the blue, in the way she did. The question she asked, and the way that she asked it, indicate that she has been successfully constituted as a sexual subject within the liberal discourse of the media in general and, specifically, in the discourse promoted by teenage magazines.

The differences between these two approaches to describing and understanding sexuality are, then, quite significant. It is important to realise that they both come from different discourses, and that young people who operate within these perspectives will see, understand and relate to sexuality differently. Each of the discourses can be seen as an attempt to dominate symbolically the field of sexuality, if not colonise it and, so to speak, the young people who operate within it. Both claim to be on the side of truth and freedom. Operating within a liberal discourse does not necessarily increase freedom. In some respects, it means that instead of being dominated and colonised by the Catholic Church, young people are dominated and colonised by a viewpoint which insists on fulfilling desires by being attractive, competitive, adventurous, and sexually active.[34] But the very existence of a liberal discourse suggests that, contrary to what the Catholic Church argues, there are no fundamental, universal truths about sexuality. There are, in effect, only different discourses. The growth of the media in Ireland shattered the myth that there was only one truth about sexuality. Once that monopoly was broken, young people were forced to operate in and between discourses and the institutions which create and maintain them.

If this argument is accepted, then the question is how there can be any freedom or emancipation from these discourses and what role, if any, education plays in such a struggle. In other words the progressive discourse, on which the Relationships and Sexuality Education programme is based, could become not a source of freedom or liberation from traditional or liberal discourses, but remain just another form of symbolic domination. Despite the best intentions of the programme, it may well be that it is just as colonising and dominating as the traditional and liberal viewpoint. The question, then, is where to begin and how best to avoid any dominating or colonising effect.

This is where the philosophy and teaching methods of certain forms of adult education, particularly those associated with Paulo Freire, have relevance. In this approach, the first task of the teacher is to avoid adding to any existing symbolic domination. This happens when the teacher introduces language and terms which do not correspond to the existing way which young people read and understand their sexual world.[35] In a Freirean approach to helping people to read, teachers begin with getting students to announce to each other what are the issues and events in their lives about which they are most concerned. Among the peasants of Brazil where Freire initiated his method, these might have been 'water', 'land', 'food', 'health', 'children', and so forth. As each of these are announced, the teacher writes down the key words. The students would use the words to make a small sentence which, again, the teacher would write down.[36] What is crucial in this process is that the students are learning to read their world by naming it. They are directing what it is they want to learn to read. The teacher becomes more of a facilitator. Instead of a set curriculum which defined what it was the children and young people had to learn, they would be given an opportunity to announce, in their own words, issues and problems about which they were concerned. They would be learning to read and understand their sexual world using their own language. This would imply, at least, that they were not wrong in they way they read or interpret the world. In the act of naming their world, they are at the same time asserting the right to self-expression. Once they have found their voices, and are able to express themselves, the task of the teacher is to help them see other ways of reading, understanding and appreciating their sexual world.

Language is, therefore, a major issue in relationships and sexuality education. If 'dick', 'cunt', 'tits' are the words which young people use to name their sexual world then, within a Freireian adult learning approach, any attempt to help them to read their world has to begin with these words. A youth project in London '*Do the Right Thing*' decided that an immediate way into discussing sexual issues was to brainstorm with the participants for various names for male and female genitalia, sexual intercourse, oral sex and other sexual activities. As one of the co-ordinators commented:

> It's a really levelling thing to do – basically if you say all the words for vagina and penis – you have to start talking about sex in your own language and this was a simple exercise to define which words we were going to use throughout the project. It's risky because to discuss sex, and to talk about what things are, is really brave and demands a lot of trust immediately.[37]

In other words, advocates of an emancipatory education approach argue that relationships and sexuality education programmes which do not enable young people to speak for themselves, to read and reveal their world to themselves, may not be just irrelevant, but a hindrance – making them less competent at making mature, responsible decisions regarding their sexuality. One of the legacies of Freire's approach to literacy is that it is inappropriate and unjust for people in developed societies to go and teach people in developing societies to read and write using words which have no relevance to their everyday lives. It adds to people's oppression to teach them to read and write through phrases such as 'the cat is on the mat' when they have neither a cat or a mat and what they are most concerned about is clean water, food and housing. Similarly, it may add to young people's oppression to teach them about sex with words which are not part of their world. A Freirean approach to learning would begin with an identification of the issues and concerns of the pupils. This involves a process of facilitation in which the issues and concerns are allowed to be revealed, announced and recognised as valid. The task of the teacher is to help pupils think through different issues and, rather than having solutions or answers presented to them, to work together and to learn from each other. This task is to create a positive learning space, where there are no hidden agendas and, most important of all, where pupils are enabled to speak in their own language. The ability to achieve this depends on teachers having no instrumental pedagogic purpose, for example, to impose a moral-ethical discourse. To be a good teacher means being able to identify closely, to sympathise if not empathise with the issues and struggles of the pupils.

Emancipatory learning is developed best when teachers have direct experience of the sexual environment and habitus in which the pupils operate. It may be difficult for those who have no experience of the sexual environment of young people, particularly priests, nuns and brothers, to help pupils read their sexual world. It is difficult for teachers to help pupils become fully mature, sexually active, pleasure-seeking, morally responsible adults if they have never been that way themselves. This may well be the most fundamental contradiction which the RSE programme has to overcome. Can an older generation of teachers, who have been brought up within, and perhaps still accept, the strict ethical teachings of the Catholic Church – who have tended to see sex as a problem rather than a pleasure – overcome the shame, guilt and embarrassment in talking about sexuality in such a way as to facilitate emancipatory learning?

Stephanie Walsh carried out a small survey of primary school teachers in north Munster in 1995. Although her final sample was small – 51 respondents – her findings suggest that many primary school teachers may be unhappy teaching RSE. Nearly three-quarters (73 per cent) of the teachers said that they did not feel comfortable teaching about sexuality. Even more, four-fifths (83 per cent) said that they did not feel confident in teaching children about sexuality. Moreover, Walsh found that levels of comfort and confidence did not change significantly – if anything they decreased – after teachers had taken the special in-service training course on RSE designed by the Department of Education.[38]

Conclusion

The first and most important lesson in Irish sexuality is that, however much we may try to escape the past, it is inscribed not just in institutions such as the state, but in the minds, hearts and bodies of Irish people.

The long nineteenth century of Irish Catholicism, in which the Church dominated not just the religious field, but many other social fields, is coming to an end. The emergence of a new field of sexuality, out from under the moral monopoly of the Church, has given rise to a number of competing discourses and, consequently, contradictions in the way we see, understand and relate to sexuality. These contradictions are not just evident in the new generation of young people, they are endemic to Irish social life. They can be seen in everyday life, among parents and grandparents, in the state, in the media, in the Church itself. Irish people are no longer confident about what is good and bad, right and wrong about sex. They no longer speak with one voice about sexuality. There are now many different perspectives and many different voices. But the move from homogeneous to a heterogeneous culture has not been an easy one. We have moved from a settled period in which, when it came to sex, everybody knew what was right and proper, and everything that was said and done sexually was in its proper time and proper place. We now live in unsettled times. There are those who wish to maintain the sanctity of family life, by keeping sex within marriage. For young people, sex has to be denied and kept at bay through chastity and modesty. But now there are competing viewpoints, voices which speak very differently about sex. As well as parents, priests and teachers, young people are listening to voices from the media and their peers encouraging them to be sexually active, experienced and adventurous.

In this chapter, I have argued that it is only by understanding the past that we can understand the contradictions of the present. Although the changes which have taken place over the last thirty years in Ireland are unique, they are part of number of long-term social processes taking place in Western society: the multiplication and differentiation of social fields, each with their own expert knowledges, the growth of secularisation, and the growth of individual moral responsibility. Overall this may be seen as a general move towards liberal individualism. It is essential to realise that these processes, and the contradictions which go with them, are etched as much in the hearts, minds and bodies of young people growing up as they are within the state, civil society and social institutions of which they are members.

The legacy of the past lives on in the hearts and minds of older Irish people. With this legacy come the contradictions of wanting to be sexually alive, but at the same time being unable to do so without becoming awkward and embarrassed. The denial of sexuality in previous generations has had the effect of inculcating in older people an incompetence in talking not just about the sexual aspects of the lives, but their pleasures, desires, feelings and emotions. There was little that could be said or discussed about sex apart from bantering, teasing and joking. The dominance of the Church in Irish society, particularly in education, had the consequence of preventing open, honest discussion about sexuality. It was censored and silenced not just in public life, but in families, between parents and children, between husbands and wives. This systematic denial prevented people from conceptualising and realising alternative ways that they might live their lives as sexual human beings. This gap has been filled by the media and the market. Young people are encouraged to be sexually alive, to discover, flaunt and realise their sexuality. The media offer them the knowledge, information, advice and know-how to enable this to take place. The market offers them the fashion clothes, beauty and health products, diet schedules, music and dance to make the realisation successful. It is the emergence of competing discourses and of the contradictions to which they give rise, which has forced the state to enter the field and provide an alternative form of discourse; something between the extremes of those put forward by the Catholic Church and the media. The problem is that unless the RSE programme begins with the existing way pupils read and understand the sexual world in which they live, unless it meets their needs and interests, unless they can participate in the decisions about what they need to learn, and unless the programme enables them to reflect critically about the different discourses and messages they receive about sex and sexuality, then it may exacerbate rather than dissolve existing contradictions. The possibility of open, honest debate, discussion and critical reflection between young people, parents and teachers, within families, schools and wider society is crucial to the ongoing creation and maintenance of an emancipatory understanding of sexuality.

9
Conclusion

Irish attitudes to sex have changed dramatically in the last thirty years. When I was growing up, any mention, display, or glimpse of sex was a source of shame and embarrassment. Sex was covered up, censored and hidden away. To think or talk about it, to dwell on it in any way – worse still to engage in it – was a mortal sin. Innocence had to be protected. If uncontrolled, sex could destroy not just individuals and families, but the very soul of Irish society.

But times have changed. Now sex is prolific. It is in the media. It is displayed openly in newspapers and magazines. Sex scandals have become regular features in news and current affair programmes. Sex scenes have become the essential ingredient which makes films, videos and advertisements successful. Sex confessions have become a major component of 'talk radio' and television chat shows. Sex has moved from the media into public and private life. It is on public display on the street, in the park, on the beach. It is in the way people dress, behave and look at each other. These changes have been occuring in Western society throughout the twentieth century and have been filtered into Irish society, primarily through the media. Irish people have become more at ease with their sexuality. There is no longer the same sense of awkwardness and embarrassment about sex. There is also a greater self-confidence in the open demonstration of love, affection and emotion. The shy, demure Irish boy and girl, uncertain of themselves and their sexuality, are gradually being replaced by bright, confident, outward-going people, able to proclaim their desires, demonstrate emotion, and anxious and willing not just to display their bodies and sexuality, but to engage in sex.

What was unthinkable thirty years ago has become commonplace. Sexual intercourse was, for most people, confined to marriage. Anyone who looked for sex – or worse had sex – outside marriage was looking for trouble. Girls who became pregnant were the scandal of the community. They had to be hidden or put away. But again, times have changed. In 1970, one in 38 births were outside marriage. By 1996, this had risen to one in four. The number of births outside marriage and the rise in teenage pregnancies are reflections of a dramatic increase in the level of sexual activity and a decrease in the age at which young people start having full sexual intercourse. In a survey in 1997, half of those aged between 17 and 20 years reported having had sexual intercourse before they were 16 years old.

I began this book by telling the tragic stories of girls who, caught in time between the old and the new, became examples of our contradictory attitudes to sex. As one part of Ireland took part in a sexual revolution in which pleasures, desires and a new sense of self were being discovered, others were still living in families and communities in which sex was hidden and silenced. Chastity and modesty are, so to speak, clothes which generations of Irish people have learnt to wear as a normal part of life. They are not easily discarded. Body and soul go together. Any unwarranted display of the body is still seen by many as an immoral and unacceptable display of the self.

The young mothers who abandoned or killed their newborn babies may be seen as victims, and their actions as inevitable consequences, of living in a contradictory culture. They were caught in time, between the virtues of modesty and purity extolled by the Catholic Church and the enticement to sex propagated by the media. Since the 1960s, the media have been sending out a steady stream of messages which have announced, as clearly and as powerfully as any parable in the Gospels, that feeling good about oneself, being physically attractive, being sexual and having sex, were not just normal, but necessary. It was, in effect, a new natural law – but very different to that taught by the Catholic Church.

The young women who killed or abandoned their newborn babies had, so to speak, taken part in the sexual revolution. They may have wanted to be lifted up by the new rising tide of sexual freedom, but they were tied down by traditional attitudes and values. They embraced sex, but did they know what they were letting themselves in for? Were they making a conscious, well-considered decision? Did they know about sexual pleasure and the way desire operates? Were they fully aware of the potential consequences of their behaviour? Were they fully informed about human biology? Did they know about contraception and safe sex? Even if they did know all these things, were they able to negotiate terms and conditions with their partners? Or were they like many passionate rebels who went before them – staunch, frustrated supporters of uncertain causes and desires?

Whatever else happened these women were caught out, not just in a moral sense, but out of time. They became pregnant, and perhaps soon realised that, despite the messages received through the media, the revolution had not started in their family or community. They were on their own, and left alone with feelings of shame, remorse and guilt.

These women were not alone. They were part of a large, unrecognised, disparate, silent community – the tip of a grotesque, unacceptable, bizarre iceberg. Between 1970 and 1996, 70,000 Irish women had abortions in England. The number is increasing each year. In 1997, it was 5,325 – an increase of almost nine per cent on the previous year.[1] There have been thousands of other women who have embraced the sexual revolution, who have lived through crisis pregnancies, and who have had to decide whether to keep the baby, have it adopted, or have an abortion.[2]

Mahon, Conlon and Dillon indicated that the main reasons Irish women had abortions were 'the shame attached to women's pre-marital sexual activity, women's fear of disclosing their pregnancies to their parents, and their anxieties about work and motherhood'.[3] Shame and loss of respect were also acute among women considering adoption. 'They had witnessed other lone mothers in their community being subjected to stigma and they were concerned about the stigma that their family would be subjected to if they were to "come out" and disclose their pregnancy.'[4]

The legacy of the past

To understand the present, it is necessary to understand the past, and to see how things came to be the way they are today. I have argued that the attempt to develop an effective sexuality education programme in the Republic of Ireland has been hampered by the legacy of the Catholic Church's monopoly over morality. That legacy arose during the nineteenth century, particularly after the Famine, when there was a need to increase standards of living by controlling population growth. The control of population was achieved by controlling sexual activity. In nineteenth-century Ireland, control of sexual activity was achieved by limiting marriage. The flaw in this social mechanism was that those who did get married had large families. This meant that the strategies by which people were encouraged to emigrate, postpone marriage, or never marry at all, had to be re-employed for successive generations. These mechanisms of sexual control persisted well into the second half of the twentieth century.

The Catholic Church became the means to the end of controlling sex and marriage. It provided the beliefs, moral values, prayers, rituals and sacraments which protected the 'sacred heart' of the family from contamination through sex and selfishness. Church teachings and rituals ensured that individual members surrendered their needs and interests to the greater common good. Children and young people learnt to sacrifice themselves for emigration, permanent celibacy or, at best, postponed marriage. These sacrifices were achieved through practices of self-denial. Self-surrender and abnegation were not just about denying sex, it was about repressing all aspects of desire and pleasure. Being selfish became a mortal sin. To do or say anything which was seen to place oneself before others incurred the wrath of mothers, fathers and priests. And so the very desire to seek things for oneself, whether they be food, clothes or material pleasures, was quietly but constantly eliminated through ridicule, teasing and censure. If these failed, stronger sanctions were employed. Those who practised self-denial willingly were honoured and respected. They became living saints, ideal role-models for others.

Within this environment, any expression of sex or desire in thought, word or deed, any movement of the body, or any look in the eyes, signalled danger and had to be eliminated. Modesty and chastity were extolled as great virtues. Children were expected to internalise these virtues to the extent that they became part of their automatic behaviour, a central element of their demeanour and outlook on life.

This control of sex – this protection of the family – became central to the modernisation of Irish agriculture in the nineteenth century, and the establishment of the new Irish state in the twentieth century. The successful implementation of the strategies which controlled sex, desire and self-fulfilment was central to the Church developing and maintaining a monopoly over morality and family life. For a long time, it was in the interest of the state and Irish Catholics to maintain this monopoly.

However, the Church's monopoly over morality could not hold forever. The type of society which was reflected the Church's vision of life – cosy homesteads within which pious, spiritual people lived in frugal comfort – was rapidly becoming out of tune with the needs and interests of a new generation of Irish people. The urban middle classes sought increased prosperity, material comforts and individual freedom. The rapid advance of world capitalism, the pursuit of economic growth by the state, the arrival of television, the rise of the women's movement, and many other changes, began to erode the Church's monopoly over morality. Being successful, self-expressive and sexually attractive became acceptable and a reflection of a healthy, positive approach to life.

But the growth of sexuality and liberal individualism has brought divisions and conflicts in Irish social life, particularly in areas such as education where the Catholic Church still exerts considerable power. For years after the media began to promote sexuality, the Church persisted in its strategy of hiding it, protecting innocence, and inculcating chastity and modesty. But with so many young people becoming sexually active, with so many teenage pregnancies, with so many births taking place outside of marriage, with so many abortions, and with so many young mothers abandoning and killing their newborn babies, the state could no longer stand idly by.

In the conclusion to their study of crisis pregnancies, Mahon, Conlon and Dillon noted that

the best way to reduce the incidence of crisis pregnancies and abortions is to reduce the incidence of unsafe sexual practices. This can only occur with the implementation of effective education and health policies on responsible sexual behaviour.[5]

The Relationships and Sexuality Education programme introduced by the state in 1997 is an attempt to provide this effective education.

State intervention

The RSE programme introduced to Irish schools has less to do with teaching children and young people about sex and sexuality, than it has with teaching them about themselves, their relationships, and how to become to self-aware, self-confident, self-assertive, and critically reflective about themselves, their family and the community and society in which they live. It is here that the centre of the Catholic Church's opposition to the RSE programme lies. Children and young people increasingly become judges of what is right and wrong, good and bad for themselves and the society in which they live. Morality is no longer something laid down by the Church. It becomes something to be debated and discussed. The formation of critically reflective, self-directed people is a crucial element in the creation of mature democratic societies. However, it is anathema to a traditional form of Catholicism in which people accepted without questioning the rules and regulations of the Church. The emergence of individual moral responsibility signals the spread of Protestantism and the demise of the Catholic Church fulfilling its role as the conscience of Irish society.

The organisational problem which the state has had in implementing the RSE programme is that the Catholic Church still has considerable power in the management and control of Irish schools, especially at primary level. As members of the Partnership in Education, representatives of the Catholic Church were actively involved in the design and implementation of the RSE programme. However, at the same time, individual bishops and Catholic interest groups have combined to oppose the introduction of RSE within schools. Their opposition has not focused on the main content of the programme which has to do with developing self-esteem, self-confidence and individual moral responsibility, but on teaching children about conception and intercourse. It is here, on the specifics of sex education, that the clash between the Catholic Church and the Irish state is now focused.

The Church has argued that the curriculum guidelines produced by the National Council for Curriculum and Assessment are just another resource for teaching children about relationships and sexuality. It has recommended that its religious education series *Children of God* would be a more suitable resource for Catholic schools. The *Children of God* series states that teaching children about sex is only an option, and that teachers can exclude it if they wish. The curriculum guidelines produced by the state are emphatic that sensitive issues such as conception, intercourse and physical changes at puberty 'will be dealt with before the end of a child's primary schooling'.[6] However, in the Church's guide to RSE, it is stated clearly that there may be situations in which teachers judge that it is not right to try to fulfil this provision.[7]

The debate about RSE may, then, be linked to another fundamental issue which has been at the centre of the debate about Church and state in modern Ireland. Does the programme represent, as some traditional Catholics would argue, not just an intrusion by the state into the fields of sexuality and morality, but into the private life of the family? Is the insistence on teaching RSE in schools an attempt by the state to take away the rights of parents to bring up their children in accordance with their beliefs and values? Does this entry by the state into the private sphere of life represent, in Donzelot's terms, an ever increasing trend towards the supervision and policing of families?[8]

In developing an RSE programme, the Irish state is following in the footsteps of its Western counterparts. What makes Ireland different – as has been the case with many other matters relating to sexuality – is not just that the state has been so late entering the field but that it has encountered such stiff opposition from the Catholic Church.[9]

But this leaves unanswered a bigger question which may be at the heart of Catholic opposition to RSE. Why has Western society developed such a fixation on sexuality? What has happened to the nature of social life in modern Western society that has made it necessary for the state to take on the task of teaching children about sexuality? Why does the state demand that sex be revealed to children, that they become sexually aware, that they develop a detailed knowledge of the sexual functions of their bodies, and that they become self-confident masters of the skills of social relationships? Is it that the state, far from promoting the freedom of the individual, is aiding the development of the most subtle, most penetrating form of self-discipline and control ever imagined? Is the state through the RSE programme not just taking over but destroying the family – the very place which has until recently been a safe haven and last refuge from the state? Is the state aiding and abetting the forces of capitalism to undermine the norms, values and customary ways of living and communicating which people in different communities have developed independently for themselves over decades, if not centuries?

On the other hand, can the state be seen as a force of emancipation which challenges and replaces outdated, inappropriate attitudes to life? In this perspective, the state acts as a force of rationalisation on traditional values, beliefs and attitudes no longer meaningful or relevant to the needs and interests of people living in a mass-mediated, consumption-driven society. In this progressive perspective, RSE can be seen as an important process of helping to rationalise traditional values, thereby enabling young people to counteract the colonising effects of the media, market forces and consumerism.[10]

Learning to live with ambivalance

We are living in sexually unsettled times, between old traditional Catholic beliefs and values and new liberal attitudes. Traditionalists want to protect family life. They want to maintain moral standards, and to safeguard the virtue and innocence of children. They want to make a stand against the ever-encroaching tide of permissive society and the diseases and social disorder which they believe goes with it. Liberals, on the other hand, want to bring an end to the repressive regime of former years. They want to eliminate the silence and taboos of the past, and the fear, shame and guilt which surrounded sex. They want to dismantle the culture of self-denial and self-mortification. They want to move away from modesty and chastity, and to create a new sense of self which is independent, confident and expressive. They want people to make up their own minds as to what is good and bad, right and wrong for themselves and others. They want people to get to know themselves through understanding and fulfilling their desires, through knowing their pleasures and, appropriately, indulging in them. They see sex as something positive and beneficial. They like and enjoy it. They want to be sexy, talk about sex, and have sex.

The reason we live in sexually unsettled times is that individuals move back and forward between these two extremes. The liberals of today, especially if they have children, can become the traditionalists of tomorrow. Many people are caught in between the two extremes of traditionalism and liberalism. They want individual freedom and choice but, at the same time, they want the security and comfort of a traditional life in which everything, including sex, is in its proper place and proper time. As Christie Davies put it personally when concluding his study of *Permissive Britain,*

I am profounding uneasy at the package deal that has been termed 'the permissive society'. I am in favour of allowing abortion, abolishing hanging, tolerating homosexuals, but I do not wish to live in the kind of society that is willing to allow changes of this kind. I accept the social and legal manifestations of the permissive society but I reject the general ethos of the society.[11]

It is not, then, that Irish people are hypocritical about sex, but that they are ambivalent. They want the best of both worlds. It may well be this ambivalence to sex is no different from our ambivalence to alcohol. In daily life the state encourages us to remain sober and in control, particularly if we are driving but, at the same time, the alcohol industry exhorts us to drink and relax.[12] It could be, as Toennies suggested, that tension between traditional and liberal viewpoints reflects not so much a conflict between irreconcilable opposites, as a healthy interdependence, as there is, for example, between city and country.[13]

It may well be that what children and young people have to learn about sexuality revolves around dealing with this ambivalence. It is not perhaps a question of them learning to be either chaste or sexually active, but of being both. In fact, what appears to be happening is that young people recognise and accept that they live in a world of ambivalent messages. There are those who tell them to hold off from sex, and there are those who tell them to let go and try it. Out of traditional and liberal Catholic culture, they develop their own sexual habitus – their own way of seeing, interpreting, reacting to and dealing with sex. From what they see, hear and learn in their homes and schools, they develop their own morality, their own values and norms about what is permissible. Learning to be sexually street-wise for young people in Ireland means growing up to realise that there are two sides to every street: the side of chastity and modesty, and the side of sexual experience. Young people have to learn to wander from one side to the other, adapt to the rules of the road and, most of all, watch out for the traffic which may knock them down. Once they become sexually active they are, so to speak, in the driving seat of a biological mechanism which can as easily create new life, as destroy an existing one.[14]

The difference between sexually active in Ireland today, compared with ten years ago, is that young people now live in a contraceptive culture. This leads to another ambivalence. Parents and teachers do not know whether to teach and promote chastity or safe sex. But even among young people there is an ambivalence about condoms. There has been a steady sexualisation of love among young people. Love and sex go together. Love is essentially a non-rational, unplanned, spontaneous activity. It may well be that for sex to be borne out of love, it too has to be unplanned and spontaneous. To carry condoms may be a sign of being responsible. But it is also a sign of a rational, deliberate, planned approach to sex. It may not be a sign of a spontaneous, loving, romantic people who are willing to surrender themselves completely to the one they love. Condoms are not romantic and may be a sign of a calculated, rational approach to sex. When carried by young women, they could be a sign of being interested in sex, not out of love, but just for the sake of sex.

Lessons in teaching sexuality

The state, through the RSE programme, is trying to help young people deal with the ambivalent messages of traditionalism and liberalism. The RSE programme aims to help young people to stay safe, happy and comfortable in the middle of the road, somewhere between chastity and sexual activity. In concentrating on developing self-esteem, the programme tries to teach children to be confident, mature and responsible in their social relationships. The message, in other words, is that when it comes to travelling the road of sexuality, they are in the driving seat of a car which can bring as much pain as pleasure and happiness. The approach of the RSE programme may be the only sensible way forward. The only problem is who is best able to teach these young people to drive on what has become a sexual superhighway. The first and most obvious consideration is that it is difficult to teach someone if you are not a good driver yourself. It is perhaps impossible if you have never driven.

Teaching children and young people about sex, sexuality and relationships is completely different from teaching them any other subject. How comfortable they feel about sex and their own sexuality will echo in everything they do and say. Young people will sniff out, quicker than a dog will a cat, if teachers are not happy with and confident about their sexuality, their bodies and their desires. Whatever else happens, it seems crucial that whoever teaches RSE has to be a special person. The pupils I talked with suggested that they would prefer to be taught in small groups, by someone a little older and more experienced than themselves. They suggested that it would be important that they did not know the teacher and the teacher did not know them. However, they emphasised that the teacher had to be someone with whom they could readily identify, who would help them read, understand and operate within the sexual world in which they lived, who could understand and sympathise with their problems, and who would help them interpret and resolve their real needs and interests.[15] Despite its merits on the long-term benefits, it may be practically and financially difficult to fulfil these requests.

As it stands, the RSE programme demands a new relationship between teacher and pupil. If the programme is to be successful, the traditional role of the teacher as the one who knows and imparts knowledge to ignorant pupils may have to be replaced by a model in which the teacher is open to learning from the pupils not just about their concerns and problems, but about the sexual world in which they live. Such a development might have long-term benefits for education in general with the teacher being able to move from being typecast as a traditional authority to be obeyed, to becoming someone who is seen as a loyal, trusted and respected ally in the struggle to know, understand and appreciate life. But to achieve this loyalty and respect, it may be necessary for the teacher to be less definite and less absolutist about sexuality, to be open to learning from the pupils, and to be willing to allow them have a say not just in the content, but in the way the programme is taught. Without this sense of ownership and control, RSE could become a frustrating, alienating imposition.

A frank, open and honest approach to teaching children and young people about relationships and sexuality may also involve critical reflection. In a world of different discourses and truths about sexuality, RSE may involve helping children and young people learn to reflect critically about themselves and the sexual world in which they live. They need to learn to ask fundamental questions such as: who is it who speaks about sex? What do they say? What is the motivation behind what they are saying? I have argued that there is no one truth about sex and sexuality. Different truths emerge from different discourses and perspectives. These divisions and contradictions make relationships and sexuality education more necessary now than ever before.

The society in which children and young people live is not of their own making. The debate about RSE has much less to do with teaching children and young people than about the morality of the society in which we are living. In other words, it is about social ethics rather than politics. People may deem it desirable that children should remain innocent about sex until puberty. This may be appropriate in a world in which there are no magazines, films, television and radio programmes. The media may not provide the best lessons in sexuality, but they are widely available, and they are presented in an easily accessible, attractive manner. It may not be desirable that such uncontrolled knowledge and information be available. But this is the world in which we live, and in which children grow up. We can debate and discuss the need for stricter censorship and a greater silencing of sex, but until there is a change in public policy and social legislation, children will grow up in a highly sexual, erotic and, increasingly, pornographic world.

Notes

Full references are given at the beginning of each chapter (including those cited in previous chapters). Second citations within chapters are given in abbreviated form.

Chapter 1. Introduction

1. See, for example, Alan Bestic, *The Importance of Being Irish*, New York: William Morrow 1969; Donald Connery, *The Irish*, New York: Simon & Schuster 1968; Rosemary Mahony, *Whoredom in Kimmage*, New York: Anchor Books 1993; John Messenger, *Innis Beag*, New York: Holt Rinehart & Winston 1969; Nancy Scheper-Hughes, *Saints, Scholars and Schizophrenics*, Berkeley: University of California Press 1981.
2. See also, T. Inglis 'From Sexual Repression to Liberation?' in *Encounters with Modern Ireland*, ed. M. Peillon and E. Slater, Dublin: Institute of Public Administration 1998, pp. 99–104.
3. Alexander Humphreys, *New Dubliners*, New York: Fordham University Press 1966, p. 139.
4. Rosita Sweetman, *On Our Backs*, London: Pan Books 1979, p. 115.
5. Miriam Wiley and Brendan Merriman, *Women and Health Care in Ireland*, Dublin: Oak Tree Press 1996, pp. 31–42.
6. M. Merrigan-Feenan, 'Contraception for Young Adults' Unpublished paper. Dublin: Rotunda Hospital 1995.
7. Evelyn Mahon, Catherine Conlon and Lucy Dillon, *Women and Crisis Pregnancy*, Dublin: Government Publications 1998, pp. 87, 514.
8. Report of Expert Advisory Group on *Relationships and Sexuality Education*, Dublin: Department of Education 1994, p. 18.
9. *The Irish Times*, 14 May 1997.

10. *The Irish Catholic,* 17 October 1996
11. Ger Casey, *Sex Education in the Primary School,* Dublin: Áras Mhuire 1996.
12. National Council for Curriculum and Assessment, *Relationships and Sexuality Education; Interim Curriculum and Guidelines for Primary/ Seconday Schools,* Dublin: Government Publications 1996.
13. Department of Education, *Relationships and Sexuality Education, Policy Guidelines,* Dublin: Government Publications 1997. Department of Education, *Going Forward Together: An Introduction to Relationships and Sexuality Education for Parents,* Dublin: Government Publications 1997.
14. Indeed it has been the failure of the Catholic Church to adapt to debate and discussion and to move from being an authority to be obeyed to being an authority to be respected, which has been at the heart of its decline in importance in civil life. See, T. Inglis 'Irish Civil Society: From Church to Media Domination'. Paper presented to the Sociological Association of Ireland, Annual Conference, 9 May 1998.
15. This is a central feature of Paulo Freire's theories. See, for example, Paulo Freire, *Pedagogy of the Oppressed,* New York, Hoder & Hoder 1970; Paulo Freire and Donald Macedo, *Literacy: Reading the Word and the World,* South Hadley [Mass.]: Bergin & Harvey 1987. For an analysis of how this translates into schooling, see Henry Giroux, *Theory and Resistance in Education,* London: Heinemann 1983.
16. Episcopal Commission for Research and Development, *A Survey of Religious Practice, Attitudes and Beliefs: Volume 3, Moral Values,* Dublin: Research and Development Commission 1975, pp. 39, 52.
17. Micheál MacGréil, *Prejudice in Ireland Revisited,* Survey and Research Unit, St Patrick's College, Maynooth 1996, p. 411. MacGréil also found a significant difference between those living in Dublin (27 per cent agreeing that pre-marital sex was always wrong) and those living outside Dublin (49 per cent agreeing).
18. Irish Marketing Surveys, *The Durex Report Ireland,* 1993, table 40/1. I am grateful to IMS and LRC London for access to this material.
19. The discrepancy between the number of sexual partners claimed by male and female respondents in social surveys has led some sociologists to claim that when it comes to sexual practices there is a tendency, particularly among men, to exaggerate if not deliberately lie about their sexual behaviour. See Anthony Giddens, 'Would I Lie To You Honey?' *The Observer,* 31 March 1996.
20. *The Durex Global Survey Report,* 28 October 1997; *Durex Irish Health Monitor Survey,* October 1997, table 40.1.
21. Lansdowne Market Research, *Survey of Sexual Attitudes and Lifestyles* 1992, table 49/1. I am grateful to the *Sunday World* and *Lansdowne Market Research* for access to these data and permission to refer to them.

22. *Durex Irish Health Monitor Survey*, October 1997, tables 37.1, 38.1, 40.1. A study of 167 Irish students in 1996 found that 67 per cent had some form of sexual experience before the age of 12 and, in comparison with American students, were more likely to have experimented with sex at an earlier age. This was a report of a study by Colman Duggan, senior social worker at the sexual assault unit at Our Lady's Hospital for Sick Children to a Child Abuse Conference. See *The Irish Times*, 22 August 1996.

23. Christine Magee and Frank Bisset, *Sex Education – Issues of Policy and Practice*, Irish YouthWork Centre: Dublin 1995, p. 25. See also Niamh Flanagan and Valerie Richardson, *Unmarried Mothers: A Social Profile*, Dublin: Department of Social Policy and Social Work, UCD 1992; Christine Magee, *Teenage Parents: Issues of Policy and Practice*, Dublin: Irish YouthWork Press 1994.

24. Quoted in Expert Advisory Group, *Relationships and Sexuality*, p. 7.

25. Lansdowne Market Research, *Survey of Sexual Attitudes and Lifestyles*, 21/1;6/1;4/1;1/1. *The Durex Report Ireland*, 1992; tables 4/1;5/1;11/1. *Durex Global Survey Report*, October, 1997. For a review of the findings of a number of other surveys on sex education in Ireland, see S. Walsh 'Relationships and Sexuality Education: The Context of New Curriculum in Primary Schools in Ireland' Unpublished Master's Thesis, University of Limerick, 1997, pp. 70–82.

26. Norbert Elias, *The Civilising Process, 1. The History of Manners*, Oxford: Basil Blackwell 1978, p. 169.

27. Elias, *The History of Manners*, p. 172.

28. Elias, *The History of Manners*, p. 180.

29. Foucault refers to this new implementation of sexuality as a 'deployment', that is an almost military organisation of bodies. See Michel Foucault, *The History of Sexuality Vol. 1*, New York: Vintage 1980, pp. 104–5. For a broader discussion of the relevance of Foucault's theories to an understanding of Irish sexuality, see T. Inglis, 'Foucault, Bourdieu and the Field of Irish Sexuality' *Irish Journal of Sociology*, 7 (1997), pp. 3–25.

30. Foucault, *History of Sexuality*, p. 100.

31. D. Carlson, 'Conflict and Change in the Discourse on Sexuality Education' *Educational Theory*, 41 (1991), pp. 343–59. Carlson presents these discourses following Foucault's methodology of producing an archaeology of knowledge. See Michel Foucault, *The Order of Things*, New York: Vintage 1973; *The Archaeology of Knowledge*, London: Tavistock 1972. There have been other, not dissimilar, classifications of sexual attitudes and practices. Pomeroy, for example, identified six different attitudes: (1) Traditional repressive asceticism which forbids any kind of sexual activity outside marriage; (2) Enlightened ascetism which emphasises the importance of debate and self-control; (3) Humanistic liberalism which rejects absolutes

and judges actions in terms of their consequences; (4) Humanistic Radicalism which argues that young people should have relatively complete sexual freedom; (5) Fun morality which emphasises for well-informed, well-adjusted people, sex is fun and good for you; (6) Sexual anarchy which seeks to remove all anti-sex taboos and ideas of sexual immorality and shame as long as no injury or violence is done to others. See Wardell Pomeroy, *Boys and Sex*, Harmondsworth: Penguin 1970, pp. 13–14.

32. Carlson, 'Conflict and Change', p. 351.

33. It is this notion of agency and how the discourses on sex and sex education are tied into other symbolic struggles and the struggle to accumulate different forms of capital which is present in the work of Bourdieu and missing from Foucault and Carlson. See Pierre Bourdieu, *The Logic of Practice*, Oxford: Polity 1990.

34. For further discussion on these concepts and how they relate to reading Irish culture and society, see Tom Inglis, *Moral Monopoly: The Rise and Fall of the Catholic Church in Modern Ireland*, 2nd ed. Dublin: UCD Press 1998; and Inglis, 'Foucault, Bourdieu and the Field of Irish Sexuality'.

Chapter 2. Being Taught to be Chaste and Modest

1. See C. S. Andrews, *Man of No Property*, Dublin: Mercier Press 1982, p. 53; Conrad Arensberg and Solon Kimball, *Family and Community in Ireland*, Cambridge [Mass.]: Harvard University Press 1968, p. 201.

2. An Irish Priest, *Quid Vobis Videtur? or A Talk to Priests on Educating Boys to Purity*, Dublin: Magnificat Press 1923, p. 10.

3. An Irish Priest, *Quid Vobis Videtur?*, p. 31. This approach was very similar to Fr O'Donnell's. 'During this early period no reference need, as a rule, be made to the sexual question properly understood. Such reference would be calculated to awaken a premature curiosity. But should children ask awkward questions, it is not advisable to put them off with a false or silly story, it is far better to answer them frankly but briefly, foreshadowing in some apt way the fuller knowledge, which time will render feasible, and reverently illustrating the mystery of motherhood from the Crib of Bethlehem.' Thomas O'Donnell, *The Priest of To-Day: His Ideals and Duties*, Dublin: Browne & Nolan 1919, p. 289.

4. See Steven Seidman, *Romantic Longings: Love in America 1830–1980*, London: Routledge 1991, pp. 13–38.

5. An Irish Priest, *Quid Vobis Videtur?*, p. 12.

6. An Irish Priest, *Quid Vobis Videtur?*, p. 78.

7. D. Carlson, 'Conflict and Change in the Discourse on Sexuality Education', *Educational Theory*, 41 (1991), p. 344.

8. Pope Pius XI, *Divini Illius Magistri. Christian Education of Youth*, London: Catholic Truth Society 1945, p. 33.

9. Norbert Elias, *The Civilising Process, 1. The History of Manners* Oxford: Basil Blackwell 1978, p. 180; Philippe Ariès, *Centuries of Childhood*, New York: Vintage 1962, p. 100.

10. Jerome O'Hea, *Sex and Innocence: A Handbook for Parents*, Cork: Mercier Press 1949, p. 25.

11. O'Hea, *Sex and Innocence*, p. 27.

12. An Irish Priest, *Quid Vobis Videtur?*, p. 46.

13. An Irish Priest, *Quid Vobis Videtur?*, p. 72.

14. An Irish Priest, *Quid Vobis Videtur?*, p. 48.

15. Pope Pius XII, *The Pope Speaks to Mothers: Allocution of Pope Pius XII 'Davanti a Questa' (1941)* London: Catholic Truth Society, 1958, p. 11.

16. An Irish Priest, *Quid Vobis Videtur?*, p. 72. The notion of self-constraint and the social constraint on people to be self-restrained is at the heart of Elias's theory of the civilising process. See, Norbert Elias, *State Formation and Civilization: Vol. 2 The Civilising Process*, Oxford: Basil Blackwell, 1982, pp. 229–50. Cas Wouters has argued that the range of differences in moral conduct has diminished in modern Europe, but that the demand and expectation of internalised self-restraint has increased. This occured in the family, between parents and children. As the balance tilts from external to internal restraint, children learn not only to restrain themselves, but to express their impulses and emotions. This was associated with a heightened awareness of self, and with a greater awareness of and sensitivity towards differences and choices. See C. Wouters, 'Formalization and Informalization: Changing Tension Balances in Civilizing Processes' *Theory, Culture and Society*, 3.2 (1986), pp. 1–18.

17. Quoted in S. MacGuaire, 'Keeping Company', *Irish Ecclesiastical Record*, Series 5, 45 (1935), p. 351.

18. J. A. McHugh and Charles Callan, *Moral Theology, ii*, No. 2629, 1930, quoted in MacGuaire, 'Keeping Company', p. 358.

19. Fr. Noldin, *Nouvelle Revue Théologique*, 1926, p. 736, quoted in MacGuaire, 'Keeping Company', p. 354.

20. For a description of how the limitation and control of marriage was central to social and economic production in the Béarn in France, see P. Bourdieu, 'Marriage Strategies as Strategies of Social Reproduction' in *Family and Society*, ed. E. Foster and P. Ranum, Baltimore: Johns Hopkins University Press 1976, p. 140.

21. P. Clancy, 'Continuity and Change in Irish Demographic Patterns' in *Ireland and Poland*, ed. P. Clancy, M. Kelly, J. Wiatr, and R. Zoltaniecki, Dublin: Department of Sociology, UCD 1992, p. 166.

22. Horace Plunkett, *Ireland in the New Century*, London, 1905, p. 285.
23. Michael O'Riordan, *Catholicity and Progress in Ireland*, London, Kegan Paul, Trench & Trubner 1905, p. 285.
24. W. Ryan, *The Pope's Green Island*, London: James Nisbet 1912, p. 79.
25. John Whyte, *Church and State in Modern Ireland 1923–1979*, Dublin: Gill & Macmillan 1980, p. 52.
26. R. Devane, 'The Dance-Hall' *Irish Ecclesiastical Record Series 5* 45 (1937), p. 170.
27. John Messenger, *Inis Beag*, New York: Holt Rinehart & Winston 1969, p. 107.
28. Messenger, *Inis Beag*, p. 109.
29. Hugh Brody, *Inniskillane*, London: Jill Norman & Hobhouse 1973, p. 180.
30. Brody, *Inniskillane*, p. 180.
31. Nancy Scheper-Hughes, *Saints, Scholars and Schizophrenics*, Berkeley: University of California Press 1981, p. 122.
32. R. Stivers, 'The Irish-American Experience with Alcohol' Paper Presented to Mid-West Sociological Association Meeting, Chicago, 1984, p. 11.
33. Arensberg and Kimball, *Family and Community in Ireland*, pp. 200–1.
34. Alexander Humphreys, *New Dubliners*, New York: Fordham University Press 1966, p. 26.
35. Humphreys, *New Dubliners*, p. 26.
36. Humphreys, *New Dubliners*, p. 232.
37. Roy Foster, *Modern Ireland 1600–1972*, London: Penguin 1988, p. 371.
38. John Murphy, in Rosita Sweetman, *On Our Backs: Sexual Attitudes in a Changing Ireland*, London: Pan Books 1979, p. 233.
39. Tom Inglis, *Moral Monopoly: The Rise and Fall of the Catholic Church in Modern Ireland*, 2nd ed. Dublin: UCD Press 1998, pp. 170–7.
40. P. Clancy, 'Irish Nuptuality and Fertility Patterns in Transition' in *Family Policy: European Perspectives*, ed. G. Kiely and V. Richardson, Dublin: Family Studies Centre, UCD 1991, p. 3.
41. C. Ó Gráda and N. Duffy, 'Fertility Control in Ireland and Scotland c. 1880–1930: Some New Findings'(Dublin: Department of Political Economy, UCD, Working Paper (1989), 89/14.
42. T. Fahey, 'Marital Fertility Control in Ireland: Some Evidence Examined', Dublin: Economic and Social Research Institute Seminar Paper 1983.
43. For descriptions of the 'bishop and the nightie' episode, see Mary Kenny, *Goodbye to Catholic Ireland*, London: Sinclair-Stevenson 1997, pp. 265–7. See also, M. Earls, 'The Late, Late Show: Controversy and Context' in *Television and Irish Society*, ed. M. McLoone and J. McMahon, Dublin: RTÉ–IFI 1984, pp. 107–22.; Gay Byrne, *To Whom it Concerns*, Dublin:

Gill & Macmillan 1972, p. 75; Joseph Dunn, *No Lions in the Hierarchy*, Dublin: Columba Press 1994, p. 39. Dunn points out that a major impetus for the whole episode was that the Bishop was not only fond of the programme but also of a drink and that left on his own on a Saturday night, he had nobody to assuage his moral indignation.

44. Daniel Lord, *M is for Marriage*, Dublin: Catholic Truth Society 1962. One of the peculiarities of traditional Catholic discourse about sex and sexual education is the ability of priests to give advice not just about sex but about married life. Baggot, for example, in the absence of any discussion about sexuality, would seem to suggest that sexual relations have little influence in creating a good marriage, Tony Baggot, *You and Your Marriage*, Cork: Mercier Press 1982.

45. John Gorey, *May I Keep Company?* Dublin: Cahill 1943, p. 21.

46. Daniel Lord, *What to do on a Date*, Dublin: Catholic Truth Society of Ireland 1962.

47. Francis Filias, *Telling Your Children: A Moderate View*, Dublin: Catholic Truth Society of Ireland 1964.

48. Mary Ryan and John Ryan, *Love and Sexuality: A Christian Approach*, Dublin: Gill & Son 1968.

49. G. Newmann, *Tell Them: What Your Child Needs to Know about Life, Love and Sex*, Dublin: Villa Books, 1979, pp. 75–6.

50. Irish Messenger, *Education in Sexuality: A Programme for Post-Primary Schools*, Dublin: Irish Messenger 1981.

51. Irish Messenger, *Education in Sexuality*, p. 18.

52. Irish Bishops Pastoral, *Love is for Life*, Dublin: Veritas 1985.

53. Pontifical Council for the Family, *The Truth and Meaning of Human Sexuality: Guidelines for Education within the Family*, Oxford: Family Publications 1995, pp. 5, 1, 19, 32.

54. Pontifical Council for the Family, *The Truth and Meaning of Human Sexuality*, p. 10

55. Pontifical Council for the Family, *The Truth and Meaning of Human Sexuality*, pp. 15, 40. Ger Casey has followed a similar line to the Council in his analysis and criticism of Irish sex education. He argues that sex education is best kept within the family. The problem with secular sex education, he claims, is that the language is indelicate. It desacralises and demystifies sex and, ultimately, creates an immodest approach to sexuality. Casey emphasises that a personalised language about sex cannot be developed in school. Most important of all he argues, following a theme developed by some psychologists, that there is a latency period between the ages of four and twelve when children have no interest in sex, almost to the point of hostility. To give them unnecessary information about

sex during this period would, he argues, destroy their innocence. He concludes emphatically that the Church teaches that: 'All detailed information on intimate matters that is deemed to be necessary is to be imparted to the child in an individualized personal dialogue, by the child's same-sex parent or an appropriate substitute, privately, and it is to correspond only to the individual needs of the moment.' Ger Casey, *Sex Education in the Primary School*, Dublin: Áras Mhuire 1996, p. 49.

56. Pontifical Council for the Family, *The Truth and Meaning of Human Sexuality*, pp. 46–50.
57. Pontifical Council for the Family, *The Truth and Meaning of Human Sexuality*, p. 56.
58. Pontifical Council for the Family, *The Truth and Meaning of Human Sexuality*, pp. 60–7.
59. Pontifical Council for the Family, *The Truth and Meaning of Human Sexuality*, pp. 78–9.
60. Pontifical Council for the Family, *The Truth and Meaning of Human Sexuality*, pp. 79–80.
61. St Brigid's National School, Greystones, Co. Wicklow, *Human Development Programme*.
62. St Brigid's National School, *Human Development Programe*, pp. 20–2.
63. St Brigid's National School, *Human Development Programe*, p. 29.
64. S. Walsh 'Relationships and Sexuality Education: The Context of New Curriculum in Primary Schools in Ireland' Unpublished Master's Thesis, University of Limerick, 1997, pp. 39–56. See also, S. Walsh, '"Who Invented Sex?": Helping Children Understand', *Doctrine and Life*, 43 (1993), pp. 593–7.
65. Mickey Quinn and Terri Quinn, *How to Talk to Your Child About Sex*, Dublin: Veritas 1981, p. 31.
66. Angela MacNamara, *Come Closer: Considerations for a Christian Relationships and Sexuality Programme* Greystones [Co. Wicklow]: Privately Circulated Document 1995.
67. Marino Institute of Education, *Relationships and Sexuality Education: Resources Guide*, Dublin: Marino Institute of Education 1997.
68. Marino Institute of Education, *Relationships and Sexuality Education: Resources Guide*, p. 34.
69. A. Heron and D. McGinley, *So You Want to Know? (About Sex and Growing Up)*, Dublin: Poolbeg 1991, p. 22 (emphasis in original).
70. K. Kearon, 'Moral and ethical issues in RSE: A Church of Ireland perspective' in *Relationships and Sexuality Education in the Primary School*, Papers presented at a Symposium of the Past Students' Association of the Church of Ireland College of Education, Dublin 1995, pp. 15–22.

71. Kearon, 'Moral and ethical issues in RSE', p. 19.
72. Kearon, 'Moral and ethical issues in RSE', p. 20.
73. Kearon, 'Moral and ethical issues in RSE', p. 21.

Chapter 3. Learning to be Independent and Responsible

1. D. Carlson, 'Conflict and Change in the Discourse on Sexuality Education' *Educational Theory*, 41(1991), p. 345.
2. For a more detailed analysis of the Catholic Church's control of Irish education see Sheelagh Drudy and Kathleen Lynch, *Schools and Society in Ireland*, Dublin: Gill & Macmillan 1993, pp. 73–82; and Tom Inglis, *Moral Monopoly: The Rise and Fall of the Catholic Church in Modern Ireland*, 2nd ed., Dublin: UCD Press 1998, pp. 57–61.
3. For a more detailed analysis of these changes, see Inglis, *Moral Monopoly*, pp. 203–42.
4. *The Irish Times*, 24 January 1995.
5. Maria Lawlor and Deidre MacIntyre, *Stay Safe Programme: User's Handbook*, Dublin: Health Promotion Unit 1991, 22. These figures are based on children aged 16 or less. In their detailed examination of Eastern Health Board records, McKeown and Gilligan found 512 reported cases of Child Sex Abuse on children aged 18 years or less. Child abusers tended to be male and to come from the child's own family or to have been a babysitter. K. McKeown and R. Gilligan, 'Child Sexual Abuse in the Eastern Health Board Region of Ireland in 1988: An Analyis of 512 confirmed cases' *Economic and Social Review*, 22 (1991), pp. 101–34.
6. Lawlor and MacIntyre, *User's Handbook*, p. 30.
7. Maria Lawlor and Deidre MacIntyre, *Stay Safe Programme: Senior Lessons*, Dublin: Health Promotion Unit 1991, p. 12.
8. Brian Gogan, *A Second Opinion: Stay Safe Child Abuse Prevention Programme*, Dublin: Education Bureau 1993, p. 15.
9. Quoted in Gogan, *A Second Opinion*, p. 12.
10. Gogan, *A Second Opinion*, p. 14.
11. See R. Cullen and P. Osborne, Papers delivered to Conference on Support Network for Professionals Working in Child Protection, 5 November 1993.
12. *The Irish Times*, 12 January 1994. In his column Fintan O'Toole cites an interview with Dr Ralph Underwager (who is quoted on the cover of Gogan's booklet and referenced for further reading and resources) in which he argues that paedophilia can be defended as the will of God and that opposition to male bonding and paedophile sex often stems from women's jealousy of male intimacy.

13. *The Irish Times*, 18 February 1994.
14. S. Gilmartin, 'Barriers to Acceptance: The Stay Safe Programme', Unpublished Master's Thesis in Education, University of Ulster 1995, pp. 51, 64–6. See also. R. Cullen, 'Child Abuse Prevention Programme: Windows on Irish Attitudes and Values', Unpublished Master's Thesis in Arts, National University of Ireland, Maynooth 1994.
15. *The Irish Times*, 11 March 1998.
16. See Gilmartin, 'Barriers to Acceptance', p. 3.
17. Ger Casey, for example, indicated his frustration with the lack of support from the Archbishop of Dublin in opposing the programme. In a letter to the *Donegal Democrat*, 30 September 1993, he claimed that as regards the Church's attitude to the Stay Safe Programme, the situation in the Dublin Archdiocese was typical. He said that the Education Secretary told him that the programme had neither been approved nor disapproved for use in the Archdiocese and that it would only be permitted to enter with the consent of the Board of Management and parents.
18. Report of Expert Advisory Group on *Relationships and Sexuality Education*, Dublin: Department of Education 1994, p. 18.
19. *Relationships and Sexuality Education: Policy Guidelines*, Dublin: Department of Education 1997, p. 4.
20. Expert Advisory Group, *Relationships and Sexuality*, p. 7.
21. *Relationships and Sexuality Education: Interim Curriculum and Guidelines for Primary Schools*, Dublin: NCCA 1997, p. 53.
22. *Relationships and Sexuality Education: Interim Curriculum and Guidelines for Primary Schools*, p. 64.
23. *Relationships and Sexuality Education: Interim Curriculum and Guidelines for Primary Schools*, p. 53. Of course the remarkable absence here is the teachers and the RSE programme itself. Nevertheless, this involves a sophisticated level of critical self-reflection which, as we shall see in Chapter 6, is often associated with radical forms of adult learning.
24. *Relationships and Sexuality Education: Interim Curriculum and Guidelines for Post-Primary Schools*, p. 25.
25. *Relationships and Sexuality Education: Interim Curriculum and Guidelines for Post-Primary Schools*, Dublin: NCCA 1996, p. 9.
26. *Relationships and Sexuality Education: Interim Curriculum and Guidelines for Post-Primary Schools*, p. 13.
27. *Relationships and Sexuality Education: Interim Curriculum and Guidelines for Post-Primary Schools*, p. 34.
28. *Relationships and sexuality eduction: Interim Curriculum and Guidelines for Primary Schools*, Dublin: National Council for Curriculum and Assessment 1996, p. 7.

29. *Relationships and Sexuality Education: Interim Curriculum and Guidelines for Post-Primary Schools*, p. 18.

30. Marino Insititute of Education, *Relationships and Sexuality Education: Resources Guide*, Dublin: Marino Institute of Education 1997, p. 61. The only reservation which the Institute had about the BBC Junior Programme was that some teachers might find the nude scene in one part of the programme inappropriate, 'although it is brief and in context'.

31. BBC Educational Publishing, *Sex Education Booklet* (Junior) 1990, p. 12.

Chapter 4. Being Encouraged to be Sexual

1. D. Carlson, 'Conflict and Change in the Discourse on Sexuality Education' *Educational Theory*, 41 (1991), p. 351.

2. Carlson, 'Conflict and Change', p. 353.

3. Alex Comfort ed., *The Joy of Sex*, New York: Simon & Schuster 1970, p. 15.

4. Comfort, *The Joy of Sex*, p. 153.

5. Steven Seidman, *Romantic Longings: Love in America 1830–1980*, London: Routledge 1991, p. 18.

6. Seidman, *Romantic Longings*, p. 18.

7. Comfort, *The Joy of Sex*, p. 168.

8. See, for example, Irwin Deutcher, *What We Say/What We Do*, Glenview [Illinois]: Scott, Foresman 1973.

9. Irish Marketing Surveys, The *Durex Report Ireland*, 1993. See also, Robert Michael, John Gagnon, Edward Laumann, and Gina Kolata, *Sex in America*, London: Little, Brown 1994; Anne Johnson, Kaye Wellings and Julia Field, *Sexual Attitudes and Lifestyles*, Oxford: Blackwell Scientific 1994; Andrew Greeley, *Faithful Attraction*, New York: Tor 1991.

10. *Durex Global Sex Survey*, 1997, p. 19.

11. John Gorey, *May I Keep Company*, Dublin: Cahill & Co. 1943, 21. There were six printings of this pamphlet; over 350,000 copies were sold.

12. D. Lowry and D. Towles, 'Soap Opera Portrayals of Sex, Contraception, and Sexually Transmitted Diseases', *Journal of Communication* 39 (1989), p. 78. It should be noted, however, that American daytime soap operas belong to the romantic melodrama genre and are quite different in style and content to the British and Irish realistic genre. For a description of this difference, see Christine Geraghty, *Women and Soap Opera*, Oxford: Polity Press 1991, pp. 25–59.

13. Lowry and Towles, 'Soap Opera Portrayals', p. 81.

14. See T. Inglis, 'Revealing Issues on Irish Sex' Paper Presented to Sociological Association of Ireland Annual Conference, Derry, 14 May, 1994, pp. 13–15.

15. This was at the heart of Foucault's argument. See, M. Foucault, *The Use of Pleasure: The History of Sexuality Vol. 2*, Harmondsworth, Penguin 1987, 138. See also, T. Inglis 'Foucault, Bourdieu and the Field of Irish Sexuality', *Irish Journal of Sociology* (1997), p. 14.

16. Pat Pinsent reports that a survey carried out by the National Centre for Research in Children's Literature, found that 77 per cent of girls aged between 14 and 16 years said that they bought teenage magazines. Bridget Knight estimates that sales of girls' teenage magazines in Britain in 1997 were £62m. See P. Pinsent, '"Lessons in Love": Girls Magazines in the 1990s, in *Teenage Girls and their Magazines*, ed. K. Reynolds, London: Roehampton Institute 1998, pp. 6–25: B. Knight, 'Teenage Magazines: Education or Titillation' in *Teenage Girls and their Magazines*, ed. K. Reynolds, London: Roehampton Institute 1998, pp. 26–32.

17. For an account of this transition, see T. Inglis, 'From Sexual Repression to Liberation' in *Encounters with Modern Ireland*, ed. M. Peillon and E. Slater, Dublin: Institute of Public Administration 1998, pp. 99–104. For an analysis of the concept of symbolic domination, see Pierre Bourdieu, *Language and Symbolic Power*, Cambridge: Polity Press 1991.

18. See Philip Meredith, *Sex Education: Political Issues in Britain and Europe*, London: Routledge 1989, pp. 102–3.

19. Meredith, *Sex Education*, p. 130.

20. D. Braeken, 'What has fun got to do with it?' Paper presented at the HIV/AIDS Seminar, Cork, 1 December 1997, pp. 4–5. This was not a random sample survey. The young people who participated in the survey were contacted through Family Planning Associations and other Non-Governmental Organisations and were interviewed through one-to-one interviews, focus-group discussions and written questionnaires.

21. Braeken, 'What has fun got to do with it?', p. 10.

22. Braeken, 'What has fun got to do with it?', p. 9.

23. C. Magee and F. Bissett, 'Sex Education – Issues of Policy and Practice', Dublin: Irish YouthWork Centre and the National Youth Federation 1995, p. 47.

24. Magee and Bissett, 'Sex Education', p. 44.

25. Again, this follows Foucault. See Michel Foucault, *Power/Knowledge: Selected Interviews and Other Writings 1972–1977*, ed. C. Gordon, New York: Pantheon Books 1980, pp. 183–93.

26. S. Lees, 'Learning to Love: Sexual Reputation, Morality and the Social Control of Girls' in *Growing Up Good: Policing the Behaviour of Girls in Europe*, ed. Maureen Cain, London: Sage 1989, p. 33.

27. See J. Mezirow, 'A Critical Theory of Adult Learning and Education' *Adult Education*, 32 (1981), p. 6. See also, T. Inglis 'Empowerment and Emancipation' *Adult Education Quarterly*, 48 (1997), pp. 3–17.

28. Peter Jarvis, *The Sociology of Adult and Continuing Education*, London: Croom Helm 1985, p. 51.

Chapter 5. Radical Sexuality

1. Quoted in Éibhear Walshe, *Sex, Nation and Dissent*, Cork: Cork University Press 1997, p. 4. It is not a question so much of whether Pearse was homosexual, or had homosexual tendencies, but rather that he produced a way of thinking about male relationships which was a radical departure or discontinuity from the way of thinking of his time. In other words, the radicalness of a viewpoint depends on the time and context in which it appears. If a political leader in contemporary Ireland wrote something similar today, it would not be radical.

2. Sigmund Freud, 'Civilization and its Discontents' in *Civilization, Society and Religion, The Penguin Freud Library* Vol. l. Harmondsworth: Penguin, 1991.

3. This corresponds, in some respects, to the traditional discourse of sexuality espoused by the Catholic Church which was described in Chapter 2, reinforcing the importance of time and place in constituting the radicalness of sexual attitudes. Nevertheless, there are, as we shall see, major differences between the Catholic Church and the 1960s popular cultural movement in the understanding of sexuality.

4. Freud, 'Civilisation and Its Discontents' p. 290.

5. Eric Fromm, *The Art of Loving*, New York: Harper & Row 1956, p. 77.

6. No longer used as a full-time instrument of labor, the body would be resexualised. The regression involved in this spread of the lidido would first manifest itself in a reactivation of all erotogenic zones and, consequently, in a resurgence of pregenital polymorphous sexuality and in a decline of genital supremacy. The body in its entirety would become an object of cathexis, a thing to be enjoyed – an instrument of pleasure. This change in the value and scope of libidinal relations would lead to a disintegration of the institutions in which the private interpersonal relations have been organized, particularly the monogamic and patriarchal family. Herbert Marcuse, *Eros and Civilization*, London: Ark 1987, p. 201.

7. Wilhelm Reich, *The Invasion of Compulsory Sex-Morality*, New York: Farrar, Straus & Giroux 1971, pp. 146–7.

8. Quoted in Carlson, 'Conflict and Change in the Discourse on Sexuality Education', *Educational Theory*, 41 (1991), p. 355.

9. Wilhelm Reich, *Character Analysis*, London: Vision 1952, p. 362.
10. I chose this example of a radical argument because it reached a much wider audience. While the pornographic industry grows by the day, the moral debate about pornography rages on. Much of this has been confined to what may broadly be defined as women's and men's studies. Most of what has been written within feminism is strongly against pornography. See Andrea Dworkin, *Pornography*, London: Women's Press 1981; C. Itzin, 'Pornography and the Social Construction of Sexual Inequality' in *Pornography*, ed. C. Itzin, Oxford: Oxford University Press 1992, pp. 57–75. Women who defend pornography tend to do so on the basis of defending individual liberty and opposing censorship. See Nadine Strossen, *Defending Pornography*, London: Abacus 1995; Gillian Rodgerson and Elizabeth Wilson, *Pornography and Feminism: The Case Against Censorship*, London: Lawrence & Wishart 1991. For a masculine viewpoint, see H. Brod, 'Pornography and the alienation of male sexuality' in *Men, Masculinities and Social Theory*, ed. J. Hearn and D. Morgan, London: Unwin Hyman 1990, pp. 124–39; A. Moye, 'Pornography' in *The Sexuality of Men*, ed. A. Metcalf and M. Humphries, London: Pluto Press 1985, pp. 44–69.
11. Sandra Lee Bartky, *Femininity and Domination*, London: Routledge 1990, pp. 71–6.
12. Bartky, *Femininity and Domination*, p. 47. See also, S. Kappeler, *The Pornography of Representation*, Oxford: Polity Press 1986.
13. A. Rich 'Compulsory Heterosexuality and Lesbian Existence' *Signs*, 5 (1980), p. 648.
14. J. VanEvery, 'Sinking into his Arms . . . Arms in his Sink: Heterosexuality and Feminism Revisited' in *Sexualising the Social: Power and the Organisation of Sexuality*, ed. L. Adkins and V. Merchant, London: Macmillan 1996, p. 49.
15. C. MacKinnon, 'Feminism, Marxism, Method and the State: An Agenda for Theory' *Signs*, 7 (1982), pp. 515–44. For a description and analysis of socophilia, the pleasure of the gaze in film, see Liesbet Van Zoonen, *Feminist Media Studies*, London: Sage 1994, pp. 43–66.
16. Bartky, *Femininity and Domination*, p. 69.
17. J. Holland, C. Ramazanoglu, S. Sharpe and R. Thomson, 'Power and Desire: The Embodiment of Female Sexuality' *Feminist Review* 46 (1994), p. 31.
18. See S. Jackson, 'Heterosexuality as a Problem of Feminist Theory' in *Sexualizing the Social: Power and the Organisation of Sexuality*, ed. L. Adams and V. Merchant, London: Macmillan 1996, pp. 15–34.
19. See Foucault, *The History of Sexuality Vol. 1*, New York: Vintage, 1980, pp. 156–7; Nancy Fraser, *Unruly Practices: Power, Discourse and Gender in Contemporary Social Theory*, Oxford: Polity Press 1989, p. 63.

20. For a history of this movement, see Kieran Rose, *Diverse Communities: The Evolution of Gay and Lesbian Politics in Ireland*, Cork: Cork University Press 1994; See also, Dublin Lesbian and Gay Men's Collectivities, *Out for Ourselves: The Lives of Irish Lesbians and Gay Men*, Dublin: Women's Community Press 1986. For a history of gay and lesbian literature, see Éibhear Walshe's introduction to *Sex, Nation and Dissent*, pp. 1–15.

21. Steven Seidman, *Romantic Longings: Love in America 1830–1980*, London: Routledge 1991, p. 18.

22. C. Wouters, 'Changes in the "lust balance" of sex and love since the sexual revolution: the example of the Netherlands' in *Emotions in Social Life: Critical Themes and Contemporary Issues*, ed. G. Bendelow and S. Williams, London: Routledge 1998, p. 230.

23. Wouters, 'Changes in the "lust balance"', p. 235.

24. Wouters, 'Changes in the "lust balance"', p. 244.

25. Luce Irigaray, *This Sex Which Is Not One*, Ithaca: Cornell University Press 1985, p. 28.

26. See, David Halperin, *Saint=Foucault: Towards a Gay Hagiography*, Oxford: Oxford University Press 1995, p. 194.

27. Jean Baudrillard, *Revenge of the Crystal*, ed. and trans. Paul Foss and Julian Pennis, London: Pluto Press 1990, p. 135.

Chapter 6. Shaping Young People's Sexuality

1. This raises a series of complex issues revolving around the debate on the relation between structure and agency which is at the heart of modern sociology. For a good overview of the issues, see Anthony Giddens, 'Agency, institution and time-space analysis' in *Advances in Social Theory and Methodology* ed. K. Knorr-Cetina and A. Cicourel, London: Routledge & Kegan Paul 1981, pp. 161–74; A. Swidler, 'Culture in Action: Symbols and Strategies' *American Sociological Review*, 51 (1986), pp. 273–86; W. Sewell, 'A Theory of Structure: Duality, Agency and Transformation' *American Journal of Sociology*, 96 (1992), pp. 1–29. For an introduction to the approach of Pierre Bourdieu, see P. Bourdieu, 'Men and Machines' in Knorr-Cetina and Cicourel, *Advances in Social Theory and Methodology*, pp. 304–17, and Pierre Bourdieu and Löic Wacquant, *An Invitation to Reflexive Sociology*, Cambridge: Polity Press, 1992.

2. This concept of *habitus* is derived from Bourdieu. He defines *habitus* as 'a system of lasting transposable dispositions which, integrating past experiences, functions at every moment as a *matrix of perceptions, appreci-ations, and actions*, and makes possible the achievement of infinitely diversified tasks, thanks to analogical tranfers of schemes permitting the

solution of similarly shaped problems.' Pierre Bourdieu, *Outline of a Theory of Practice*, Cambridge: Cambridge University Press, 1977, 83 (emphasis in original). See also, *The Logic of Practice*, Cambridge: Polity Press, 1990, pp. 52–65.

3. For a description of how the engagement in social life is like playing a game, see Bourdieu, *The Logic of Practice*, pp. 66–8; Bourdieu and Wacquant, *An Invitation to Reflexive Sociology*, pp. 98–100.

4. For a discussion of the different types of captial which people struggle to accumulate in social life, see P. Bourdieu, 'Forms of Capital' in *Handbook of Theory and Research for the Sociology of Education*, ed. J. Richardson, Westport C.T.: Greenwood Press, 1986, pp. 252–3. For a desciption of how the different forms of capital operate in Irish social life in relation to religious capital, see Tom Inglis, *Moral Monopoly: The Rise and Fall of the Catholic Church in Modern Ireland*, 2nd ed., Dublin: UCD Press, 1998, pp. 65–76.

5. The use of the term 'field' here follows Bourdieu. See Pierre Bourdieu, 'Some Properties of Fields' in *Sociology in Question*, London: Sage 1993, pp. 72–7; 'The Intellectual Field: a world apart' in *In Other Words*, Cambridge: Polity Press 1990, pp. 140–9. Pierre Bourdieu, *The Logic of Practice*, Cambridge: Polity Press 1990, pp. 66–8. A social field, such as the sexual field, consists of a set of objective, historical relations between individuals, organisations and institutions which are based on certain forms of power, or capital. Bourdieu often uses the analogy of a game to describe a social field. Consequently, the sexual field centres around people playing or struggling to be attractive and desireable. There is a certain logic to the sexual field. It has its definite patterns and regularities which mark it out as different from other social fields. Even though attitudes and practices change within different cultures, it is almost universally recognised that being sexy means being attractive and desirable. This is not to deny that playing at or struggling to be sexy in Ireland requires a knowledge of local logics and regularities. Success in the sexual field – that is, being able to control if not dominate the game – depends on the accumulated capital which players bring. Obviously the media now dominate the sexual field, as the Catholic Church once did. Not only do the media determine what is attractive and desireable, they influence the beliefs, values, attitudes and practices necessary for others to acquire sexual capital and be seen as a desirable and attractive person. For a more detailed discussion of a 'game' being an analogy for what takes place in a social field, see Pierre Bourdieu and Löic Wacquant, *An Invitation to Reflexive Sociology*, Cambridge: Polity Press 1992, pp. 94–115.

6. For a description and analysis of censorship in Ireland, see Michael Adams, *Censorship, the Irish Experience*, Alabama: Alabama University Press 1968; Kieran Woodman, *Media Control in Ireland 1923–1983*, Carbondale: University of Southern Illinois Press 1985; Ciarán Carty, *Confessions of a Sewer Rat*, Dublin: New Island Books 1995; J. A. Murphy, 'Censorship and the Moral Community' in *Communications and Community in Ireland*, ed. B. Farrell, Cork: Mercier Press 1984, pp. 51–63.

7. Ger Casey, *Sex Education in the Primary School*, Dublin: Áras Mhuire 1996, p. 10.

8. Casey, *Sex Education in the Primary School*, p. 25

9. Casey, *Sex Education in the Primary School*, p. 23

10. Casey, *Sex Education in the Primary School*, p. 63.

11. Casey, *Sex Education in the Primary School*, p. 65.

12. *Relationships and Sexuality Education in Catholic Schools: A Resource for Teachers and Boards of Management*, Dublin: Veritas 1997, p. 5.

13. Sean McEntee, Kathleen Glennon and William Murphy, *Workers for the Kingdom: Children of God Series, 5th Class Primary (teachers)*, London: Geoffrey Chapman 1987, p. 229.

14. Sean McEntee, Kathleen Glennon, William Murphy, *Walk in My Presence, Children of God Series, 6th Class Primary (Pupils)*, London: Geoffrey Chapman 1987, p. 42.

15. This is an enormous and complex area within the sociology of communications. See, for example, Jürgen Habermas, *The Structural Transformation of the Public Sphere*, Oxford: Polity Press 1989; J. Habermas, 'Further Reflections on the Public Sphere' in *Habermas and the Public Sphere*, ed. C. Calhoun, Cambridge [Mass.]: MIT Press 1992, pp. 421–61; J. Curran, 'Rethinking the Media as a Public Sphere' in *Communication and Citizenship*, ed. P. Dahlgren and C. Sparks, London: Routledge 1991, pp. 28–57; N. Garnham, 'The Media and the Public Sphere' in *Communicating Politics*, ed. P. Golding, G. Murdock and P. Schlesinger, Leicester: Leicester University Press 1986, pp. 37–53.

16. *The Irish Times*, 30 March 1998.

17. Carmel Wynne has argued along similar lines, see *The Irish Times*, 5 May 1998.

18. The influence of the media on children and young people has been the subject of intensive study and debate. Television has been the major focus of attention. For an overview of the debate about television, see Barrie Gunter and Jill McAleer, *Children and Television*, 2nd ed. London: Routledge 1990. See also, Brian Clifford, Barrie Gunter and Jill McAleer, *Television and Children*, Hillsdale [N.J.]: Lawrence Erlbaum 1995; Gordon Berry and Joy A. Asamen, *Children and Television*, London: Sage 1993.

In relation to the media and the construction of self-image and self-identity, see Karl Eric Rosengren and Sven Windahl, *Media Matter: TV Use in Childhood and Adolescence*. Norwood [N.J.]: Ablex 1989, p. 234; Thomas Johansson, 'Late Modernity: Consumer Culture and Lifestyles', in *Media Effects and Beyond*, ed. K. Rosengren, London: Routledge 1994, pp. 265–94; Robert Fiske, *Television Culture*. London: Routledge 1987, pp. 48–83. For a description of children interpreting sex scenes, see David Buckingham, *Children Talking Television*, London: Falmer, 1993, p. 179. Less attention has been given to the influence of teenage magazines. Angela McRobbie has carried out some classic studies. For an overview, see Angela McRobbie (ed.), *Feminism and Youth Culture: from 'Jackie' to 'Just Seventeen'*. London: Macmillan, 1991. For a recent description and analysis of the sexual content of magazines, see Pat Pinsent and Bridget Knight, *Teenage Girls and their Magazines*, London: National Centre for Research in Children's Literature, 1998.

19. There is evidence which suggests that nonvirginity in youths is associated with non-authoritative parenting, permissiveness and lack of parent support. A link has also been found between a mother's own sexual experience as a teenager and that of her adolescent daughter. Finally, girls from single-parent families have been shown to be more likely to become sexually active at an earlier age than those who grow up in two parent families. Moore and Rosenthal, *Sexuality in Adolescence*, p. 65.

20. Freud was the first to analyse the complex relation between adult sexual behaviour, personality formation, and identification and bonding with parents. The theory of adolescent sexuality was developed by his daughter Anna, Peter Blos and Erik Erikson. See, A. Freud, 'Adolescence as a developmental disturbance' in *Adolescence*, in G. Caplan and S. Lebovici, New York: Basic Books 1969; Peter Blos, *On Adolescence*, New York: Free Press 1962; Erik Erikson, *Childhood and Society*, 2nd ed., New York: Norton 1963. For a good overview of this complex area and a summary of research findings on in the influence of parents, see Susan Moore and Doreen Rosenthal *Sexuality in Adolescence*, London: Routledge, 1993, pp. 22–40, 62–6.

21. The influence of friends, teenage groups and youth subculture has been long recognised as an important factor in young people's sexual knowledge, attitudes and practices. This was a central finding of Schofield's classic study in the 1960s. See Michael Schofield, *The Sexual Behaviour of Young People*, Harmondsworth: Penguin 1968, pp. 132–9. See also, Christine Farrell, *My Mother Said. . . : The Way Young People Learned about Sex and Birth Control*, London: Routledge & Kegan Paul 1978. Similar conclusions were reached in America. See C. E. Lewis and M. A. Lewis,

'Peer Pressure and the risk-taking behaviours in children' *American Journal of Public Health* 74 (1984), pp. 580–4. For ethnographic accounts of the influence of peer groups, see Máirtín Mac an Ghall, *The Making of Men*, Milton Keynes: Open University Press 1994, pp. 51–88; S. Lees, 'The Policing of Girls in Everyday Life' in *Growing Up Good*, ed. M. Cain, London: Sage 1989, pp. 19–37. For an overview of the research findings in relation to peer groups and youth subculture, see Susan Moore and Doreen Rosenthal *Sexuality in Adolescence*, London: Routledge 1993, pp. 62–71.

22. Moore and Rosenthal, *Sexuality in Adolescence*, p. 67

23. For a discussion of the importance of biological factors, see David Barash, *The Whisperings Within: Evolution and the Origin of Human Nature*, Harmondsworth: Penguin 1981, pp. 46–90; Richard Posner, *Sex and Reason*, Cambridge [Mass.]: Harvard University Press 1992, pp. 85–110; Sarah Hardy, *The Woman that Never Evolved*, Cambridge [Mass.]: Harvard University Press 1981, pp. 16–168. For an overview of gay and lesbian adolescence, see M. Goggin, 'Gay and Lesbian Adolescence' in Moore and Rosenthal, *Sexuality in Adolescence*, pp. 102–23.

Chapter 7. Views of Parents, Teachers and Pupils

1. For a detailed discussion of the place of focus group interviews in social research, see D. L. Morgan, *Focus Groups as Qualitative Research*, London: Sage 1988. For a useful guide and summary, see A. Gibbs, *Social Research Update 19*, Guildford: Department of Sociology, University of Surrey, 1997.

Chapter 8. Putting Contradictions into Context

1. This concept of civil society follows that developed by Cohen and Arato. See Jean Cohen and Andrew Arato, *Civil Society and Political Theory*, Cambridge [Mass.]: MIT Press 1992; A. Arato and J. Cohen, 'Civil Society and Social Theory' *Thesis Eleven* 21 (1988), pp. 40–64

2. For a discussion as to how the media have colonised debate and discussion in the public sphere see N. Garnham, 'The Media and the Public Sphere' in *Habermas and the Public Sphere* ed. C. Calhoun, Cambridge [Mass.]: MIT Press 1992, pp. 359–76 ; J. Curran, 'Rethinking the media as a Public Sphere' in *Communication and Citizenship*, ed. P. Dahlgren and C. Sparks, London: Routledge, 1991, pp. 28–57. Peter Dahlgren, *Television and the Public Sphere*, London: Sage 1995. For an analysis of this issue in relation to Ireland, see S. O'Sullivan, '"The Ryan Line is Now Open . . ."':

Talk Radio and the Public Sphere' in *Media Audiences in Ireland*, ed. M. Kelly and B. O'Connor, Dublin: UCD Press 1997, pp. 167–90; M. Kelly, 'Participatory Media and Audience Response' in *Media Audiences in Ireland*, ed. M. Kelly and B. O'Connor, pp. 17–40; S. Ryan, 'Divorce Referendum Coverage, Programme Formats and Television Audiences' in *Media Audiences in Ireland*, ed. Kelly and O'Connor, pp. 191–211.

3. A. Swidler, 'Culture in Action: Symbols and Strategies' *American Sociological Review* 51 (1986), pp. 273–86.

4. Margaret Archer, *Culture and Agency*, Cambridge: Cambridge University Press 1988, p. 148. Archer takes the classic example of the contradiction between Christian beliefs and scientific thought as an example. With the advancement of scientific knowledge it has been increasingly difficult for people to hold on to creationist beliefs. This has been unsettling not just in terms of teaching religion in school, but in terms of people's knowledge and understanding of themselves. Another example – taken from Durkheim's *The Evolution of Educational Thought* – is the persistence of pagan beliefs and practices within Christianity, even though they are mutually contradictory moral systems.

5. *The Irish Times*, 18 February 1994.

6. MRBI poll for *The Irish Times*, 16 December 1996.

7. For a more detailed analysis of these changes, see Tom Inglis, *Moral Monopoly: The Rise and Fall of the Catholic Church in Modern Ireland*, 2nd ed. Dublin: UCD Press 1998, pp. 208–11.

8. See Inglis, *Moral Monopoly*, pp. 243–59.

9. See Max Weber, 'Religious Rejections of the World and Their Directions', in *From Max Weber*, ed. H. Gerth and C. Wright Mills, New York: Oxford University Press 1946, pp. 323–59.

10. As Weber puts it, while the fulfilment of sexual-erotic interests has always throughout history ranked equal to seeking economic and political power, it has always stood in stark contrast to fulfilling salvationary religious interests. Weber, 'Religious Rejections', p. 345.

11. For a review and analysis of the secularisation literature and how it applies to Catholic Ireland, see Inglis, *Moral Monopoly*, pp. 202–8.

12. For a detailed description of the background and activities of Fr Brendan Smyth, see Chris Moore, *Betrayal of Trust: The Fr Brendan Smyth Affair and the Catholic Church*, Dublin: Marino Books 1995.

13. See Max Weber, *The Protestant Ethic and the Spirit of Capitalism*. (New York: Charles Scribner, 1958). For a detailed discussion of Weber's theories of rationalisation and modernity see S. Whimster and S. Lash (eds) *Max Weber's Rationality and Modernity*, London: Allen & Unwin 1987.

14. Wolfgang Schluchter, *The Rise of Western Rationalism*, Berkeley: University of California Press, 1981, p. 45.

15. See J. Habermas, 'Three Normative Models of Democracy' *Constellations*, 1 (1994), pp. 1–10.

16. Pope John Paul II, *Veritatis Splendor*, London: Catholic Truth Society 1993, pp. 97–8.

17. Pope John Paul II, *Veritatis Splendor*, p. 120.

18. Pope John Paul II, *Veritatis Splendor*, p. 122.

19. Patrick Hannon, *Church, State, Morality and Law*, Dublin: Gill & Macmillan 1992, p. 76.

20. Transcripts of advertisements for AIDS Prevention Campaign, May 1993, Health Promotion Unit.

21. See R. Thomson, 'Moral Rhetoric and Public Health Pragmaticism: The Recent Politics of Sex Education' *Feminist Review*, 48 (1994), p. 45.

22. A similar situation has occured in Britain, see S. Lees, 'Talking about Sex in Education' *Gender and Education*, 6, 3 (1994), p. 281.

23. Michel Foucault, *The Order of Things*, New York: Vintage 1973.

24. Michel Foucault, *The Use of Pleasure: The History of Sexuality Vol. 2*, Harmondsworth: Penguin 1987, p. 6.

25. C. Wouters, 'Changes in the Lust Balance: Love and Sex Since the Sexual Revolution: The Example of the Netherlands' in *Emotions in Social Life*, ed. G. Bendelow and S. Williams, London: Routledge 1998, pp. 228–49.

26. See Norbert Elias, *The Civilising Process, 1. The History of Manners*, Oxford: Basil Blackwell 1978; C. Wouters, 'Formalization and Informalization: Changing Tension Balances in Civilizing Processes', *Theory, Culture and Society*, 3, 2 (1986), pp. 1–18.

27. In some respects, the present postmodern era of sexuality reproduces many elements of ancient society. Foucault argues that the ethic and practice of care for the self through which we can determine what is sexual pleasure and our erotic, loving, passionate relationships with others, have been important phenomena since Greek and Roman times but that, particularly in the present era, they have been laid siege to by religious, pedagogical, medical and psychiatric institutions. See Michel Foucault, *The Use of Pleasure*, pp. 25–32; M. Foucault, 'the ethic of care for the self as a practice of freedom: an interview with Michel Foucault on January 20, 1984' in *The Final Foucault*, ed. J. Bernauer and D. Rasmussen, Cambridge [Mass]: MIT Press 1991, pp. 2–3.

28. See J. Mezirow, 'How Critical Reflection Triggers Transformative Learning', in Jack Mezirow and Associates, *Fostering Critical Reflection in Adulthood*, San Francisco: Josey-Bass 1990, pp. 1–20; J. Mezirow, *The Transformative Dimensions of Adult Learning*, San Francisco: Jossey-Bass 1991.

29. See Michael Collins, *Adult Education as a Vocation*, London: Routledge 1991.
30. See Ralph Brockett and Roger Hiemstra, *Self-Direction in Adult Learning*, London: Routledge 1991.
31. Christine Magee and Fran Bisset, *Sex Education: Issues of Policy and Practice*, Dublin: Irish YouthWork Centre/ National Youth Federation 1995, p. 44.
32. Mickey Quinn and Terri Quinn, *How To Talk to Your Child About Sex*, Dublin: Veritas 1981, p. 26.
33. *Just Seventeen*, 30 November 1994. Pat Pinsent has argued that 'in' language reassures readers that they are part of a group from which their teachers and parents are excluded. See P. Pinsent, 'Lessons in Love: Girls' Magazines in the 1990s' in *Teenage Girls and their Magazines*, ed. K. Reynolds, London: Roehampton Institute 1998, p. 23.
34. For an analysis of language and symbolic domination in general, and how it operates in different social fields, see Pierre Bourdieu, *Language and Symbolic Power*, Cambridge: Polity Press 1991.
35. P. Freire, *Pedagogy of the Oppressed*, Harmondsworth: Penguin 1972, pp. 46–7.
36. For a discussion of the difference between Freire and a traditional approach to literacy, see T. Inglis, 'Could We All Come Down from the Clouds Again?; Frank C. Laubach and World Literacy', *International Journal of University Adult Education*, 29, 3 (1990), pp. 1–22.
37. Theatre Venture, *Doing the Right Thing*. London n.d.
38. S. Walsh, 'Relationships and Sexuality Education: Context of a New Programme in the Primary School Curriculum in the Republic of Ireland' Unpublished Master's Thesis, University of Limerick 1997, pp. 199–211.

Chapter 9. Conclusion

1. See, Evelyn Mahon, Catherine Conlon and Lucy Dillon, *Women and Crisis Pregnancy*, Dublin: Government Publications 1998, pp. 27–35. *The Irish Times*, 26 May 1998.
2. As part of their study, Mahon, Conlon and Dillon received completed questionnaires from 2,053 women and conducted in-depth, one-to-one interviews with 353 women having had a crisis pregnancy decided *(a)* to have an abortion in England, *(b)* to pursue lone motherhood or *(c)* to have the baby adopted. See Mahon, Conlon and Dillon, *Women and Crisis Pregnancy*, pp. 52–75. For a discussion of the political background to these issues, see E. Mahon, 'From Democracy to Femocracy: the Women's Movement in the Republic of Ireland' in *Irish Society: Sociological*

Perspectives, ed. P. Clancy, S. Drudy, K. Lynch, L. O'Dowd, Dublin: Insitute of Public Administration 1995, pp. 675–708.

3. Mahon, Conlon and Dillon, *Women and Crisis Pregnancy*, p. 528.
4. Mahon, Conlon and Dillon, *Women and Crisis Pregnancy*, p. 530.
5. Mahon, Conlon and Dillon, *Women and Crisis Pregnancy*, p. 518.
6. *Relationships and Sexuality Education: Interim Curriculum and Guidelines for Primary Schools*, Dublin: NCCA 1997, p. 13.
7. *Relationships and Sexuality Education in Catholic Schools: A Resource for Teachers and Boards of Management*, Dublin: Veritas 1997, p. 5.
8. Jacques Donzelot, *The Policing of Families*, London: Hutchinson 1980. See also P. Aggleton, 'Sexuality In and Out of School', *British Journal of Sociology of Education* 15 (1994), pp. 279–82; Isobel Allen, *Education in Sex and Personal Relationships*, Oxford: Policy Studies Institute 1987, p.184; M. Wyness, 'Schooling and the Normalisation of Sex Talk within the Home' *British Journal of the Sociology of Education* 13 (1992), pp. 89–103.
9. See, for example, C. Haywood, 'Sex Education Policy and the Regulation of Young People's Sexual Practice', *Educational Review*, 48, 2 (1996), pp. 121–9; R. Johnson, 'Sexual Dissonances: or the Impossibility of Sexuality Education', *Curriculum Studies* 4, 2 (1996), pp. 163–89; S. Lees, 'Talking about Sex in Sex Education', *Gender and Education* 6 (1994), pp. 281–92. M. Reiss, 'What are the Aims of School Sex Education?' *Cambridge Journal of Education*, 23 (1993), pp. 125–36.
10. Jürgen Habermas, *The Theory of Communicative Action, Vol. 2*, Cambridge: Polity Press 1987, pp.153–97; A. Arato and J. Cohen, 'Civil Society and Social Theory' *Thesis Eleven*, 21 (1988), pp. 42, 44; Jean Cohen and Andrew Arato, *Civil Society and Political Theory*, Cambridge [Mass.]: MIT Press 1992, p. 435.
11. Christie Davies, *Permissive Britain: Social Change in the Sixties and Seventies*, London: Pitman 1975, p. 200. Ernest Gellner progressed this further and suggested that the fundamental contradiction in contemporary society is between fundamentalism, which he associated with Islamic society, and relativism, which he associated with postmodern society. He himself was an adherent of a neo-Habermasian position 'which retains the faith in the uniqueness of truth, but does not believe we possess it definitively, and which uses, as the foundation for practical conduct and inquiry, not any substantive conviction, but only a loyalty to certain procedural rules.' Ernest Gellner, *Postmodernism, Reason and Religion*, London: Routledge 1992, p.vii.
12. For a recent discussion of the Irish ambivalence to alcohol, see T. Cassidy 'Alcoholism in Ireland' in *The Sociology of Health and Illness* ed. A. Cleary

and M. Treacy, Dublin: UCD Press, 1997, pp. 175–92; T. Cassidy, 'Just Two Will Do' in *Encounters with Modern Ireland*, ed. Michel Peillon and Eamonn Slater, Dublin: Institute of Public Administration 1998, pp. 165–73.

13. Ferdinand Toennies, *On Sociology: Pure, Applied and Empirical*, Chicago: Chicago University Press 1971, pp. 211–16. The concept of ambivalence has recently been redeveloped by Neil Smelser. He notes that the 'nature of ambivalence is to hold *opposing affective orientations* toward the same person, object or symbol.' In other words, people are excited and disgusted by sex. This can be related to Durkheim's concept of sacred and profane. Sex is something sacred because it is the great testimony of love and intimacy between humans. Yet at the same time, sex is profane because it involves a surrender to reason and rationality to animality. See N. Smelser, 'The Rational and the Ambivalent in the Social Sciences', *American Sociological Review*, 63, 1 (1998), p. 5.

14. The ambivalence in adolescence between being chaste and sexually active, is, as Gaffney points out, part of a series of tensions between being progressive-regressive, active-passive, dependent-independent. See Maureen Gaffney, *The Way We Live Now*, Dublin: Gill & Macmillan 1996, pp. 17–20.

15. The practice of using outsider teachers has been recommended by others. See Isobel Allen, *Education in Personal Relationships*, Oxford: Policy Studies Institute 1987, p. 58; Carmel Wynne, *Relationships and Sexuality*, Cork: Mercier Press, 1997, p.100; Stephanie Walsh, 'Relationships and Sexuality Education', Unpublished Master's Thesis, University of Limerick, 1997, p. 189.

Index

Lightning Source UK Ltd.
Milton Keynes UK
UKOW04f1808131213

222965UK00001B/26/P

9 781900 621168